The Campus History Series

TORRANCE HIGH SCHOOL

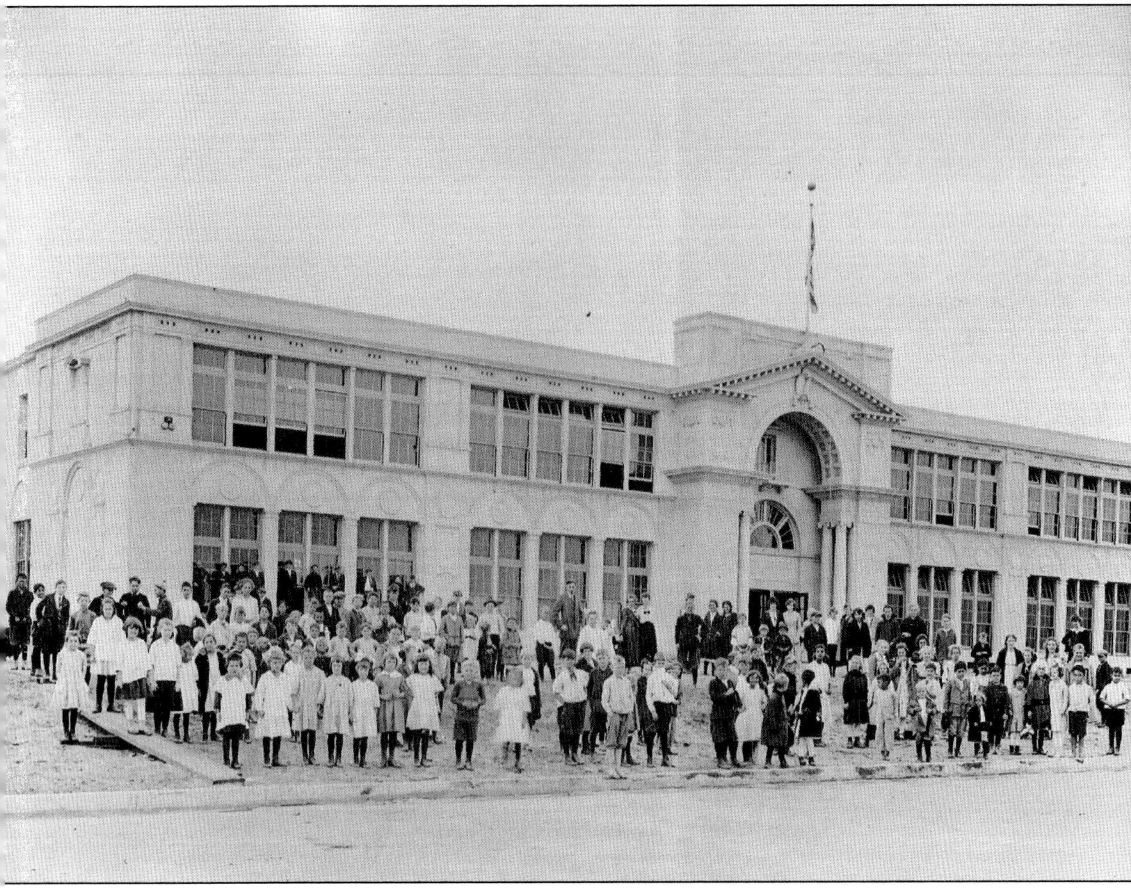

This 1918 image of Torrance High School shows the entire student body in front of the school. For the first six years, from 1917 to 1923, the single building with 10 rooms served all school-aged children in Torrance. In 1923, the elementary children (kindergarten through sixth grade) moved into their own school. That building would later become part of Torrance High. (Courtesy of Claudia Wolverton.)

On the Front Cover: The unidentified students in this image are sitting in an A10 biology class. The A10 refers to the students as being sophomores. The photograph was taken sometime in the early 1930s. Torrance High students took classes in English, sciences, history, shorthand, and bookkeeping. By 2016, students were taking classes in multiple foreign languages, such as Spanish, Korean, and Japanese, as well as engineering classes. (Courtesy of Torrance Historical Society.)

On the Back Cover: This photograph depicts the main building of Torrance High School in the 1930s. It is this building that is the most recognized feature of the campus. (Courtesy of Torrance Historical Society.)

The Campus History Series

TORRANCE HIGH SCHOOL

LORALEE SPRADLIN

ARCADIA PUBLISHING

ISBN 978-1-4671-2589-5

Published by Arcadia Publishing
Charleston, South Carolina

Printed in the United States of America

Library of Congress Control Number: 2016957460

For all general information, please contact Arcadia Publishing:
Telephone 843-853-2070
Fax 843-853-0044
E-mail sales@arcadiapublishing.com
For customer service and orders:
Toll-Free 1-888-313-2665

Visit us on the Internet at www.arcadiapublishing.com

To all Tartars,
May you continue to honor the past, celebrate the present,
and dream of the future.

Contents

ACKNOWLEDGMENTS

This book could not have been completed without the assistance of many people. To Liz Gurley, my editor at Arcadia, thank you for navigating me through the publication process. I appreciate the e-mails, insights, and encouragement that have led to this collection.

To Janet Payne, Cleoan McComas-Ferm, and Debbie Hays from the Torrance Historical Society, thank you for your kindness and patience with a novice researcher and writer. Gail Morgan at the Torrance High School (THS) Alumni Association, thank you for trusting me with the very special Torrance High memorabilia.

Thank you to Karen, Terry, Sue H., Sharon, Gail, Jerry, Mark, and Ann for the support, ideas, research, and dedication.

To the THS Centennial Committee, thank you for your support: Edith Coit, Karen Gebhard, Karim Girgis, Debbie Hays, Sue Herbers, Theresa Hollis, Nathan Jones, Sharon Jones, Gwen Knapp, Deena Koda, Gail Morgan, Jerry Ronan, Ann Strong, and Sue Trutanic.

My family's patience, especially when I was worried about completing this special task, is especially appreciated. I love you all: Charlene (Mom), Jay, Jeff, Brian, Jennifer, Sarah, Joshua, Benjamin, and Jordyn. Dad, I wish you were here to see this.

To the members of the Tartar community who graciously let me borrow your personal photographs and information, I cannot express how much enjoyment I had in sharing your memories: Danish Akmal, Mary Basile, Traci Liston Castro, Paul Comon, Casie Duvall, Kelly Gasset, Janis Gragg, Christy Gustafson, Theresa Hollis, Jerry Johnson, Nathan Jones, Jill Kingsmill, Betty Knapp, Devin Kushi, Kathy Nelson, LifeTouch Photo, Kris Radcliffe, Jerry Ronan, John and Norma Sibley, Charles Slater, Charlene Spradlin (Mom), Torrance High School Associated Student Body (ASB), Dottie Towle, Jim Weyant, Claudia Wolverton, and Leah Wolverton. Much of the information for the text came from the book *Historic Torrance* by Dennis F. Shanahan and Charles Elliot Jr. and *The History of Torrance Schools, 1890–2000* by Thomas Rische, the *Torrance High School Torch*, and *Torrance News Torch*.

A portion of the author's royalties from the sale of this publication will go to Torrance High School. Thank you all for your confidence and trust in me to accomplish this endeavor. I accept responsibility for any errors that may appear.

INTRODUCTION

Standing in front of Torrance High School, it is hard to imagine that the land was once part of a large rancho owned by a single family. The Dominguez family, whose origins in Southern California date back to the 18th century, owned much of the land situated between Los Angeles and San Pedro. Through the 19th century, the Dominguez family became part of the fabric and industry of the region, dealing in oil, real estate, and cattle. By the end of that century, parcels of land were sold, including one to Ben Weston. The Weston Ranch comprised 3,000 acres, much of what would eventually become the city of Torrance. Weston's nephew became the manager of the land holdings in the 1890s and built a one-room schoolhouse for his own children and the children of the hired men. Though it was under control of the Los Angeles school system by 1909, the little ranch schoolhouse was the foundation of education in the area. In 1905, a second schoolhouse was built in the area. The Perry School served children for 76 years, both as an independent school and part of the Torrance Unified School District.

Between the two small schools, the city of Torrance developed. As president of the Dominguez Land Company, Jared Sidney Torrance's real estate and business acumen led him to develop a planned community, with El Prado as the backbone, that would ultimately bear his name. In 1912, the Union Tool Company had established themselves as a leading employer, and labor unrest in Los Angeles encouraged more businesses to move to the idyllic town. In 1913, in order to encourage local workers to relocate to Torrance, a small, two-room elementary school began operating in an existing building on Cabrillo Avenue. Though this new school was listed, in part, as a high school, the oldest students were eighth graders. By 1916, the student population of Torrance had increased enough to warrant a larger school, particularly for secondary students. Prompted by this growing population, city leaders convinced Los Angeles school officials to purchase land on which to build a school in Torrance. The site chosen for the new school was at the end of El Prado, on a slight rise that was to originally house a civic center.

Situated on nine acres today, the initial building consisted of 10 rooms, 7 of which were used for classrooms. Designed by Robert Allen Farrell in the Beaux-Arts style, the building cost about $34,300. When the school opened on September 11, 1917, the student body consisted of only 19 students in the high school classes, including two seniors. Thomas Elson, who had been administering the schoolhouse on Cabrillo Avenue, served as principal. The student population grew significantly in just a few short years, justifying more classroom space. The main building, as it is known to most, was designed to accommodate additions, including the 1921 rear addition designed by E.H. Cline. This addition included a patio with a small tiled fountain. By 1923, two additional buildings were added on either side of the main building. The home economics wing and auditorium were connected to the original wing with symmetrical colonnades. As the population of high school students continued to increase, it was decided that another building would be needed to house the elementary-aged children. Cline designed a two-story L-shaped building with a cafeteria forming the bottom of the "L." Opened as Torrance Elementary, this building remained an elementary school until 1963, when it was annexed by Torrance High School.

While those first six years formed the foundation of Torrance High, it was not until 1923, when the elementary students got their own building, that Torrance High was able to carve out its own identity. It is thought that the class of 1923 changed the school colors from red and gray to maroon and gray and chose the Tartar as the mascot. By 1922, students were publishing a small newspaper called the *Tentacle*. In 1926, the student body published its first yearbook, *The Torch*. That same year, the school newspaper was changed to the *Torrance News Torch* to better connect with *The Torch*. Other buildings were added to the campus, including a gymnasium and a print shop, whose responsibility it was to print the yearbook and newspaper, thereby contributing to the unique character of Torrance High.

Both nature and a growing population resulted in additional changes to the campus. Just before six o'clock on the evening of March 10, 1933, an estimated 6.4-magnitude earthquake shook the community. Centered in Long Beach, the quake caused significant damage to the campus. The auditorium was so severely damaged that, along with the colonnade connecting it to the main building, it had to be torn down. Some classes were temporarily housed in tents. For many years, Tartars referred to the area where the original auditorium stood as the "sunken garden." As part of the Works Progress Administration, a new auditorium was constructed in 1938 near the site of the original. Called the Assembly Hall, the new auditorium served as the only space large enough in the city to host civic events.

In the years following World War II, the population of the city of Torrance grew significantly. Active members of the community like Evelyn Carr, argued that the city of Torrance should have its own district. In 1947, voters in Torrance chose to remove themselves from the auspices of Los Angeles's school district and form Torrance Unified School District. Much of this population growth may be attributed to the aerospace industry, which was a predominant part of the southern California economy through the 1950s to the 1980s. According to population statistics at the Torrance Historical Society Museum, the population of Torrance in 1940 was 9,950. In 1955, that population had grown to 67,459. A year later, the population reached 82,238.

This continued growth again put pressure on Torrance High to include more space for its student body. Classroom bungalows were added in the early 1950s. Additionally, between 1955 and 1962, three more high schools opened in Torrance. By 1963, the student body at Torrance High was large enough to warrant claiming the building housing Torrance Elementary, now affectionately referred to as the Annex. In 1966, a music building was added, as the old gymnasium was demolished. A larger school library replaced the small one located adjacent to the senior patio and main building. At the midpoint of campus, another structure was added and would eventually house the science and industrial arts. Throughout the 1980s and 1990s, the campus did not witness new construction, but a ballot measure in the early 2000s allowed for modernization.

While the buildings provided the foundation of Torrance High, it is the people who have truly defined the school. The school's motto is "Enter to Learn, Go Forth to Serve." Many Tartars have epitomized this motto in their service to the country. Countless alumni have left the safe halls of Torrance High to join the armed forces. Some of these, like Louis Zamperini and Ted Tanouye, left well-known legacies. But there were many other heroes of this Greatest Generation whose names and stories have been lost to all but their families. Very few remember that John Fess from the class of 1938 was killed aboard the USS *Arizona* during the attack on Pearl Harbor. Students at Torrance High did their part for the war effort, making checkerboards and jigsaw puzzles for injured servicemen. In keeping with the government rationing programs, the yearbooks during the war years were decidedly shortened to save paper. These everyday heroes included faculty members like Irene Mills, who wrote to Tartars serving abroad, providing some memories of home. The next generation of Tartars also served in the military during the Vietnam War. Again, many of their names are lost to history, but young men such as Rodney and Brian Strobridge, Larry Robillard, and Dennis Purcell paid the ultimate sacrifice, losing their lives in the line of service.

Teachers and faculty members have also been instrumental in creating the fabric of Torrance High. Early classes included history and English, commercial, science, and math.

As more teachers were hired, more subjects were included in the curriculum, including agriculture classes, added in the 1920s. European languages like French and German have been replaced with Korean and Japanese. Typing classes gave way to word processing and media design. Home economics evolved to fashion construction. Current faculty members who attended Torrance High themselves keep those legacies alive by sharing stories of how Will Boerger, Richard Hulse, Pat Wright, John Radcliffe, and many others contributed in shaping them into who they are today.

Athletics have always been a part of high school life, and throughout the last century, many of the same sports continued field teams. Others, such as golf, gymnastics, and soccer, were later added. But for many years, only boys played these sports competitively. Girls participated in sports under the Girls' Athletic Association (GAA). Title IX, passed by the federal government in 1972, called for gender equity in educational settings of any program receiving federal funds. Female participation in sports continued to increase through the end of the 20th century, as they participated in basketball, soccer, and track events, to name a few. By the early 2000s, Torrance High's athletic program expanded to include swim teams and a water polo team.

Other aspects of campus life continued to evolve. Like athletics, student organizations have long been a part of how the Tartar community bonds. Early clubs included boys' and girls' glee, Scholarship Society, the Madrigals, and a few language-based clubs. Many of these evolved to include more about the culture and less about the language. The Scholarship Society is now the California Scholarship Federation. Two of the most significant and long-standing student organizations are the Tartar Knights (1936) and Tartar Ladies (1943). Many of the changes on campus throughout the years are reflected in how the student body dressed. The early decades saw boys wear slacks with button-down shirts and even ties, while girls typically wore dark skirts and white blouses. By the late 1950s, as the campus grew, the style changed to reflect what was made popular by film stars such as James Dean. Letterman sweaters as well as leather jackets were popular for the boys. Despite the popularity of pedal pushers, girls were expected to wear skirts and dresses. Long-legged pants like pedal pushers were only acceptable on a special activity day. By the turn of the 20th century, the standard uniform consisted of jeans, T-shirts, and hoodies.

In some ways, being a student or faculty member at Torrance High is like being part of a truly special family. As each new generation walks through the doors of Torrance High, their names are added to the family tree. Some of those branches are multigenerational, with roots dating back to the 1920s. While there is pride in the past, there is always hope for a bright future. And while members of the family sometimes lose touch, there is no denying that the branches of the Tartar tree remain strong and "shall ne'er be broken."

One

Enter to Learn

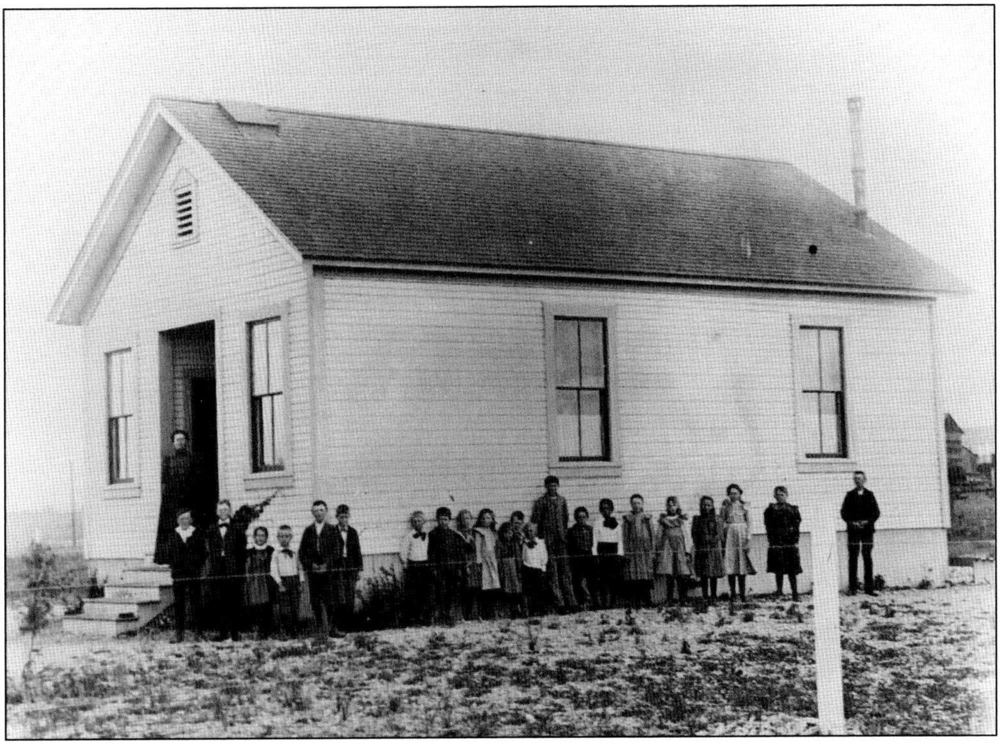

The Weston Ranch school started sometime in the 1890s. Set on the 3,000-acre Weston Ranch, the school served the children of the ranch hands. To get to the one-room schoolhouse, teachers, and students walked or rode horses. Despite the day-to-day ranch operations, the teacher instructed students in grades first through eighth in basic spelling, reading, and arithmetic, as well as history. (Courtesy of the Torrance Historical Society.)

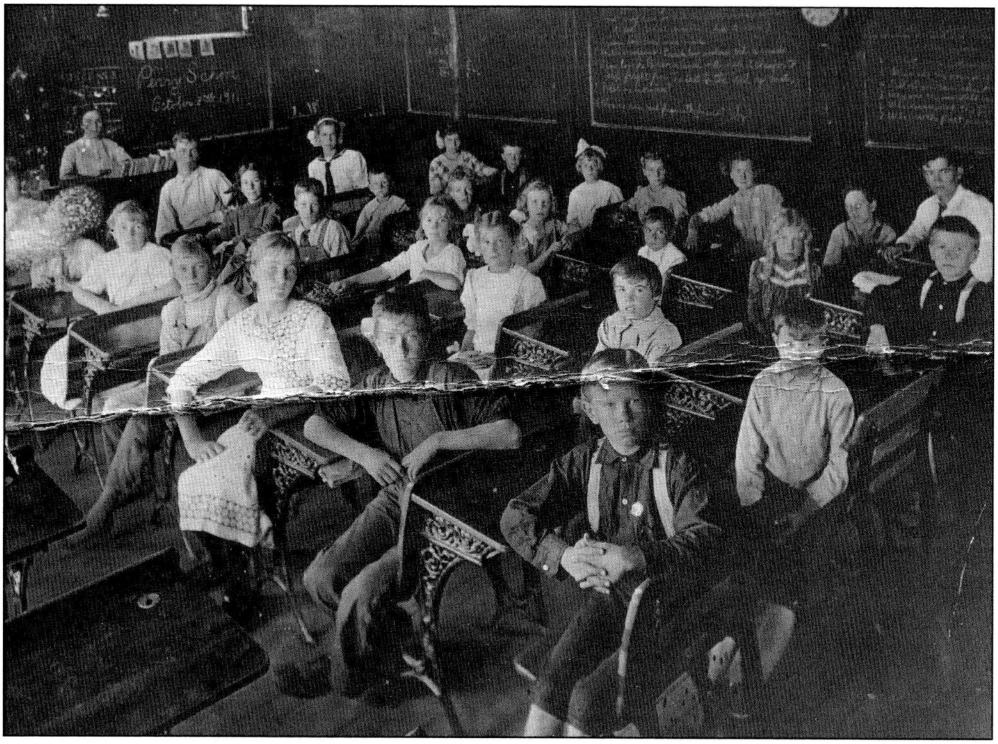

The Perry School opened sometime in 1905. Located near present-day Prairie Avenue and 179th Street, the school remained in operation for 76 years. In this c. 1911 image, Elizabeth Smith instructs her young pupils in subjects such as geography and agriculture. For many years, the Perry School operated as a separate district with only one school. (Courtesy of Torrance Historical Society.)

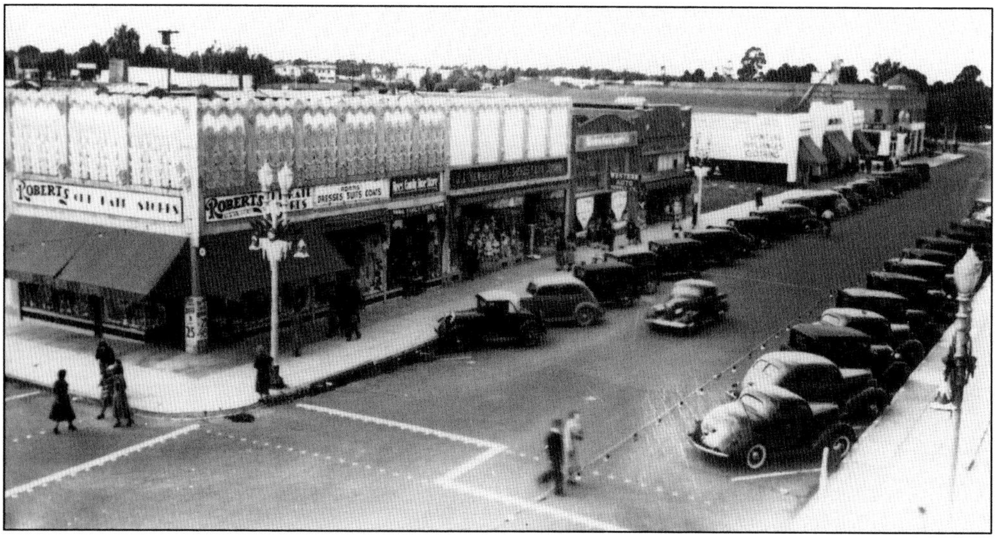

In this image, the downtown area of Torrance has grown significantly. Sartori Avenue featured many shops for the community to conduct business, including J.J. Newberry, as seen on the left of this 1940s photograph. J.J. Newberry carried a lot of different items, from pots and pans to clothes. (Courtesy of the Torrance Historical Society.)

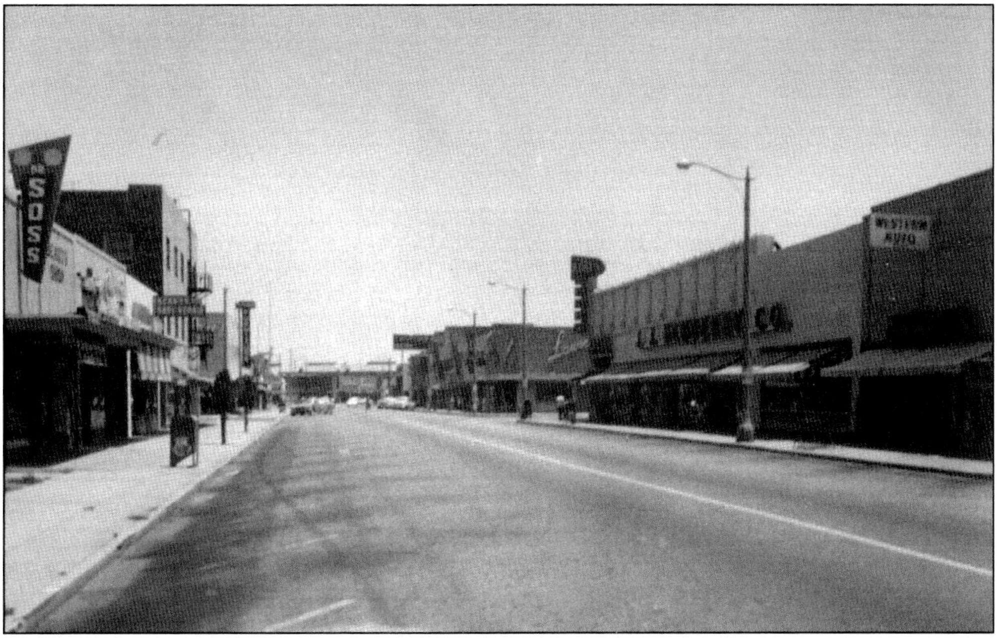

This image shows Sartori Avenue from a different corner. J.J. Newberry store has expanded to include the smaller shops and stretches to the corner. The growth of the city throughout the first half of the 20th century justified the opening and expansion of Torrance School. (Courtesy of the Torrance Historical Society.)

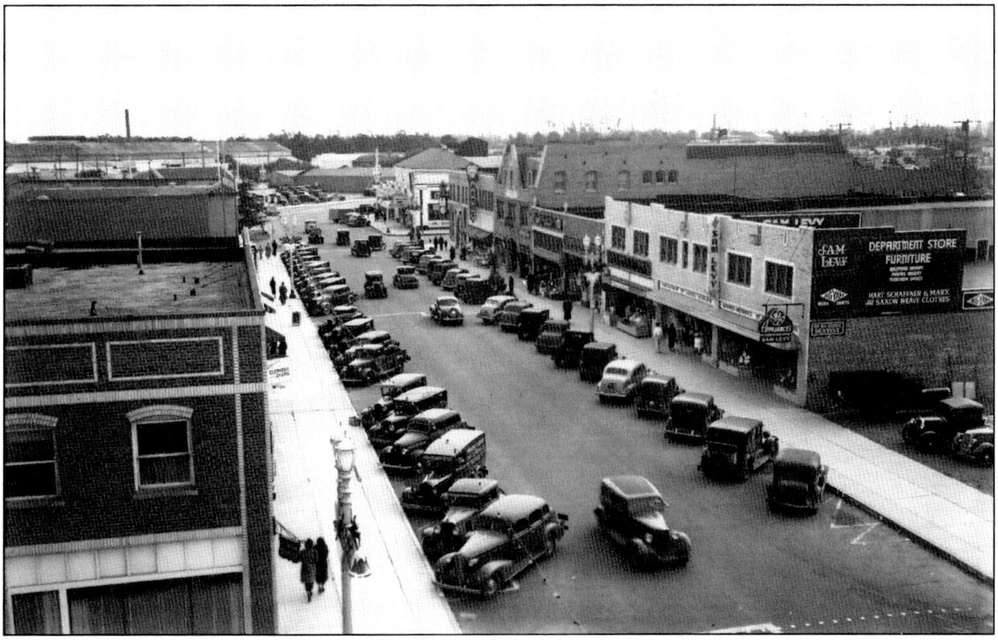

This photograph provides another view of Old Torrance. On the right side of the photograph is the Sam Levy department store, which was located on Sartori. This store catered to the local working-class economy. After his death, a school was named in his honor. His daughter took over the department store and, in 1989, converted it to a women's boutique called Ella's. (Courtesy of the Torrance Historical Society.)

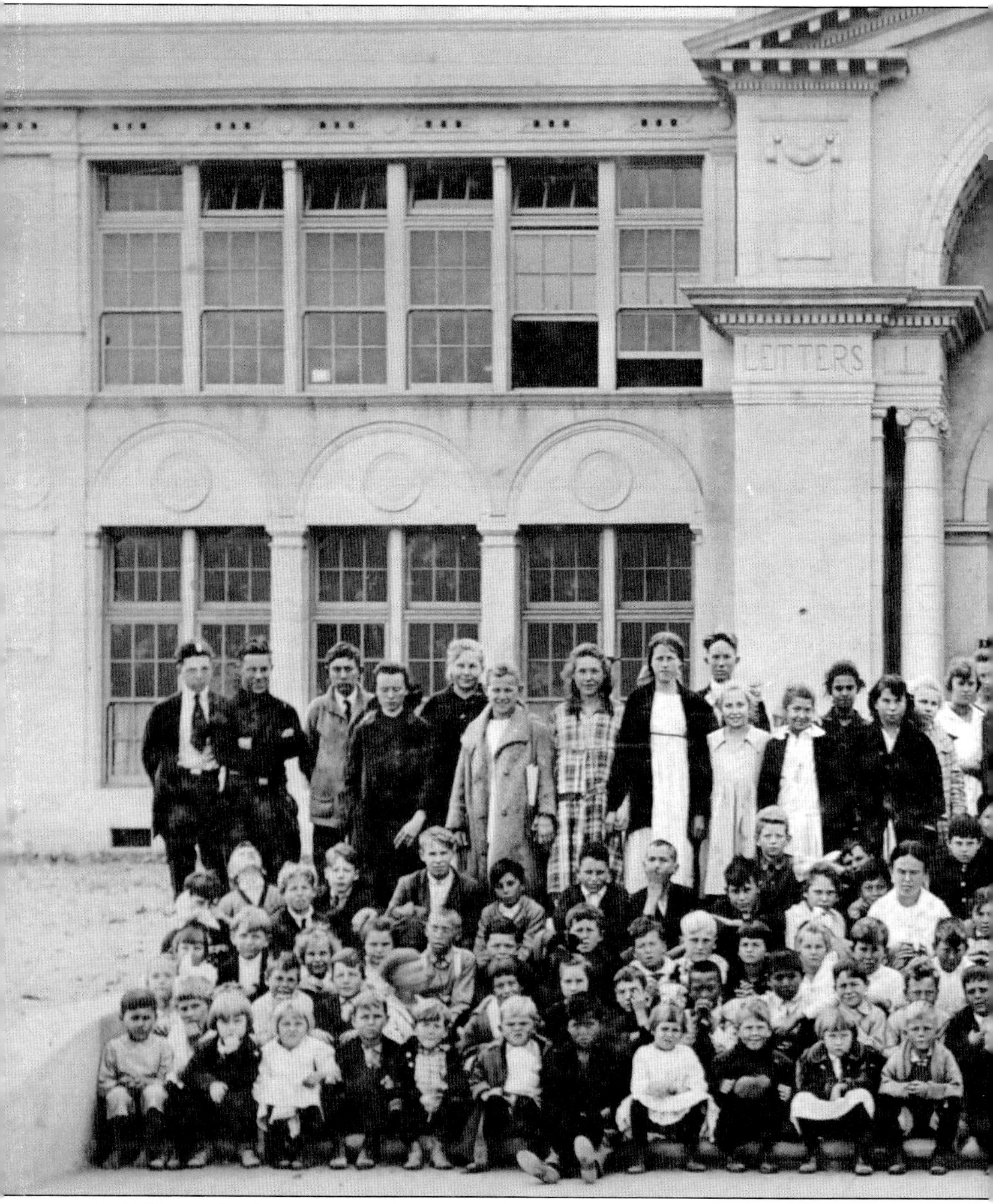

In 1917, city leaders convinced Los Angeles School District that a larger school was necessary in the growing city of Torrance. The site chosen for the new school was located at the end of El Prado Avenue. This land was originally intended to showcase a city hall. The necessity of a school received priority over a new city hall. When Torrance School opened on September 11, 1917, it served schoolchildren of all ages. With a price tag of

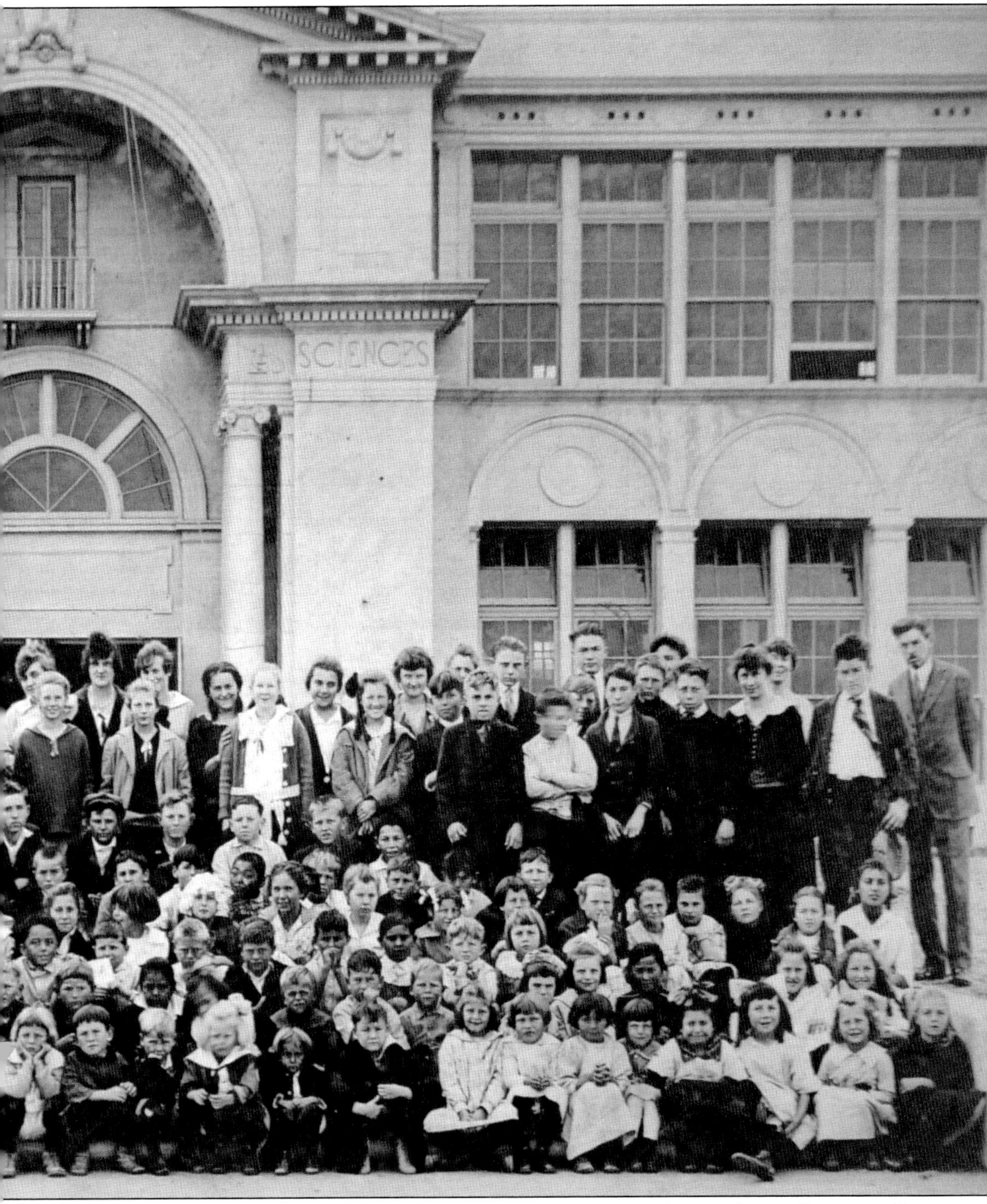

nearly $34,300, the Beaux-Arts, 10-room school was designed by Robert Allen Farrell and featured seven classrooms. This 1918 image shows the entire student body in front of the school. Above the facade was a rampart of sorts that featured the words "Torrance School." (Courtesy of Claudia Wolverton.)

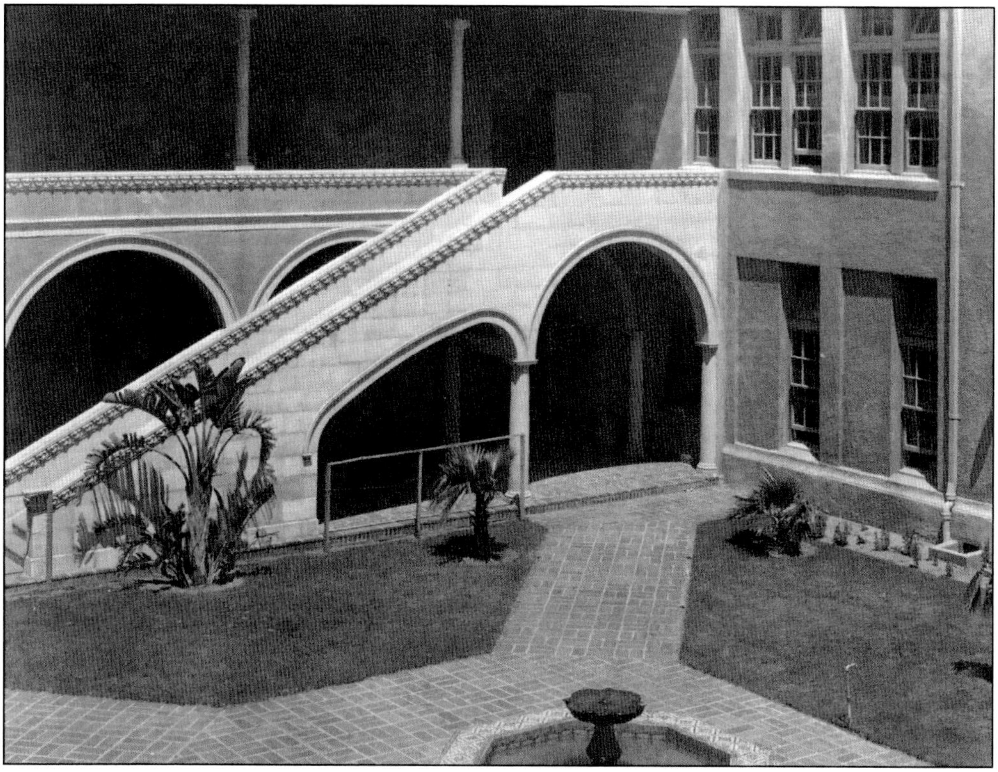

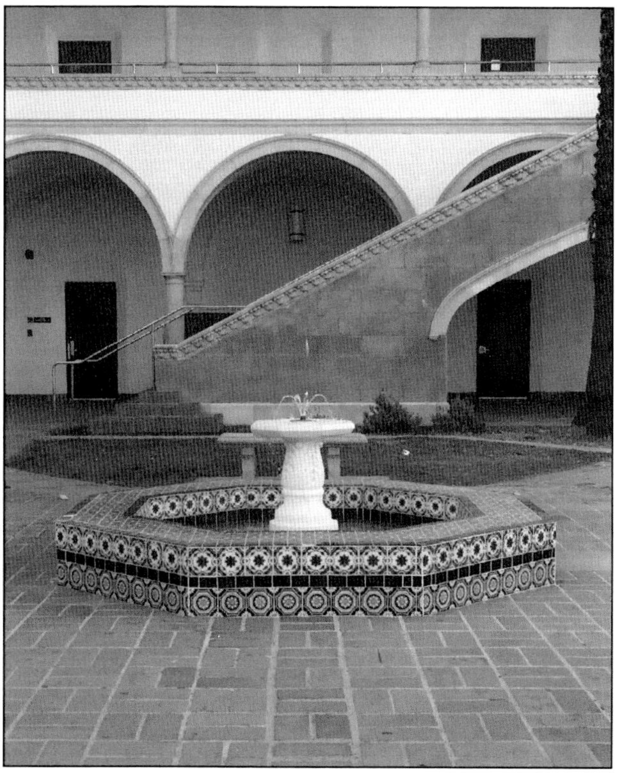

The design of the school encouraged expansion, and in 1921, a rear addition was added to the main building, creating a patio area (above). Included on the senior patio was a small tiled fountain in the center (left). In the early 2000s, the fountain was refurbished, and a new pump was installed. The bowl in the middle of the fountain has also been replaced. In 2012, in preparation for modernization, the senior patio area was closed off. Construction workers carefully removed sections of the arches and staircase in order to replace weakened rebar. Each section that was removed was painstakingly labeled in order to be put back in exactly the correct position and to maintain the historical integrity of the building. (Both, courtesy of Paul Comon.)

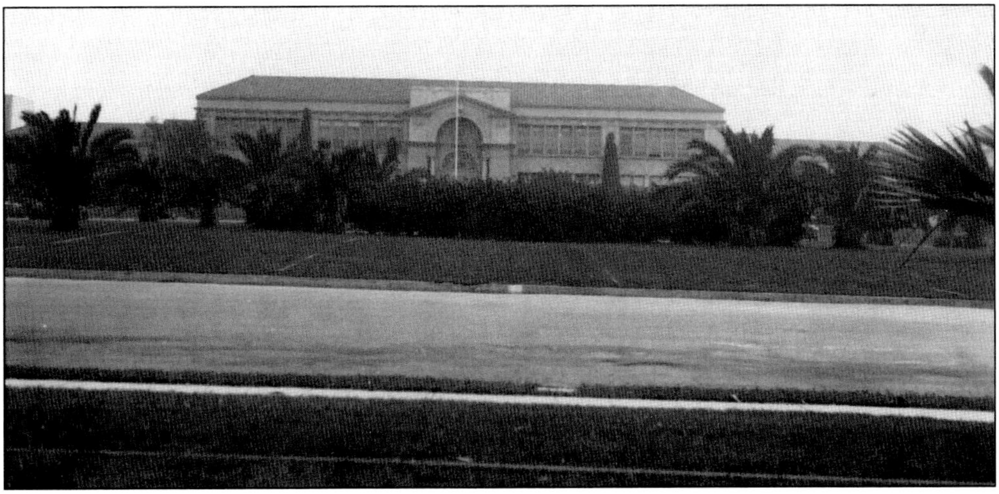

The home economics building and auditorium were constructed in 1923 and connected to the main building with symmetrical colonnades. In this image, mostly likely taken from El Prado Park in the late 1920s, these additions are visible behind the trees. The expanse of grass in front of the school was later altered to allow for Carson Street to cut through. (Courtesy of Torrance Historical Society.)

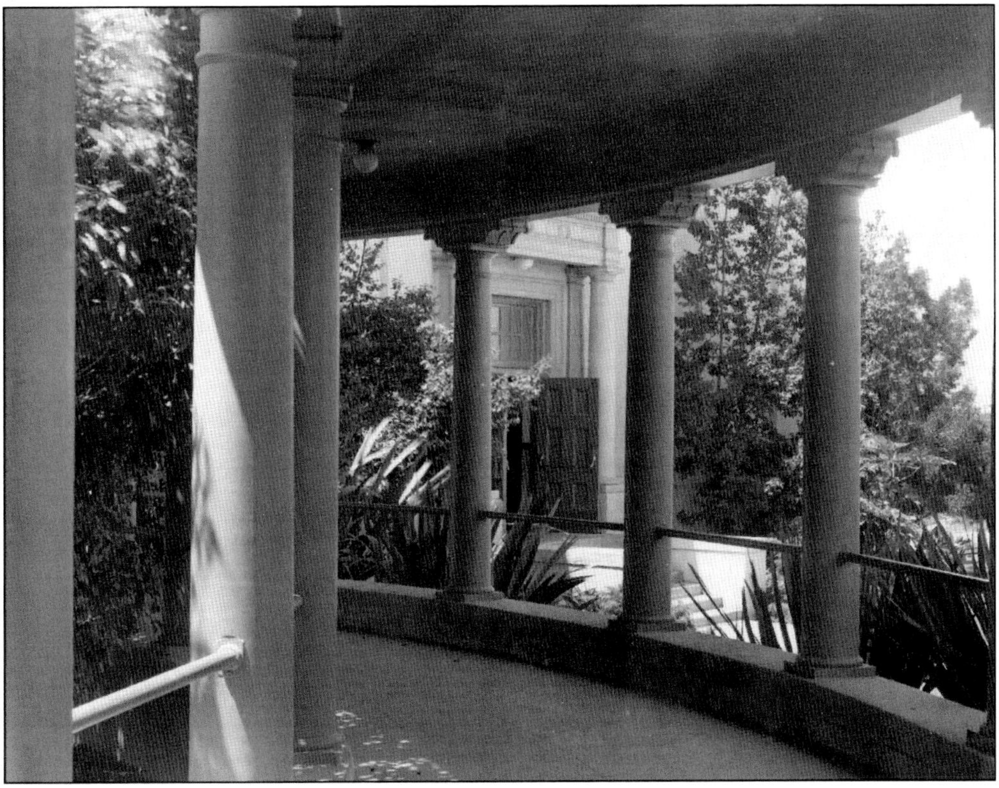

Only one set of colonnades remains, linking the main building to the home economics building. The area between the main building and home economics buildings became known as the junior patio. It remains a favorite place for students to gather at lunch. (Courtesy of Paul Comon.)

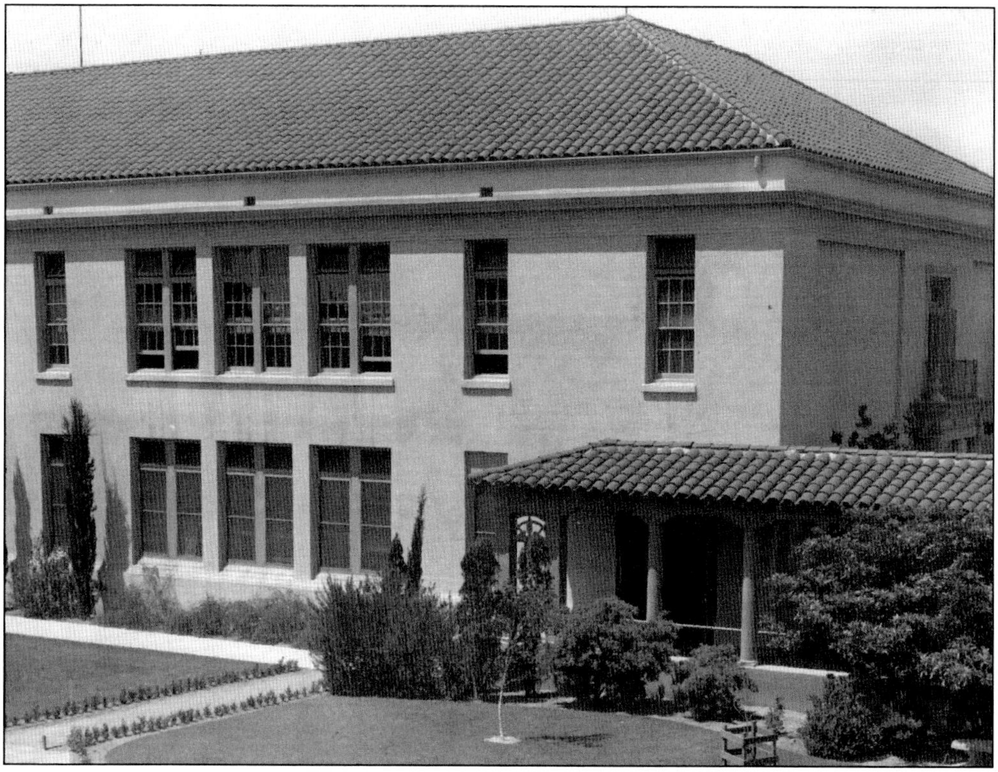

This c. 1950s photograph was taken from upstairs in the main building and looks down on the junior patio. The colonnade can be seen on the left. The home economics building is still in use, though the curriculum has changed. Today, instead of classes about homemaking, students participate in fashion construction classes, in which they learn how to design and sew their own creations. (Courtesy of Paul Comon.)

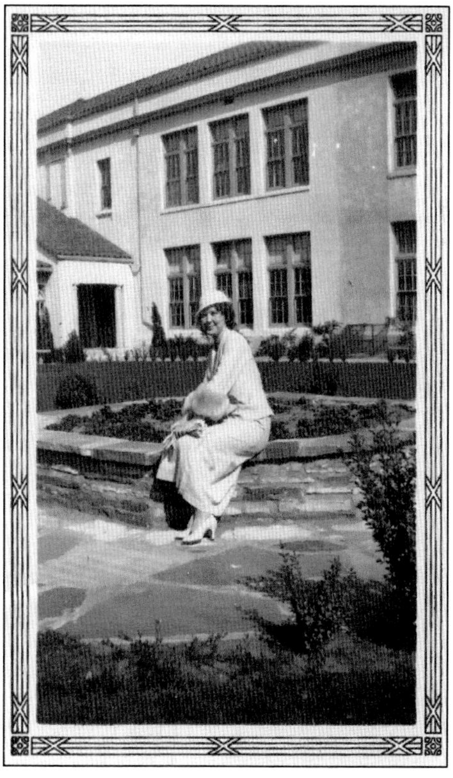

Mildred Holland Halter, a graduate of Torrance High, sits on the junior patio. A planter was added and a palm tree planted in the late 1940s or early 1950s. The palm tree and planter are still a popular location for students during lunch. Behind Halter is the main building. (Courtesy of Torrance Historical Society.)

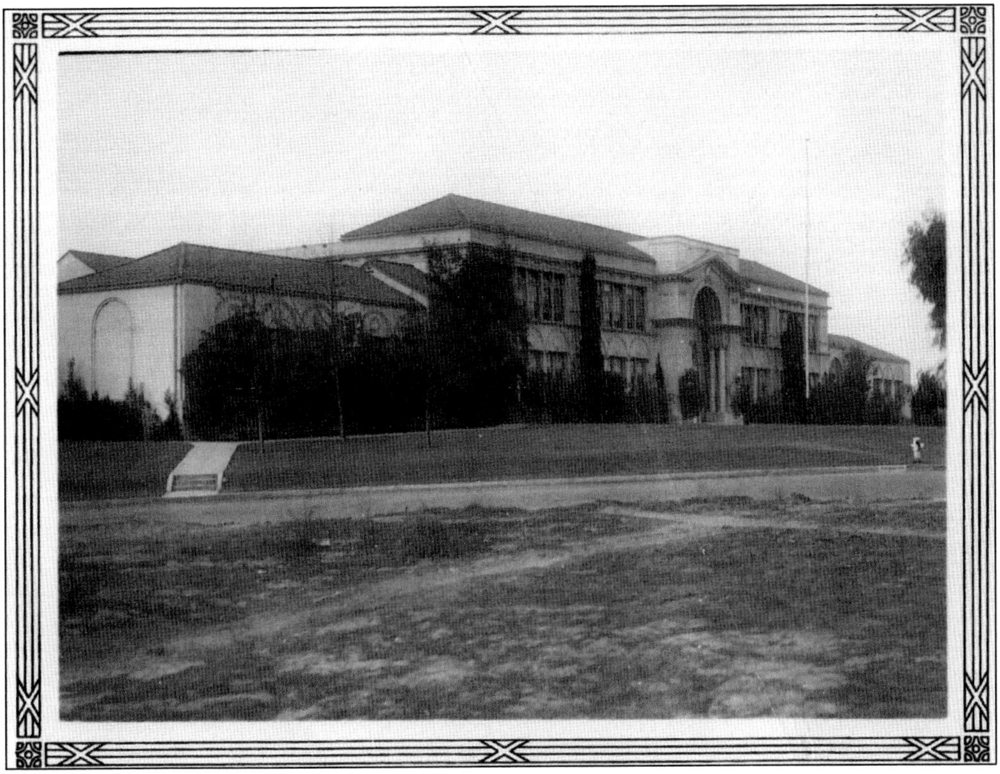

In this side view of the main building, most likely taken prior to 1923, the single-story additions on either side of the original are evident, but the colonnades do not appear to be constructed yet. It is also interesting to note the changes in landscaping, as different trees were added or removed. (Courtesy of Torrance Historical Society.)

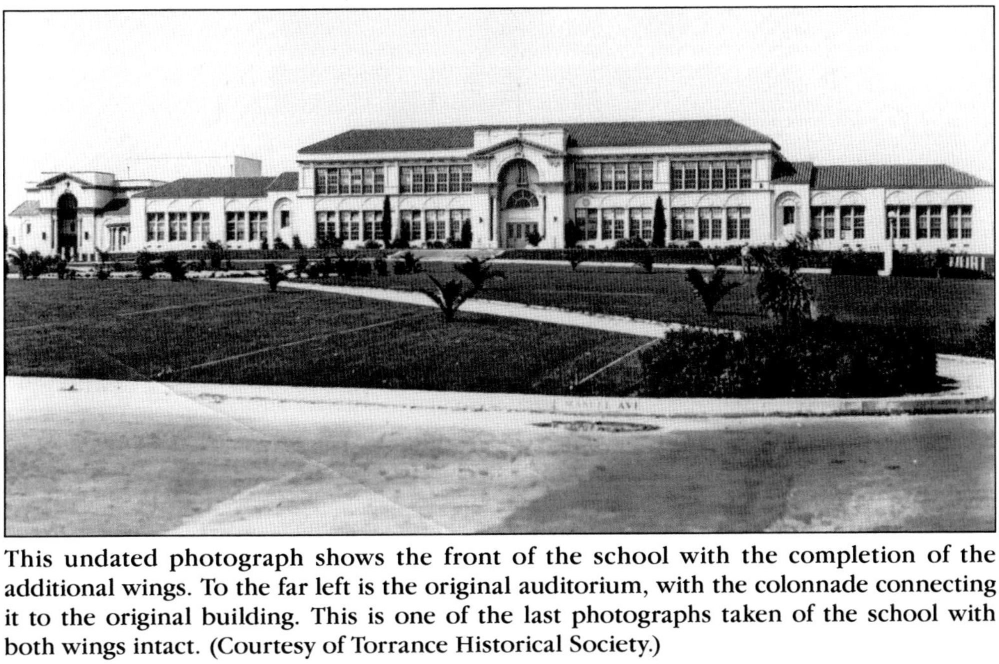

This undated photograph shows the front of the school with the completion of the additional wings. To the far left is the original auditorium, with the colonnade connecting it to the original building. This is one of the last photographs taken of the school with both wings intact. (Courtesy of Torrance Historical Society.)

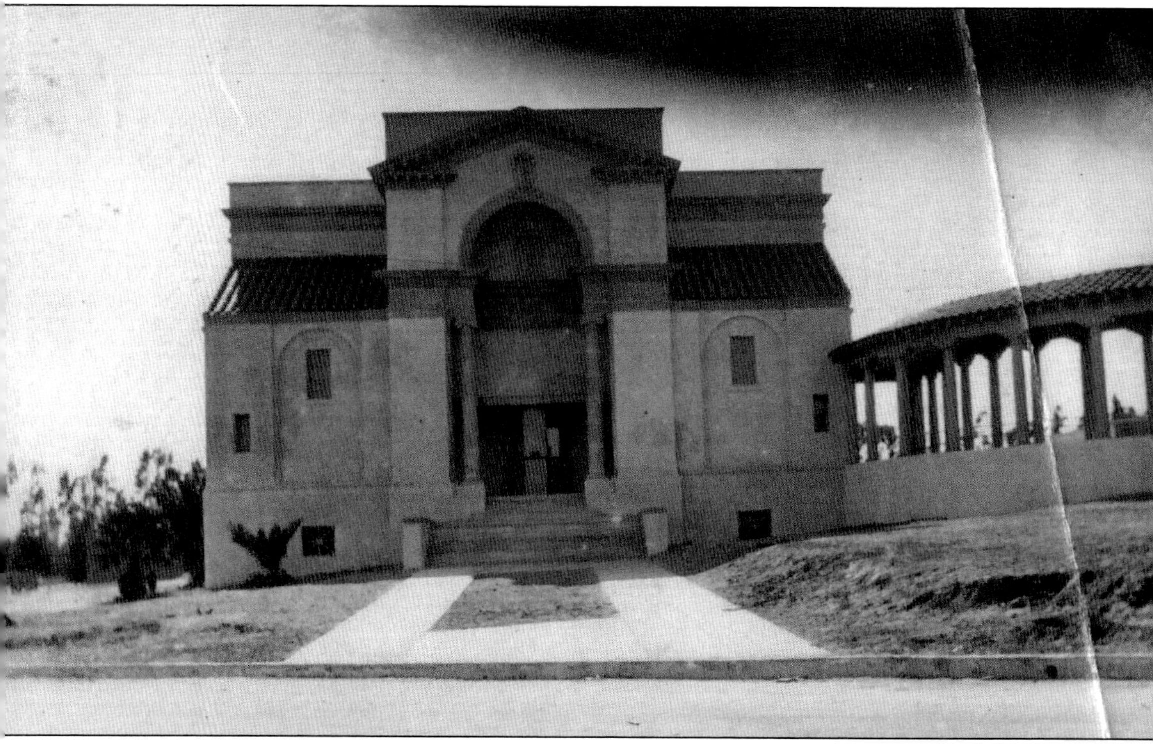

This rare image from the early 1930s showcases the front of the original auditorium, built in 1923. In order to utilize the space efficiently, a cafeteria was included in the basement of the auditorium. It is rumored that during the first years of the Great Depression, Walt Disney sent his animators to various schools in the South Bay to create illustrations and that some of those paintings were on the walls of the cafeteria. Unfortunately, no photographic evidence has emerged to corroborate this information. Sadly, on March 10, 1933, just before 6:00 p.m., an estimated 6.4-magnitude earthquake struck. Centered in Long Beach, the earthquake caused substantial damage to the South Bay. The damage to the auditorium was significant, and it was determined that the building and adjacent colonnade would have to be demolished completely. It would be several years before another auditorium would be constructed. (Courtesy of Torrance Historical Society.)

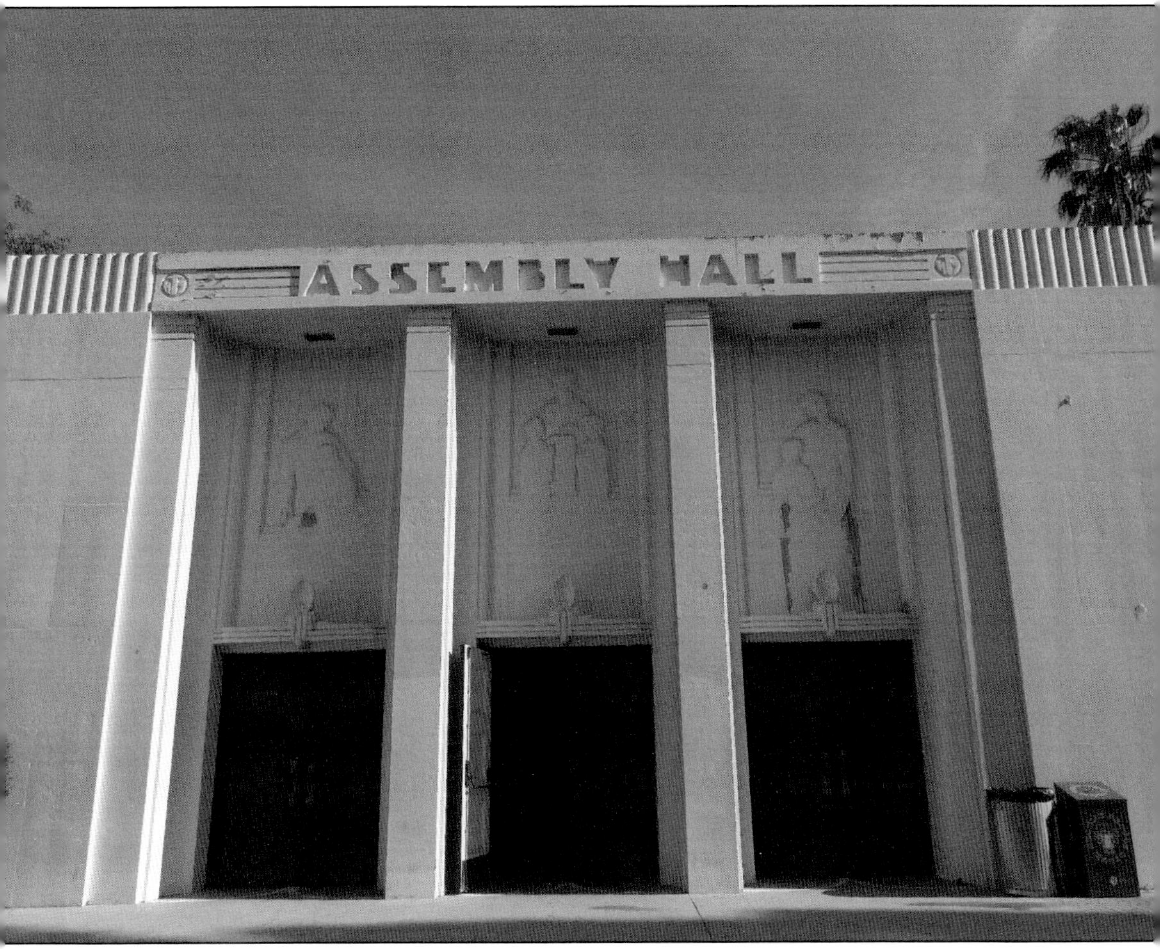

After the original auditorium was fatally damaged in the 1933 earthquake, it was several years before another auditorium was constructed. In the 1930s, Pres. Franklin Roosevelt implemented the New Deal to help the nation recover from the Great Depression. Many government agencies were created with the intention of putting Americans back to work. Included in these was the Works Progress Administration (WPA). In 1938, the WPA completed a beautiful assembly hall on the campus at a cost of just over $100,000. Until the 1950s, this auditorium served as a community gathering place. Hanging in the foyer is a mural titled *Home Life in Old Taos*, completed by A. Katherine Skeele. Originally displayed in the school library, the mural was moved to the auditorium in the 1970s following modernization in the main building. (Courtesy of Lori Spradlin.)

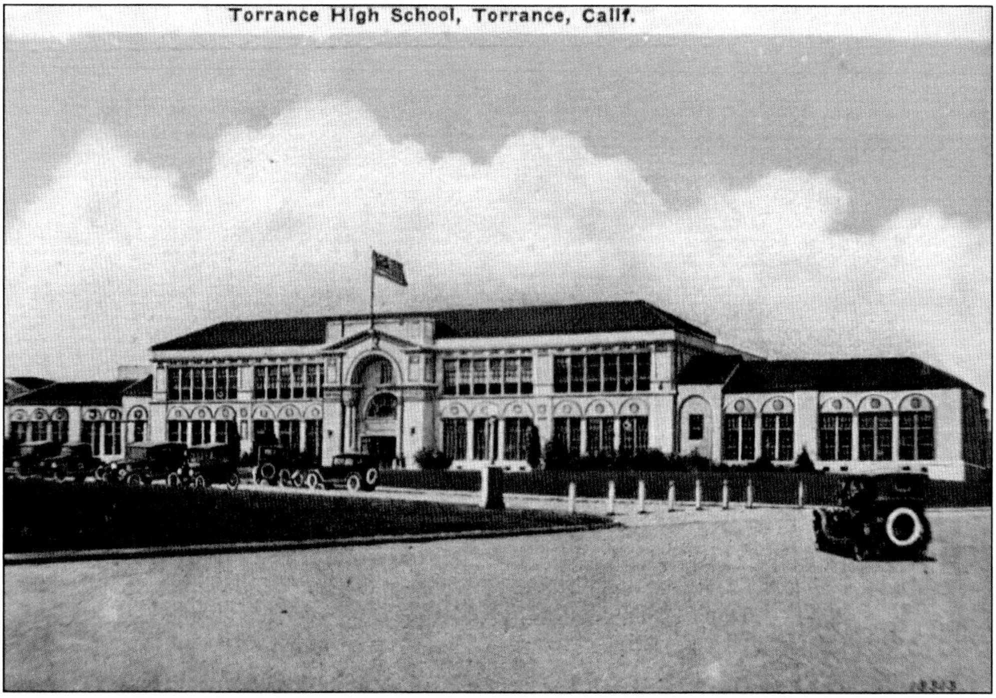

As depicted in the postcard showing Torrance High from the 1920s, the facade of the school shows a picturesque building. The number of vehicles in the postcard seemingly indicates the prosperity of the city of Torrance. The red tiled roof was added in the mid-1920s, replacing the flat roof that was part of the original construction. (Courtesy of Torrance Historical Society.)

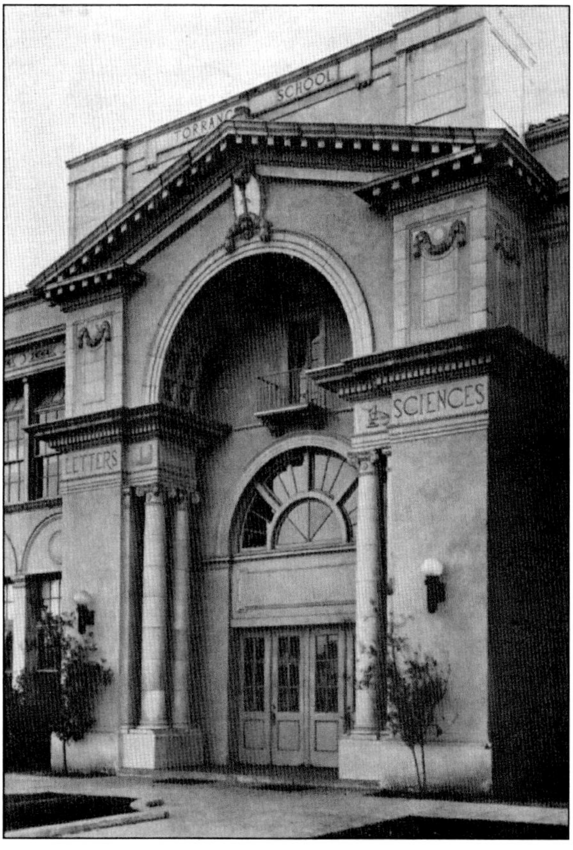

This close-up, pre-1933 image of the exterior of the main building clearly shows the architectural design. The columns, in keeping with Beaux-Arts style, were included, not so much as a supportive function, but for aesthetics. The arched fanlight sits at the landing between the first and second floors. In keeping with one of the mottos of Torrance High ("Let there be light"), near the top cornice is a small medallion featuring a torch. (Courtesy of Torrance Historical Society.)

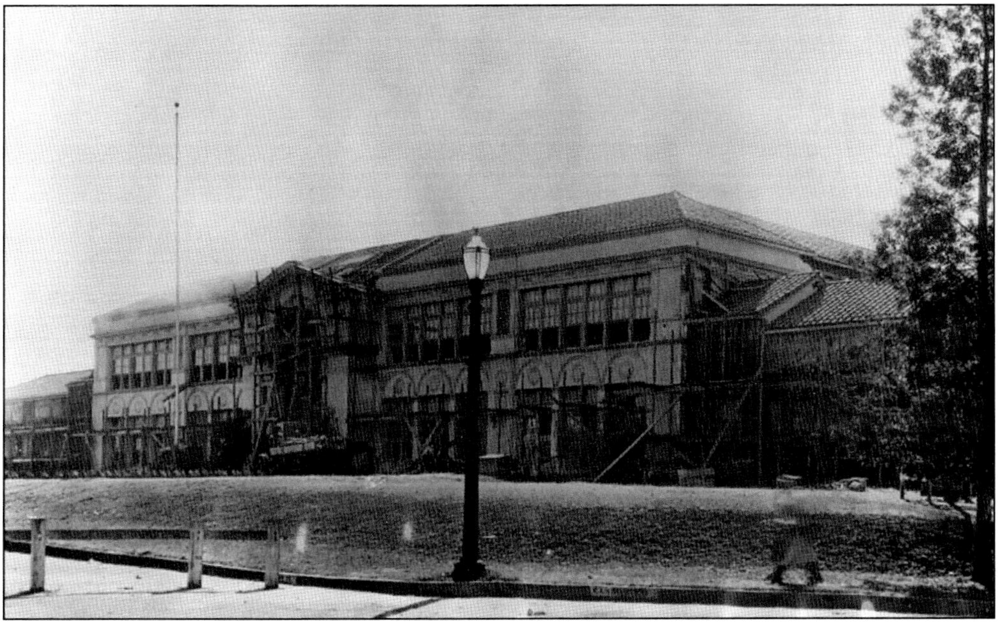

Though it is an undated image, this photograph presumably was taken following the 1933 earthquake that destroyed the original auditorium. The piece on top that proclaimed the site as "Torrance School" is no longer evident. Scaffolding surrounds the lower part of the building and the doors of the school. (Courtesy of Theresa Hollis.)

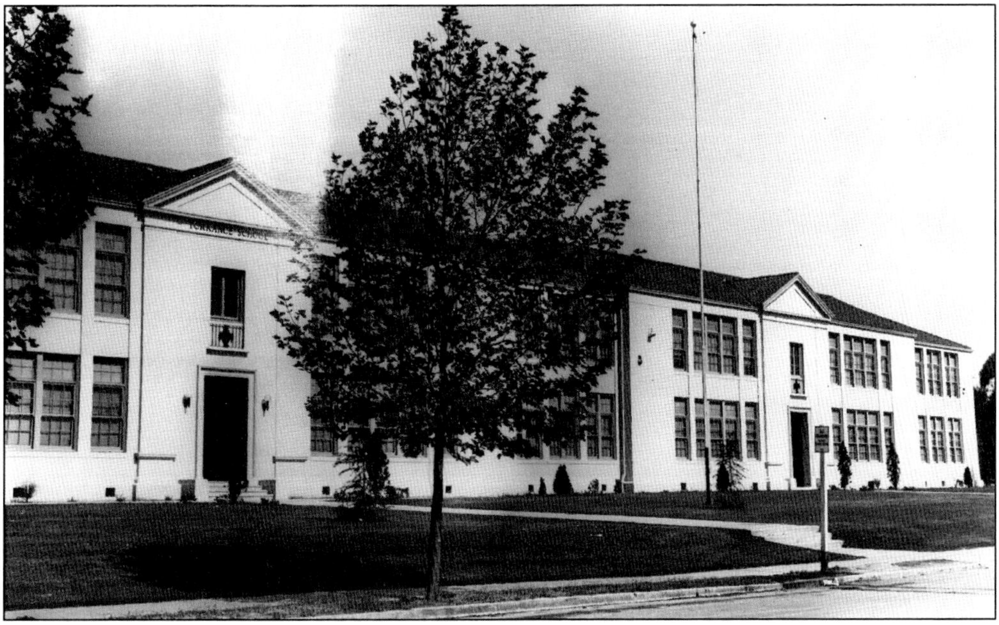

By 1923, the student body at Torrance School had increased substantially, and it was decided that a new building should be constructed for the elementary children. Constructed near the site of Torrance School and designed by E.H. Cline, the two-story L-shaped structure was simply called Torrance Elementary. The new school housed the kindergartners through sixth graders until 1963, when the building was annexed to Torrance High. (Courtesy of Torrance Historical Society.)

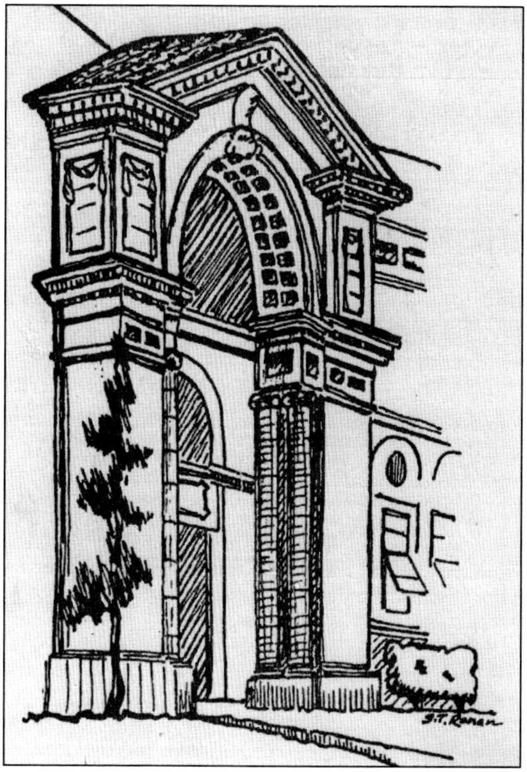

Jerry Ronan, who began his career at Torrance High in 1955, created this beautiful pen drawing of the main building. In the 37 years he worked at Torrance High, Ronan took on many roles to support Tartars. He taught world heritage (a combination of English II and world history) for several years before becoming the boys' advisor. When the counseling program was created, he seamlessly transitioned to being a counselor, which he continued doing until his retirement in 1992. (Courtesy of the Torrance High Alumni Association.)

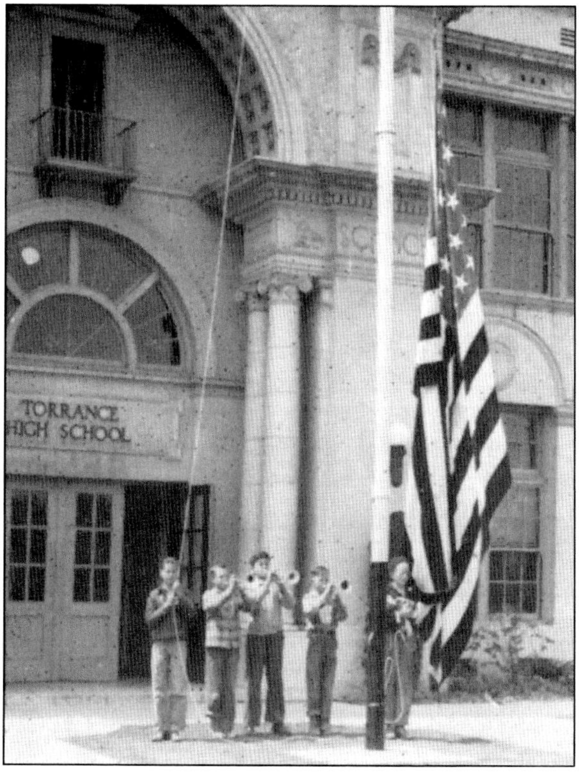

Many Tartars served in World War II. While most returned stateside, some did not. Each morning, the bugle corps would honor the men who served by playing their bugle as the flag was raised. In the 1943 yearbook, a page gives honor to those that were lost in the war. (Courtesy of Torrance High Alumni Association.)

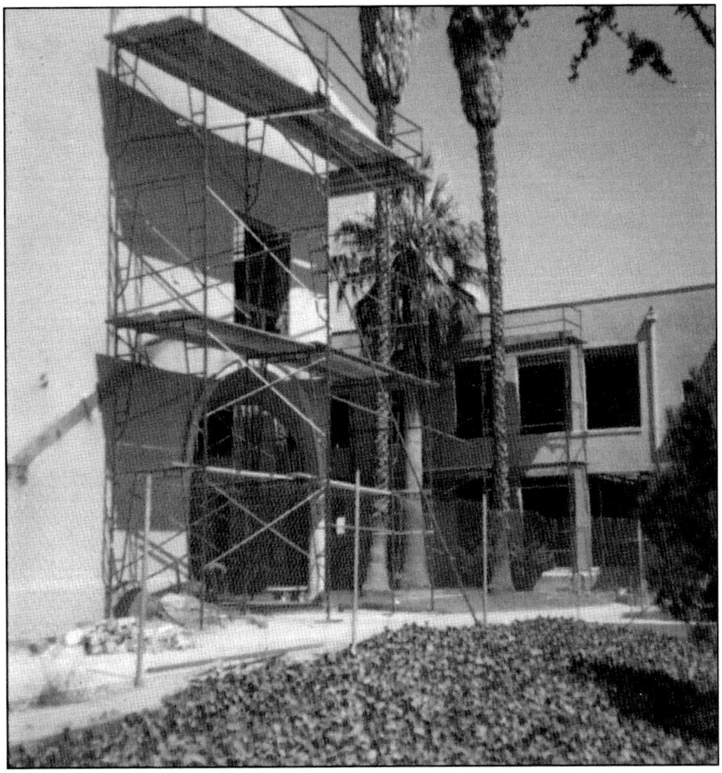

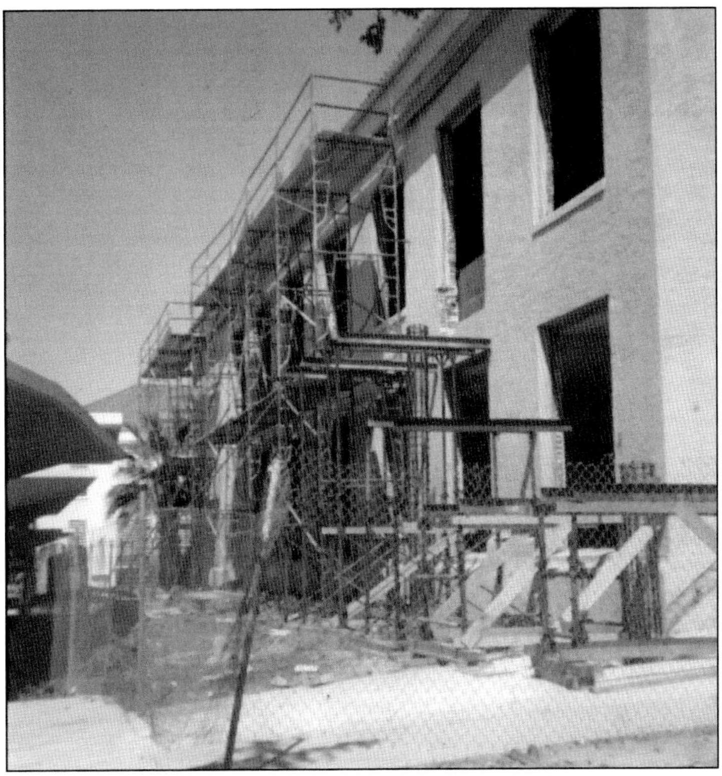

In 1974, the main building underwent significant restoration work, costing nearly $2 million. The interior was retrofitted for earthquakes, particularly near the staircase of the main building. Additional modifications were added to the exterior areas surrounding the senior patio, including near the original school library. Now called the Little Theater, this room has a stage and serves as a meeting place for faculty and clubs. The theater department has also staged productions here, including a dinner theater experience for their production of *Rumors* in the 1990s. In the image above, another exit and exterior steel staircase were added to the Little Theater. In the image below, the side of the Little Theater, as well as downstairs classrooms, show windows being replaced. The home economics building is visible in the background. (Both, courtesy of Torrance High School Associated Student Body.)

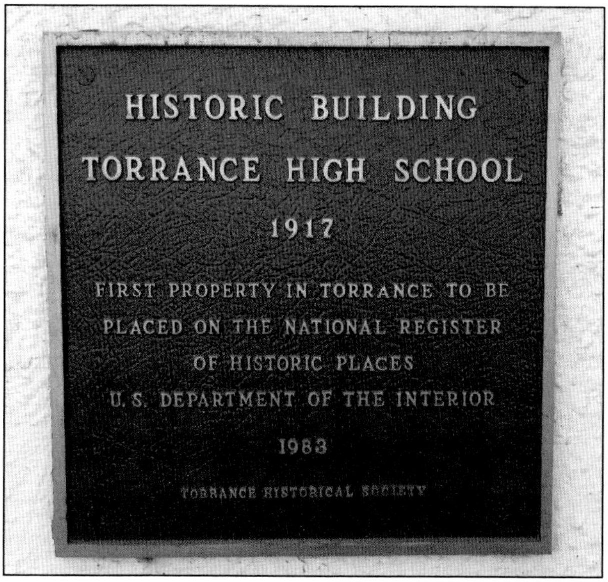

In February 1983, Torrance High graduate Don Fulton led a team in preparing an application for specific buildings at Torrance High School to be listed in the National Register of Historic Places. The buildings included in the documentation are the main building, the home economics building, the auditorium, and the Annex. The plaque is affixed near the doors of the main building. (Courtesy of Torrance High School Associated Student Body.)

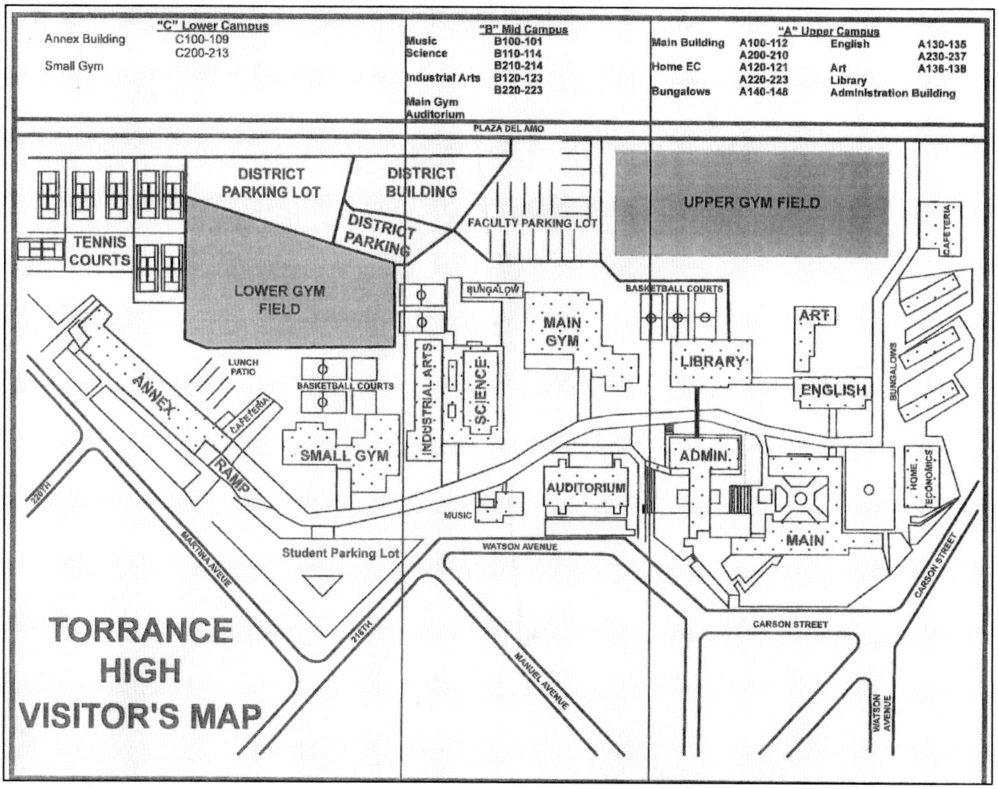

As the population of the city of Torrance grew significantly in the 1950s, other high schools were opened in other parts of the city. Over the next two decades, Torrance High gained several new buildings, including the classroom bungalows (1952), the main cafeteria (1954), new administration offices (1963), science and industrial arts (1965), the music building (1966), a larger library (1970) and the English building (1970). (Courtesy of Torrance High School.)

Two

Let There Be Light

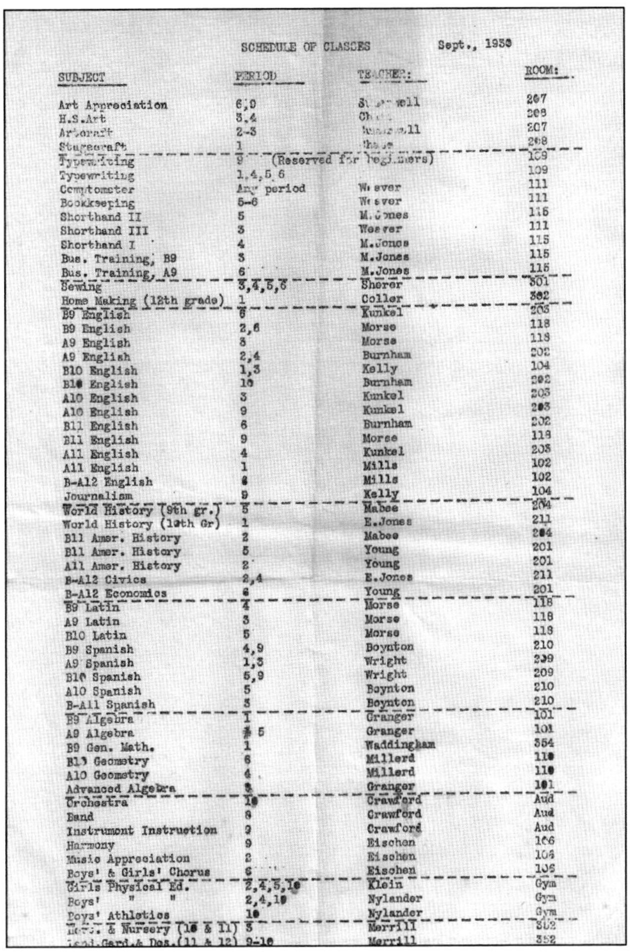

SCHEDULE OF CLASSES Sept., 1930

SUBJECT	PERIOD	TEACHER:	ROOM:
Art Appreciation	6,9	[illegible]well	207
H.S.Art	3,4	[illegible]	208
Artcraft	2-3	[illegible]well	207
Stagecraft	1	[illegible]	208
Typewriting	9 (Reserved for beginners)		109
Typewriting	1,4,5,6		109
Comptometer	Any period	Weaver	111
Bookkeeping	5-6	Weaver	111
Shorthand II	5	M.Jones	115
Shorthand III	3	Weaver	111
Shorthand I	4	M.Jones	115
Bus. Training, B9	3	M.Jones	115
Bus. Training, A9	6	M.Jones	115
Sewing	3,4,5,6	Sherer	301
Home Making (12th grade)	1	Coller	302
B9 English	6	Kunkel	203
B9 English	2,6	Morse	118
A9 English	8	Morse	118
A9 English	2,4	Burnham	202
B10 English	1,3	Kelly	104
B10 English	10	Burnham	202
A10 English	3	Kunkel	203
A10 English	9	Kunkel	203
B11 English	6	Burnham	202
B11 English	9	Morse	118
A11 English	4	Kunkel	203
A11 English	1	Mills	102
B-A12 English	6	Mills	102
Journalism	9	Kelly	104
World History (9th gr.)	5	Mabee	204
World History (10th Gr)	1	E.Jones	211
B11 Amer. History	2	Mabee	204
B11 Amer. History	5	Young	201
A11 Amer. History	2	Young	201
B-A12 Civics	2,4	E.Jones	211
B-A12 Economics	6	Young	201
B9 Latin	4	Morse	118
A9 Latin	3	Morse	118
B10 Latin	5	Morse	118
B9 Spanish	4,9	Boynton	210
A9 Spanish	1,3	Wright	209
B10 Spanish	5,9	Wright	209
A10 Spanish	5	Boynton	210
B-A11 Spanish	3	Boynton	210
B9 Algebra	1	Granger	101
A9 Algebra	3 5	Granger	101
B9 Gen. Math.	1	Waddingham	354
B10 Geometry	6	Millerd	110
A10 Geometry	4	Millerd	110
Advanced Algebra	3	Granger	101
Orchestra	10	Crawford	Aud
Band	8	Crawford	Aud
Instrument Instruction	9	Crawford	Aud
Harmony	9	Eischen	106
Music Appreciation	2	Eischen	106
Boys' & Girls' Chorus	6	Eischen	106
Girls Physical Ed.	2,4,5,10	Klein	Gym
Boys' " "	2,4,10	Nylander	Gym
Boys' Athletics	10	Nylander	Gym
[illegible] & Nursery (10 & 11)	3	Merrill	352
[illegible] Gard.& Des.(11 & 12)	9-10	Merrill	352

In 1930, the master schedule of classes was a single typed sheet of paper. Classes included those typical of the era: English, history, algebra, Latin, and shorthand. By the late-20th century, the master schedule was done through a computer program. While many of the same classes are still taught, new classes continue to be added, such as the Project Lead the Way Engineering program. (Courtesy of Torrance High Alumni Association.)

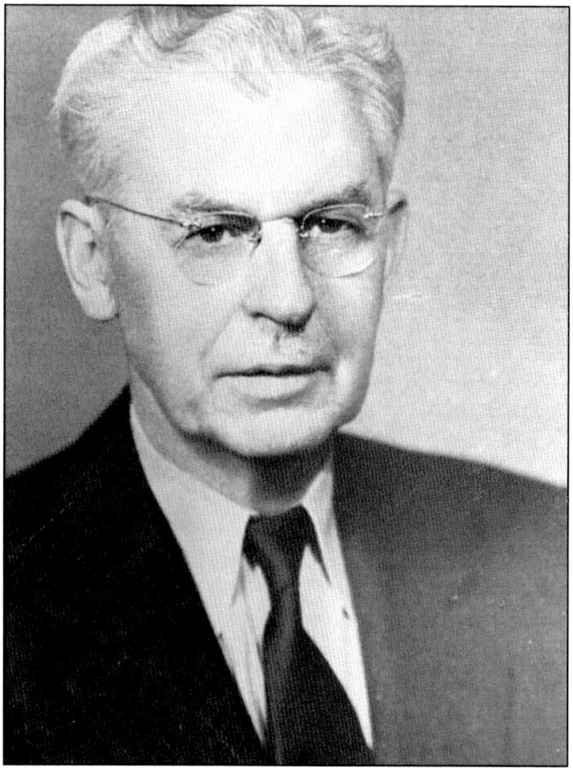

Thomas Elson had been principal of the little school on Cabrillo when he became the principal of Torrance School in 1917. He stayed at Torrance School until 1919, when the elementary classes moved to their own building. Elson returned to Torrance High School in 1935 and was the principal again until his death in 1942. (Courtesy of the Torrance High School Alumni Association.)

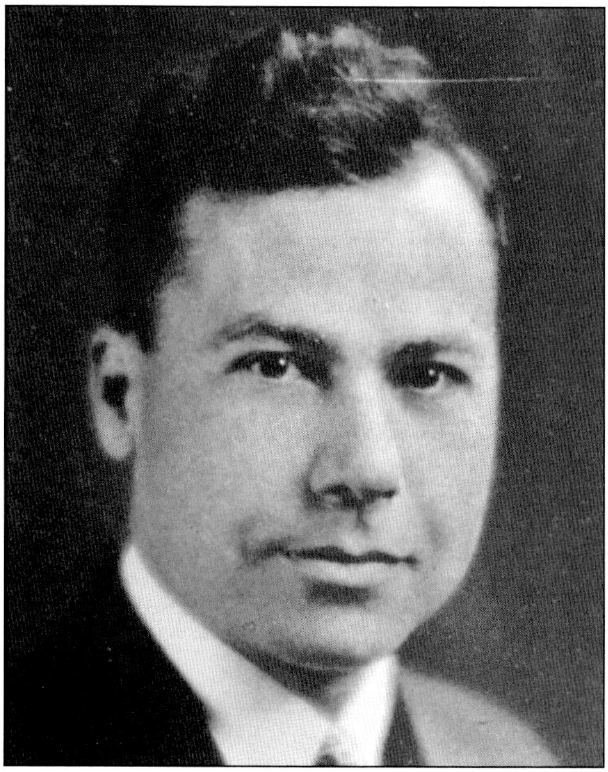

Herbert Sidney Wood began serving as principal of Torrance High School in 1923. Prior to Wood, Thomas Elson had served as the principal of Torrance School. Elson had previously been the principal at the school on Cabrillo Avenue. When the new Torrance Elementary opened in 1923, he assumed the role of principal, and Wood was selected as principal of the secondary school. Wood served as principal until 1932. (Courtesy of the Torrance High Alumni Association.)

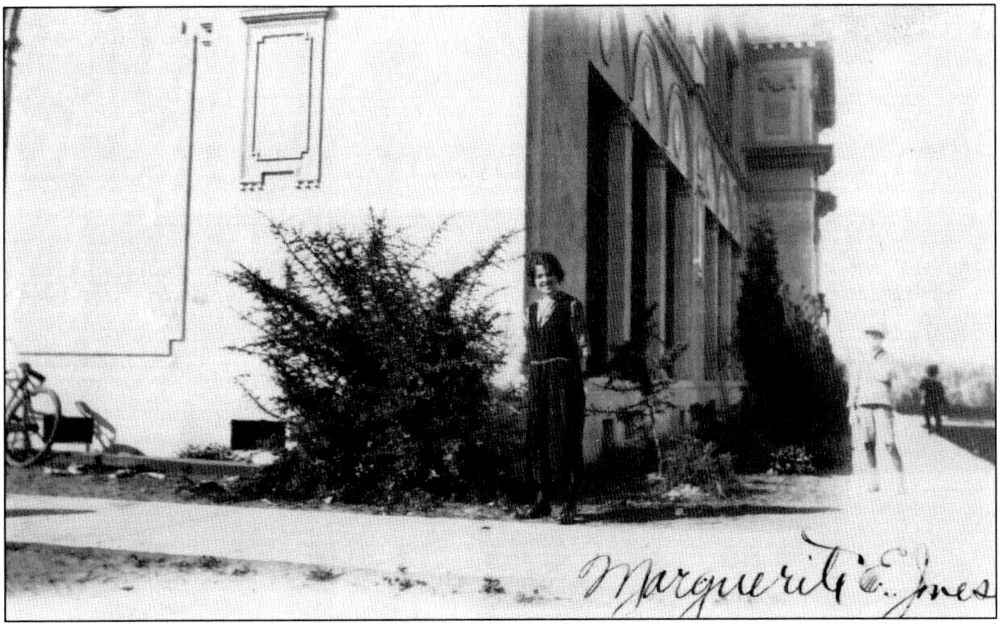

In this image from the early 1920s, Marguerite Jones stands at the corner of the main building, prior to the additional wings being added. Jones taught at Torrance High from the 1920s through 1946. She taught English, history, and commercial, which may have been similar to some form of vocational education. (Courtesy of Torrance Historical Society.)

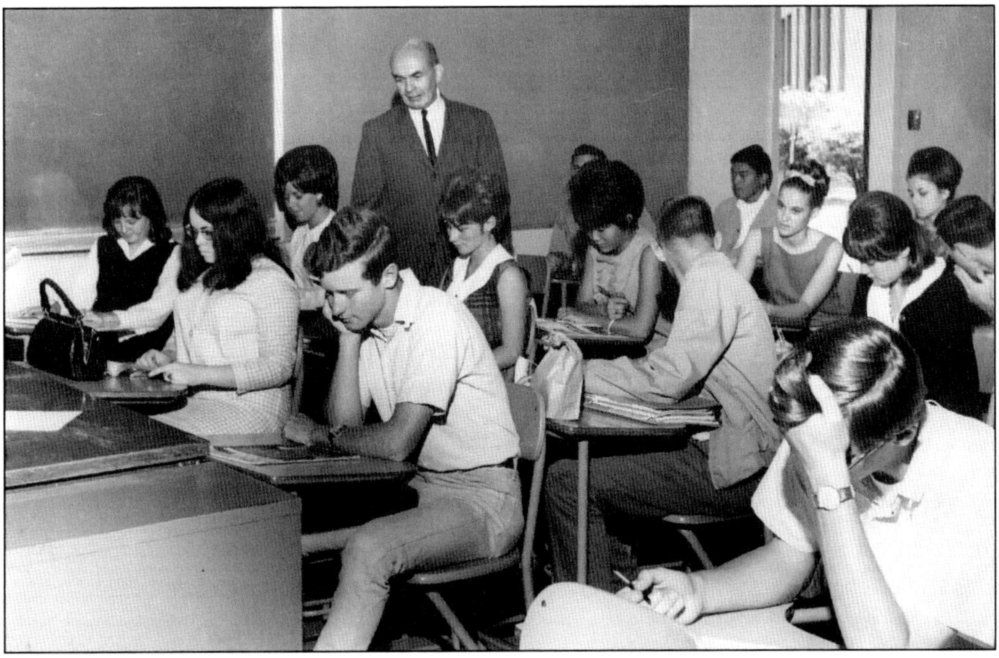

Wes Peterson spent three decades at Torrance High, teaching history. Throughout his years at Torrance High, Peterson witnessed many changes, such as the addition of new buildings on campus and the enforcement of a dress code. New elective courses were added to the history and English programs, including Law and the American Citizen, international relations, and novel and motion picture studies. (Courtesy of Torrance Historical Society)

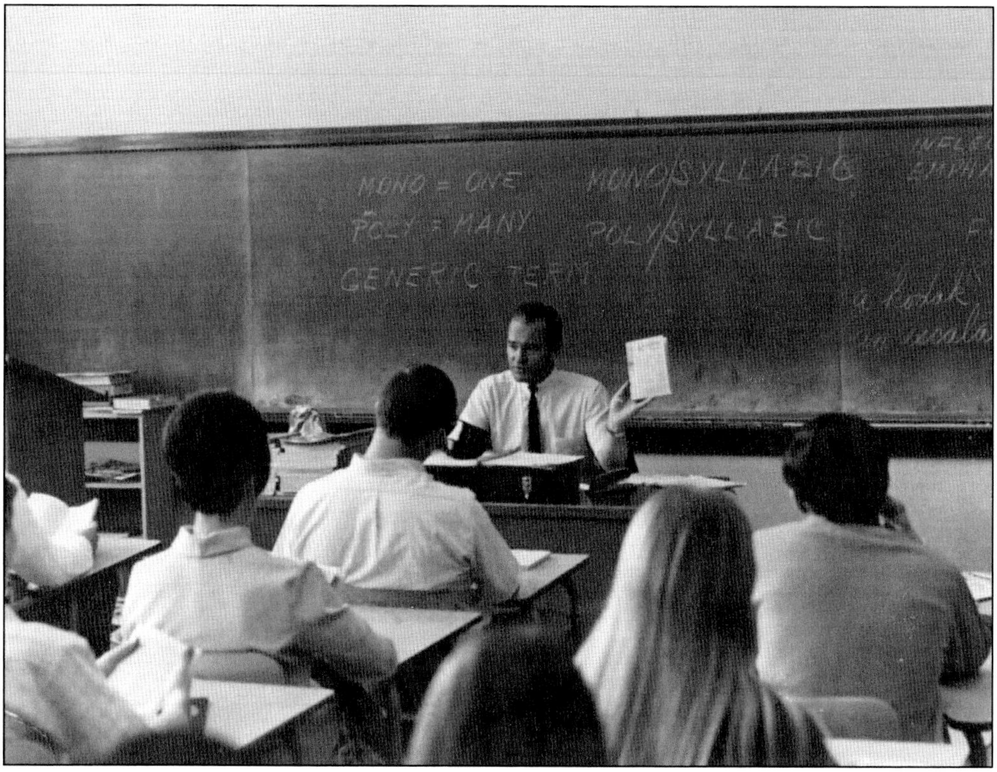

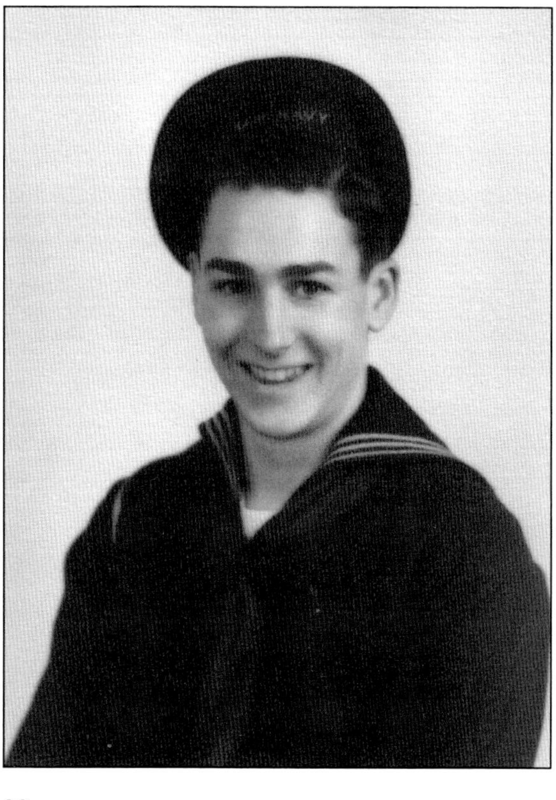

Howard Towle taught English from the mid-1950s until 1990. Like many teachers, Towle also coached athletic teams, including tennis, and worked with the drivers' education program. According to one past student, what made Towle a great teacher was that "he made it fun. He had a great sense of humor, he was able to connect with most every student. He enjoyed what he taught and that made it infectious." (Courtesy of Dottie Towle.)

After serving the United States in the Navy, Jack Knapp moved from the Midwest to Southern California with his wife, Betty. Jack began teaching science at Torrance High in 1958 and remained a teacher at THS through the late 1980s. Students remember him fondly for his sense of humor. (Courtesy of Betty Knapp.)

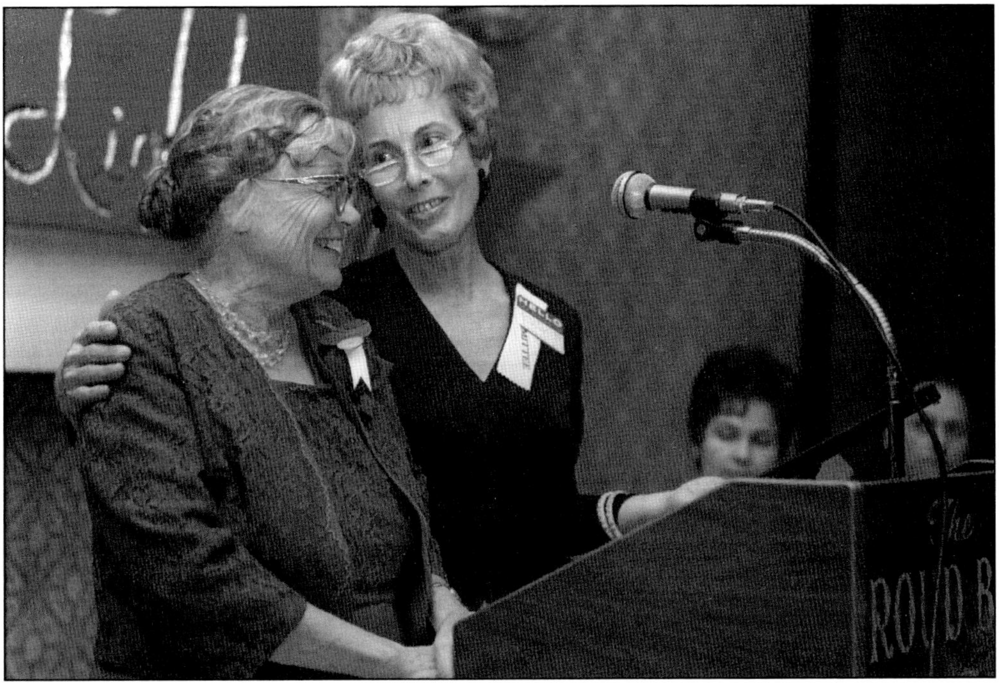

Between 1924 and 1947, Irene Mills touched the lives of thousands of students. She has been described as a "tough cookie" and someone who earned the respect of her students. During World War II, she wrote to Tartars serving overseas, sending them news of home. In 1971, she was recognized for her dedication to her students. Mills is seen here with former student Florence Summers. (Courtesy of the Torrance Historical Society.)

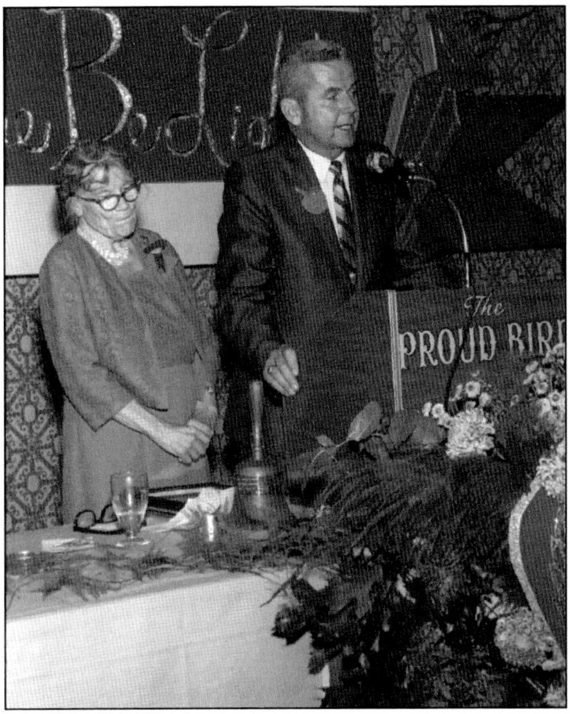

James Armstrong provided real-life experience for his government students. He began teaching at THS in 1958. Armstrong served on the planning commission for the city of Torrance before becoming a city council member. In 1978, Armstrong was elected as the mayor of Torrance. Though he was offered an administration position at the school, Armstrong turned it down, because he wanted to keep teaching. (Courtesy of Torrance Historical Society.)

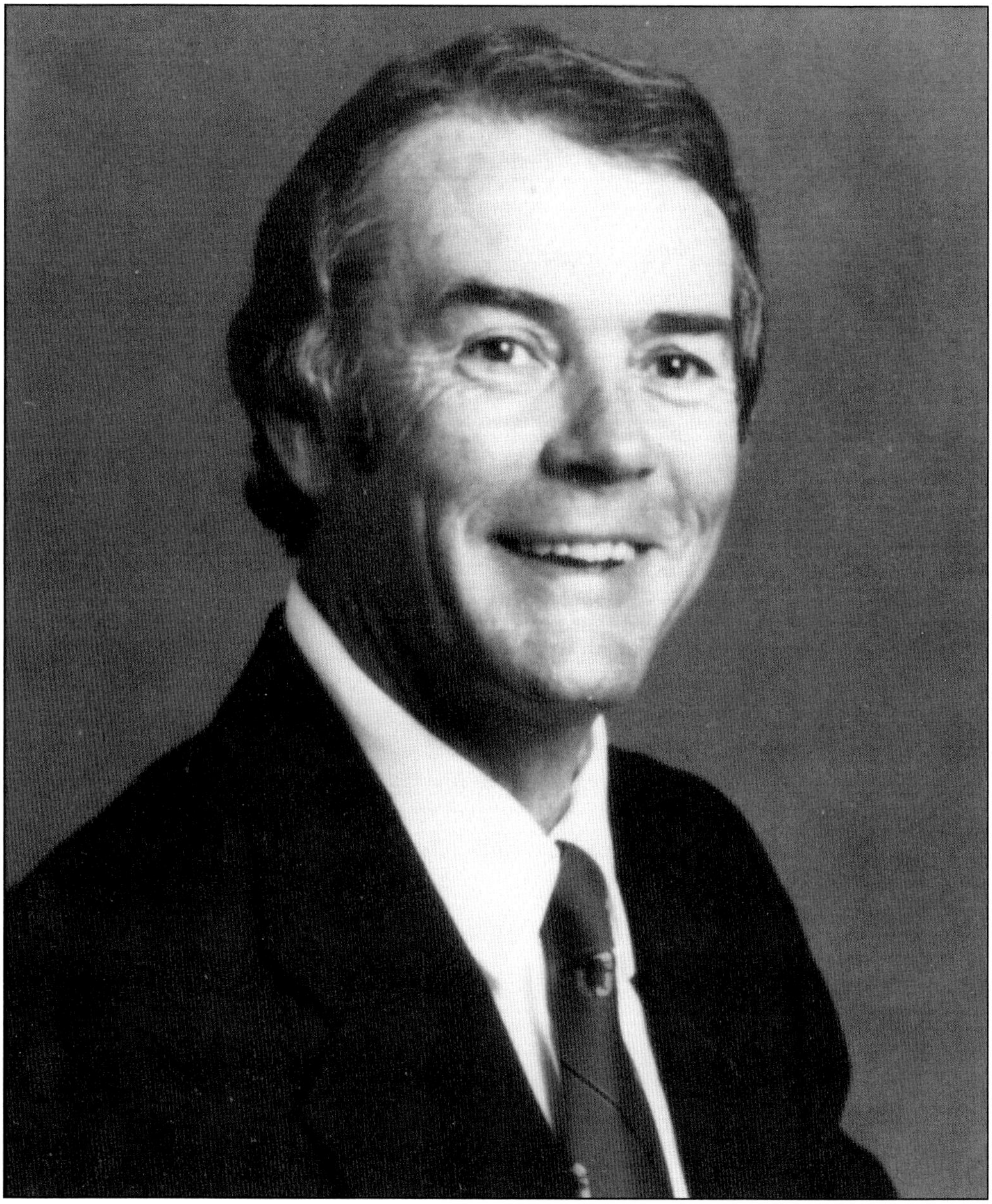

Will Boerger is among the most beloved of Tartars. His teaching career spanned from 1957 to 1992, but he continued to serve as a substitute teacher into the early 2000s. He taught physical education, health and drivers education, coached baseball, golf, and basketball. "Boerger's Bombers," as the basketball team was known, were the California Interscholastic Federation (CIF) runners-up in 1965. Boerger is also known as the Snickers man. He would ask questions on various topics, including historical or current events and students with correct answers received Snickers. After his retirement, Boerger continued to be an active member of the Tartar community, showing up at holiday lunches and other events. In 2012, he was named a Tartar Living Legend. Boerger passed away in 2015, and his memorial service was attended by many former students and faculty members. (Courtesy of Torrance High Alumni Association.)

After serving in the US Navy, Carl Ahee earned multiple degrees, including a doctorate. He worked as an administrator for the armed services and then as an assistant principal at North High School in Torrance. In 1956, Dr. Ahee began a 14-year tenure as principal at Torrance High. From there, he continued to work in the school district until 1978. (Courtesy of Torrance High School Alumni Association.)

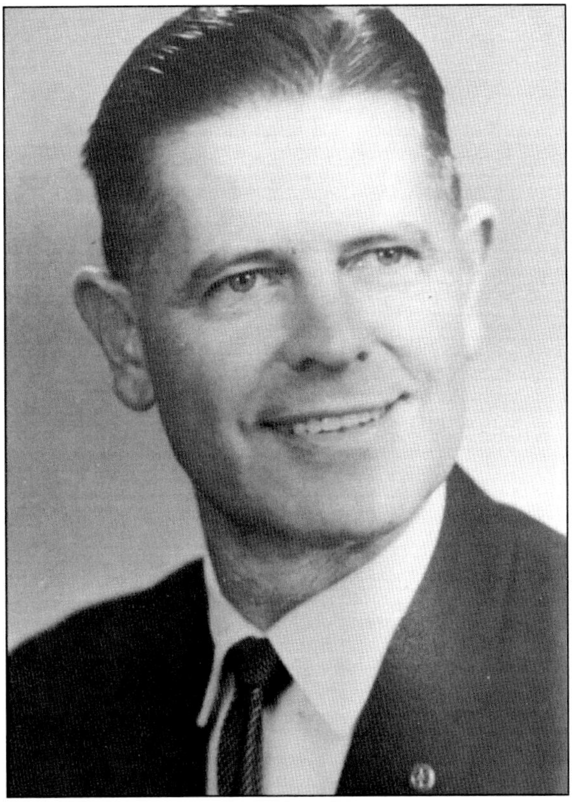

Pat Wright (center) started teaching government in 1966 and continued until her retirement in 2001. She was also a longtime sponsor of Tartar Ladies. She is seen here in this photograph with Bora Song (left) and Tiana Birmingham. Many seniors will recall Wright reminding them to "walk with pride" at baccalaureate. As a "super fan," Wright was at every home football and basketball game. (Courtesy of Tracy Langley Clark.)

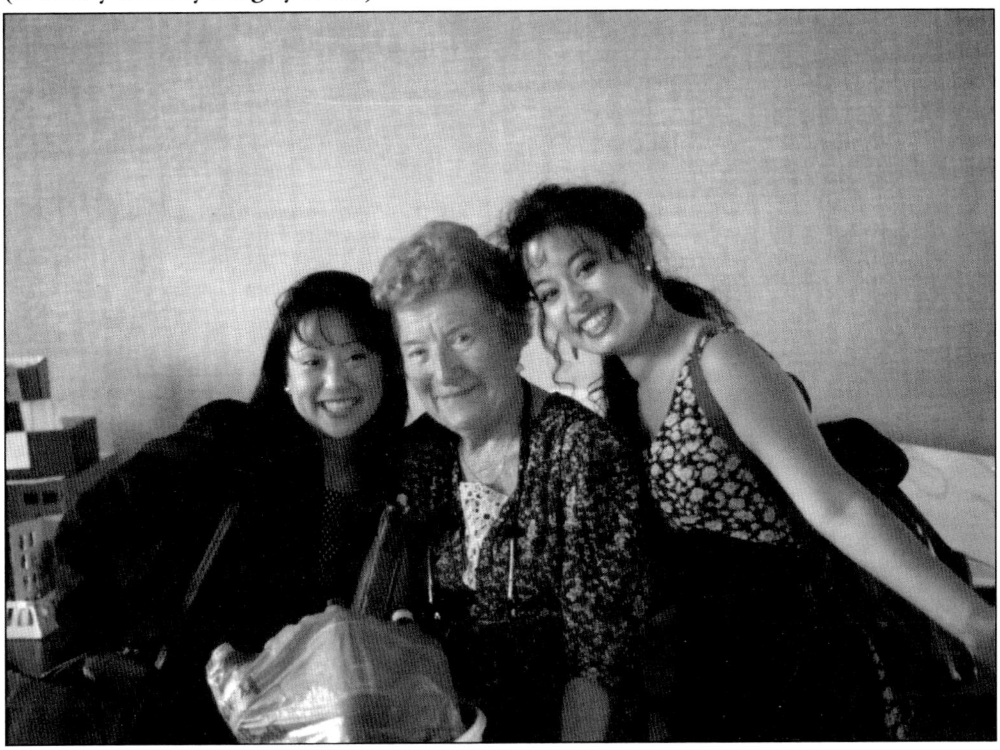

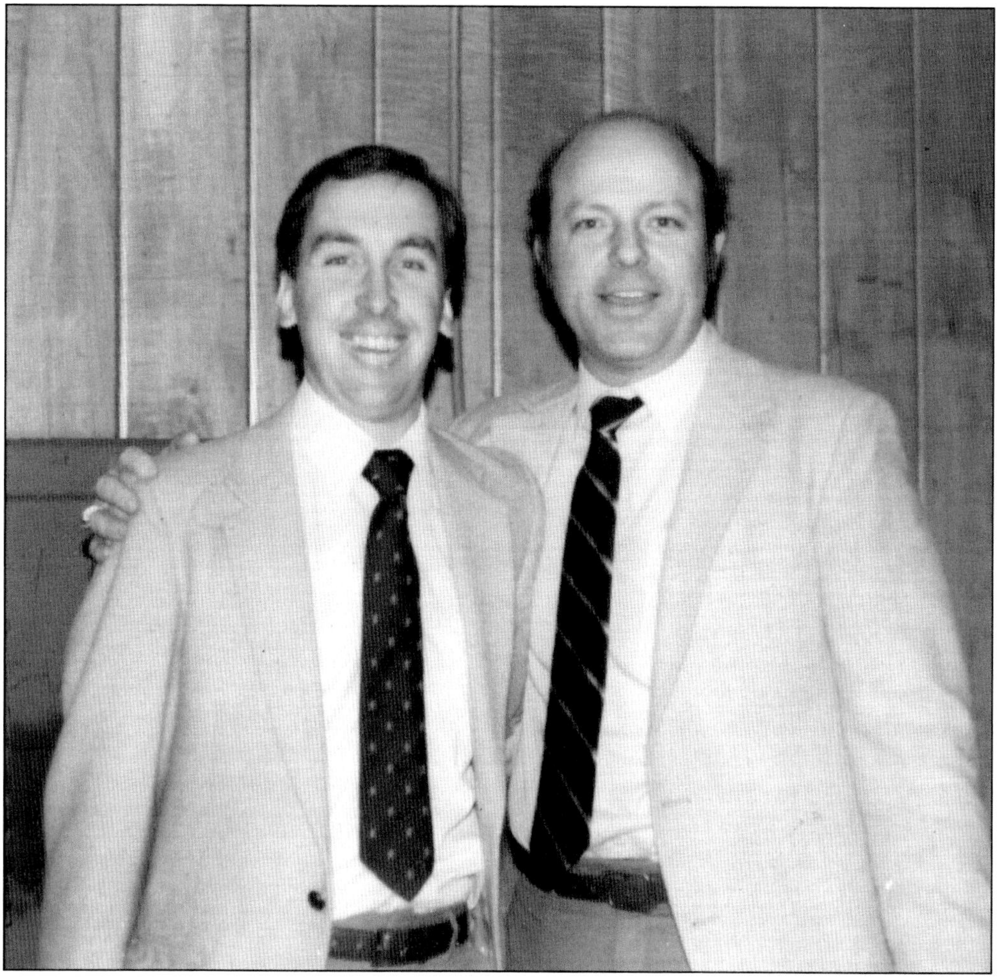

John O'Brien (right) taught history at Torrance. He became the student activities director in 1984 and was promoted to assistant principal in 1985. O'Brien was an administrator at a sister school in Torrance before returning to Torrance High in September 2001 to serve as principal, where he remained until his retirement in 2010. Gary Breese (left) began teaching English in 1975. Over the years, he taught 9th-, 10th-, and 11th-grade English. Breese also served as the yearbook advisor from 1983 until 1993, and he also coached softball. In 1989, he played the iconic role of Daddy Warbucks in the THS production of *Annie*. He retired in 2009. (Courtesy of Torrance High Associated Student Body.)

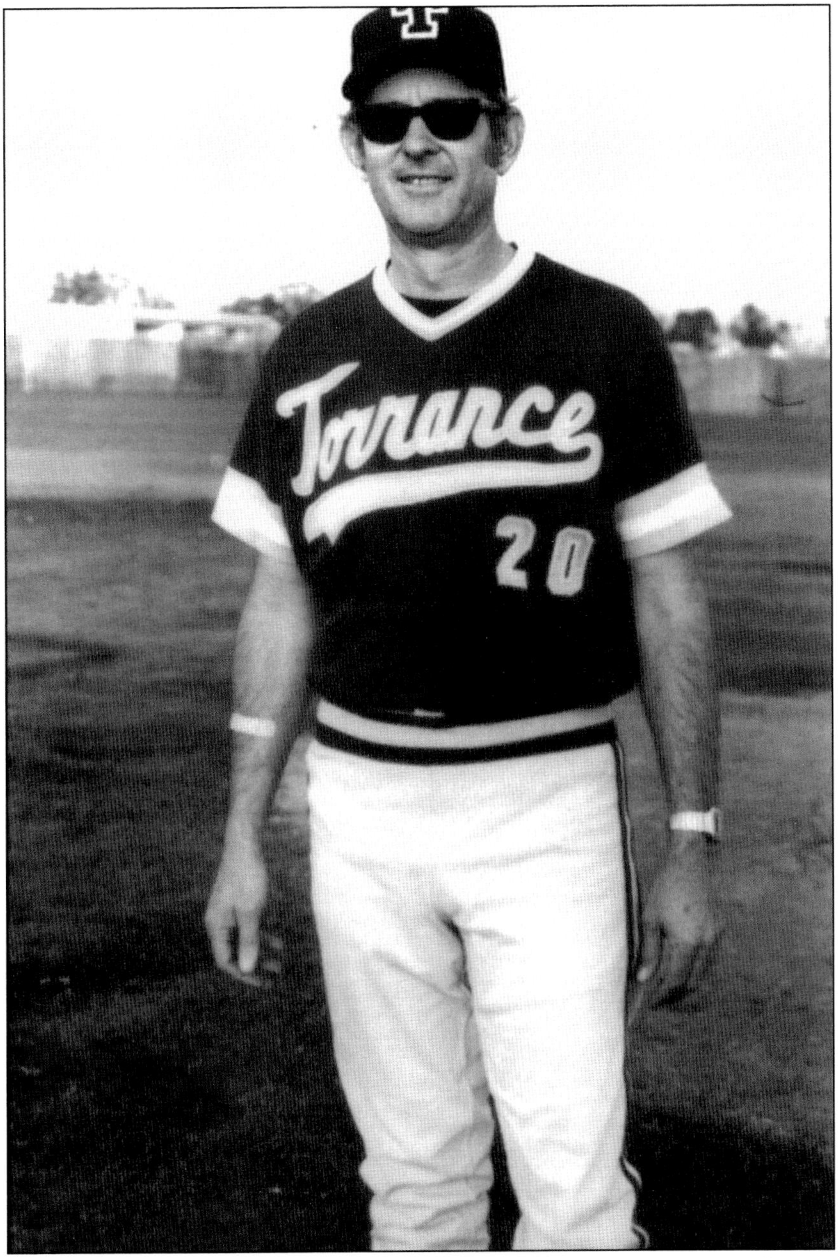

John Radcliffe was a sort of athletics Renaissance man. From the time he joined the faculty in 1969, Radcliffe coached track, baseball, football, tennis, and volleyball. As a teacher, he taught physical education, drivers education, and math. In the late 1980s, Radcliffe assumed the activities director position. At the time, the ASB worked independently from the activities director. However, the principal at the time, Joe Rotcher, asked Radcliffe to combine the ASB leadership class with student activities. One period a day is the leadership class, in which the ASB officers are able to take care of the duties of their office and help plan rallies and other activities. Radcliffe also worked as the official scorekeeper for the Los Angeles Lakers from 1961 through 1999. (Courtesy of Kris Radcliffe.)

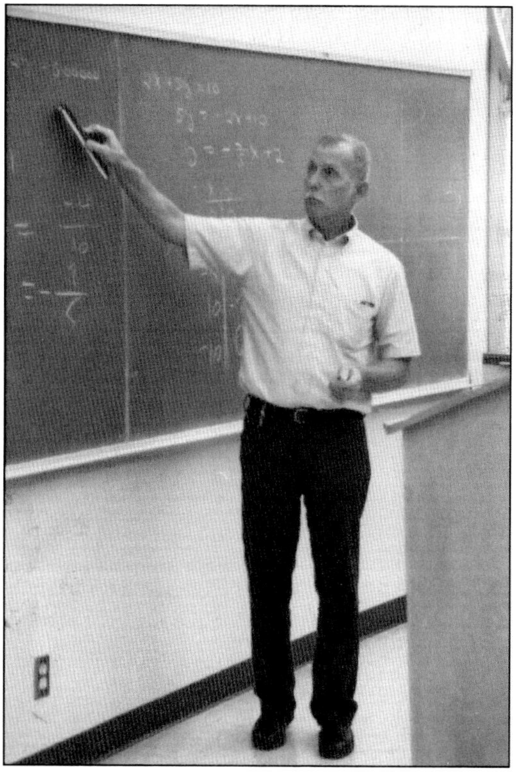

Richard Hulse taught algebra I and II for many years, from 1958 until 1991. He had a strict daily routine, but students learned how to properly solve equations. In this 1991 image, Hulse is carefully instructing students on examples of each type of math problem they would encounter on their homework. (Courtesy of Torrance High Associated Student Body.)

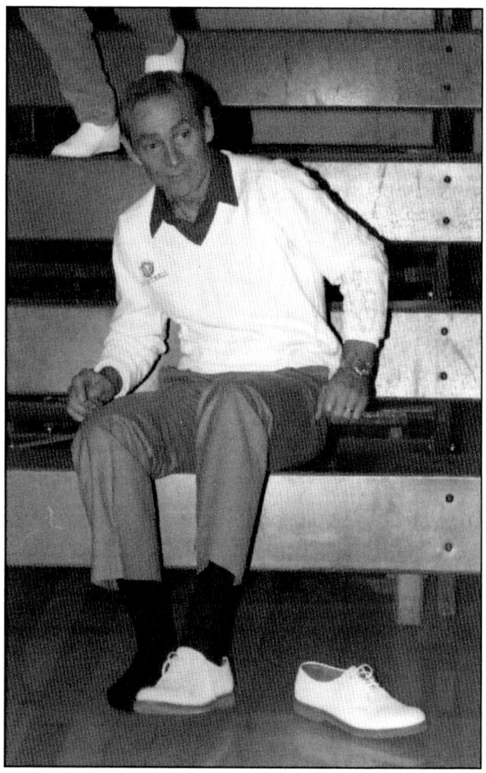

Carl Strong started at Torrance High in 1969, teaching geography. Freshmen were introduced to his infectious spirit at the first pep rally of the year. Known as the "Dean of Spirit," Strong would to take the microphone and run around the gym, stopping in front of each grade level to get that class involved in the rally. (Courtesy of Torrance High Associated Student Body.)

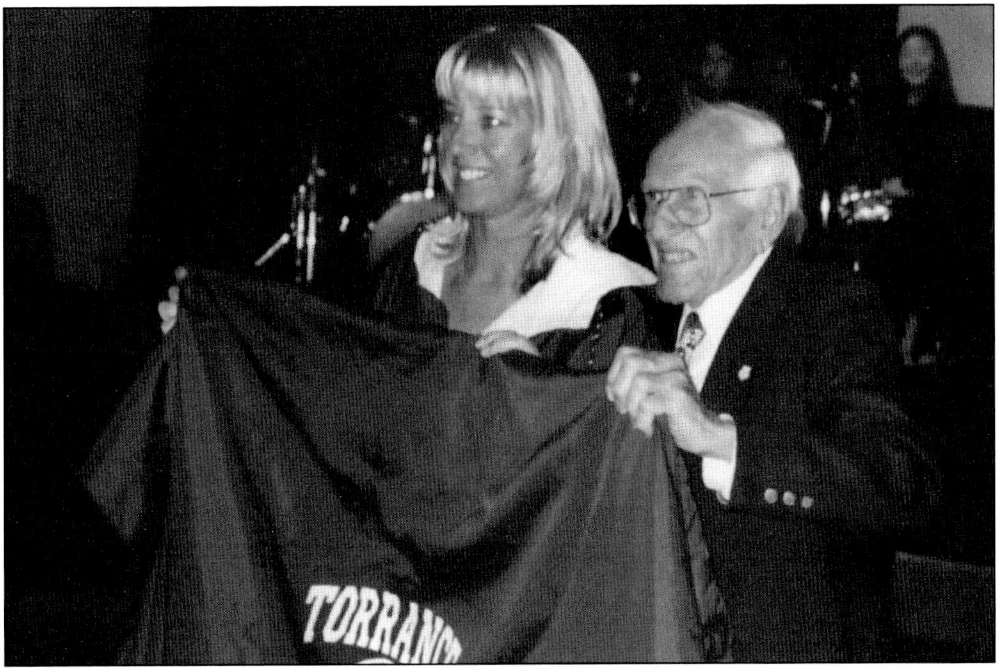

In this image from 2007, Traci Liston Castro (class of 1981) celebrates with Louis Zamperini (class of 1935) at his 90th birthday party, hosted by the alumni association. Castro teaches in the math department and coached the girls' soccer team for several years. (Courtesy of Traci Liston Castro.)

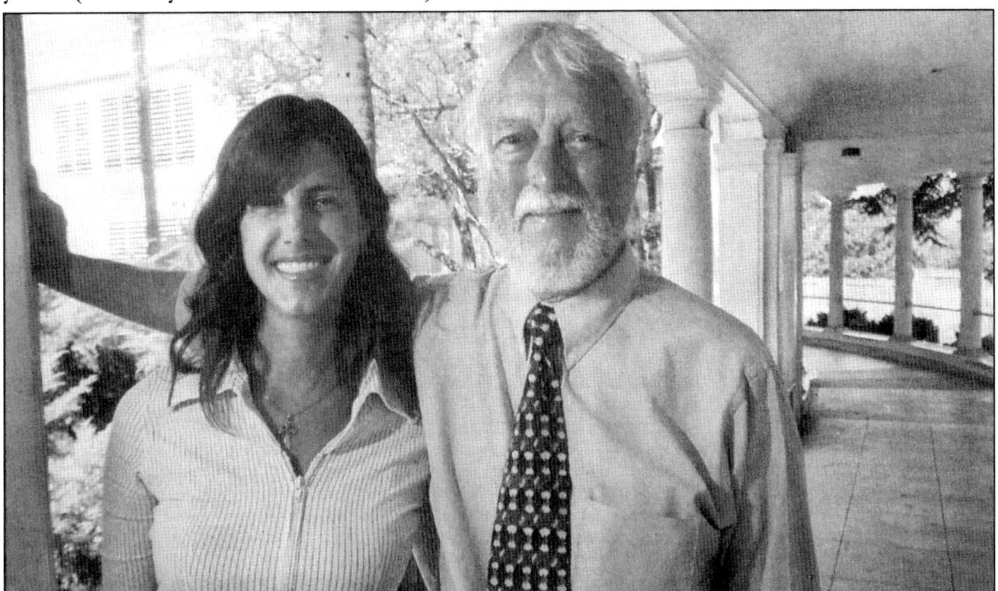

Charles Slater began working at Torrance High in 1962. For many years, he staged impressive productions of some of the most well-known dramas, comedies, and musicals. Upon his retirement, his daughter Casie Slater Duvall assumed the role of theater teacher. She has followed in her father's footsteps, staging such productions such as *Little Shop of Horrors* and *High School Musical.* She also teaches English. (Courtesy of Casie Slater Duvall.)

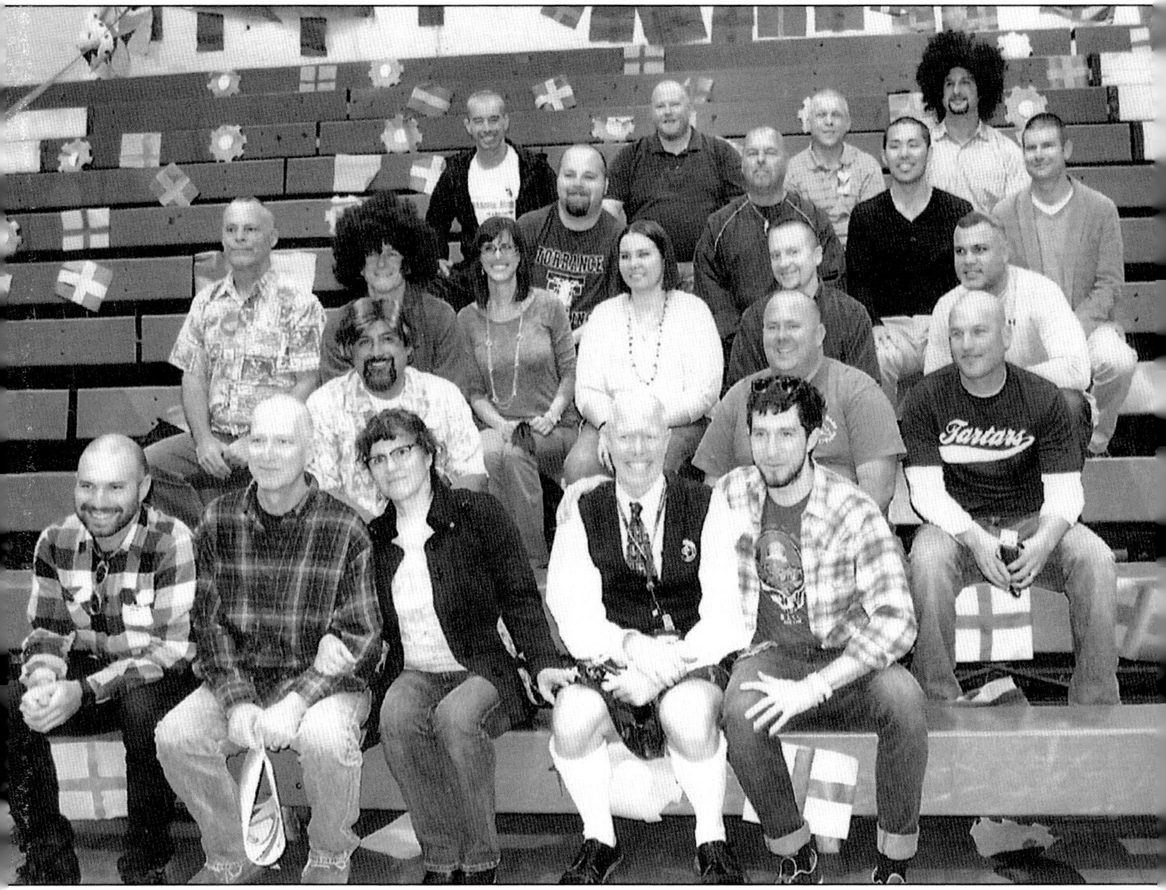

In 2012, history teacher Jeff Jones was diagnosed with cancer. The faculty came together to raise money to help Jones by offering to shave their heads. Students donated money to specific teachers; if teachers raised over $100, they pledged they would let students shave their heads. Students then bid for the opportunity to wield the hair clippers. In total, $5,000 was raised in just over a month. A few female teachers had a few inches cut from their hair. Pictured from left to right are (first row) Michael Villalobos, Jeff Jones, Michelle Villalobos, Charles Griffin, and Perrin Jones; (second row) Don Glavich, Nathan Jones, and Ollie Turner; (third row) Robert Zuliani, Mark Duvall, Casie Duvall, Kristen Spence, David Wright, and Danny Jimenez; (fourth row) Chad Greendale, Roger Hedgepeth, Paul Nitake, and Steve Love; (fifth row) Ben Sagolla, Wes Black, Tom Snider, and Karim Girgis. (Courtesy of Don Glavich.)

The Tartar faculty is supportive of one another in many ways. As part of the head-shaving fundraiser, Mark Duvall of the English department takes a turn with the clippers on Paul Nitake's hair, who teaches in the science department and is the head basketball coach. (Courtesy of Torrance High Associated Student Body.)

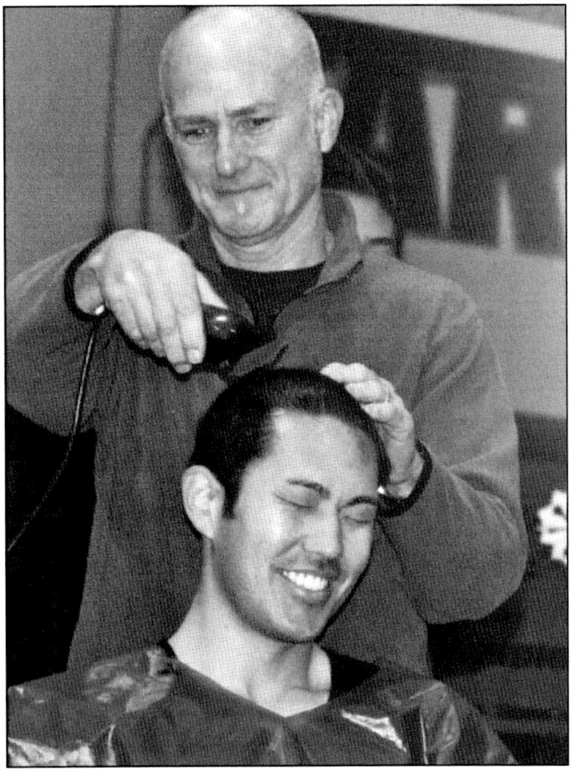

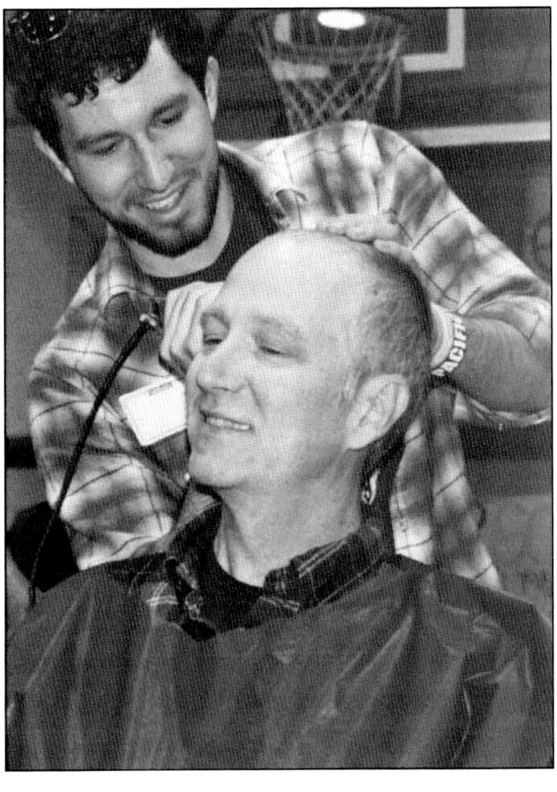

On the day of the head shaving in honor of Jeff Jones, an all-school rally was held. When Jones entered, the students erupted into loud cheers and applause. Jones took the microphone to speak, and the gym went silent. In this image, his son Perrin does the honor of shaving his dad's head. Sadly, Jeff succumbed to his illness in March 2014. (Courtesy of Torrance High Associated Student Body.)

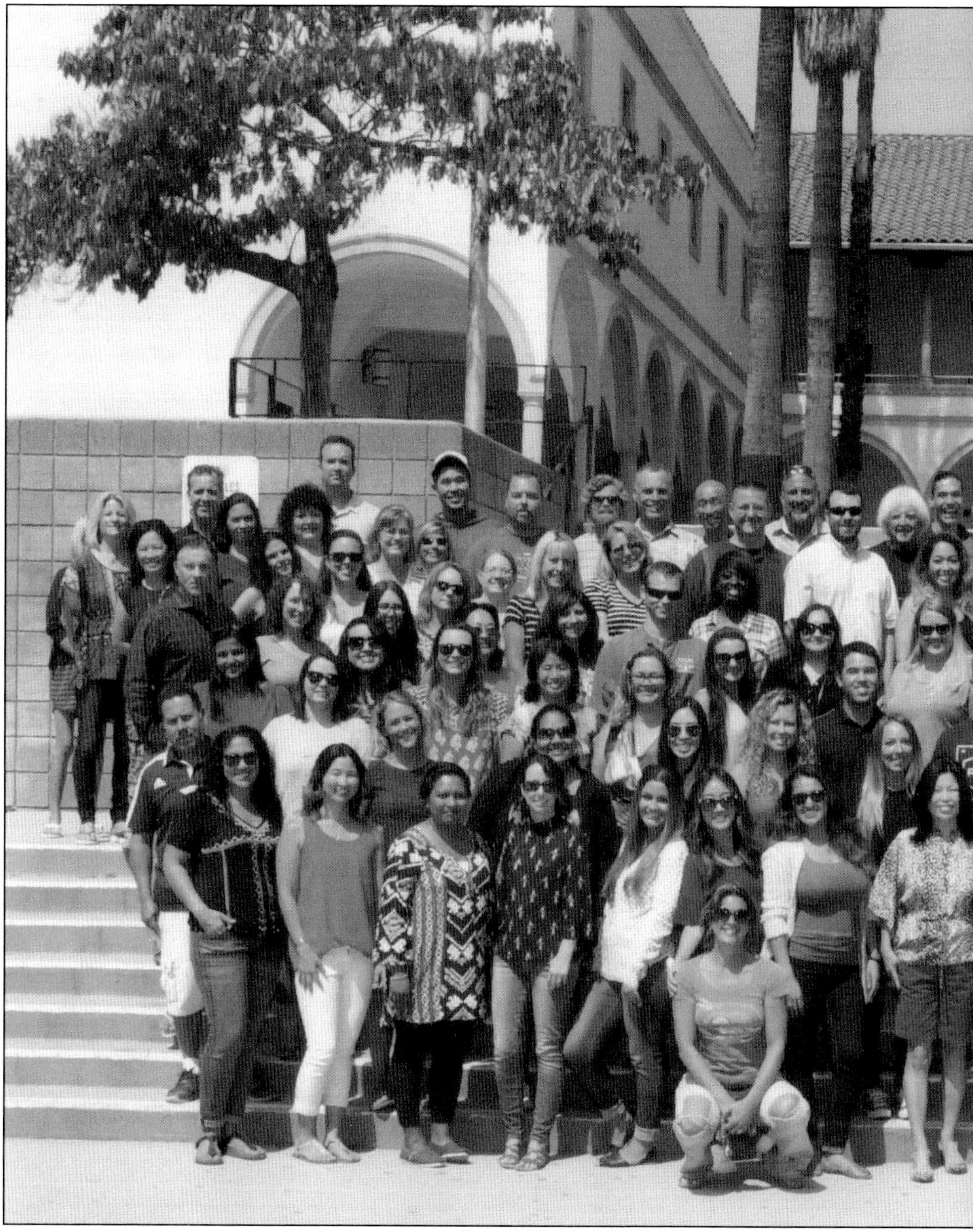

In 1917, when Torrance School first opened, there were only 19 students in the high school classes. According to Dr. Thomas Rische's book *The History of Torrance Schools, 1890–2000*, there were only three high school teachers at Torrance School. Principal Thomas Elson "taught mathematics, German, and science." Additionally, W.M. Ward taught commercial, Spanish, history, and English; and Mary E. Ward, sewing. More teachers had

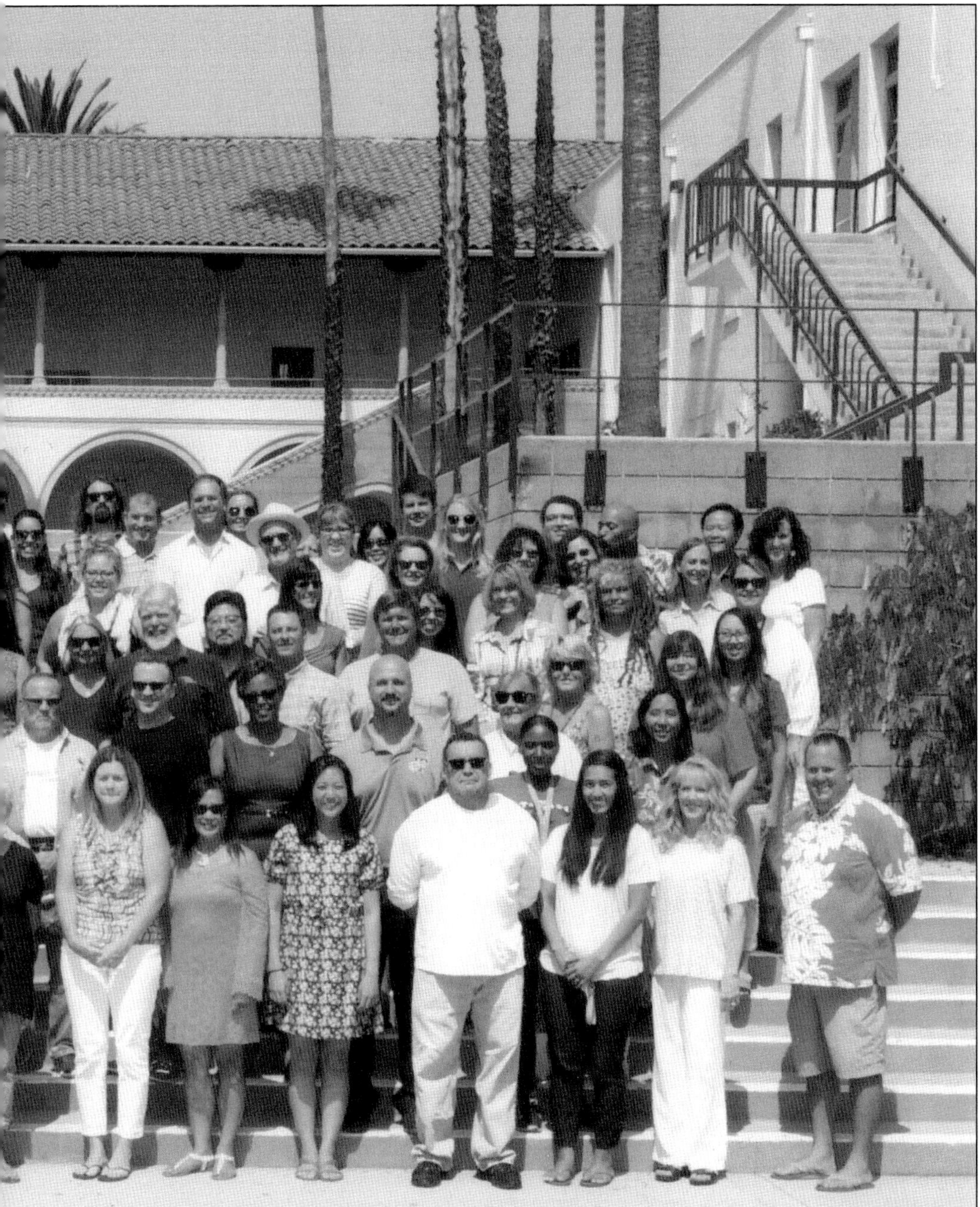

been added by 1918, and in 1927, the faculty totaled 28. In 2016, the faculty, including clerical, certificated, custodial, and administration, numbered well over 100. There are nine departments represented in curricular areas: English, mathematics, science, social science, fine arts, physical education, world languages, special education, and career development. (Courtesy of LifeTouch.)

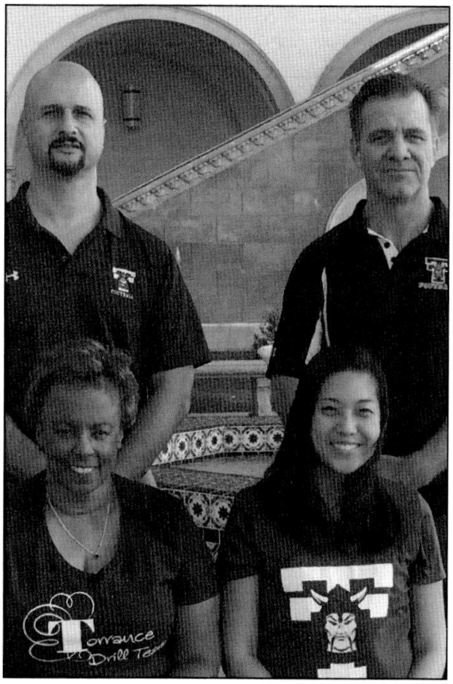

The Torrance High administration team has changed significantly over the years. As the student population went through stages of increasing or decreasing numbers, assistant principal positions were altered. Schools went from having three assistant principals to having only two. In 2016, each of the four high schools in Torrance gained an additional assistant principal. The administration team works closely with various faculty groups to ensure the priority remains student learning. The administrative council consists of the counselors, student activities director, athletic director, site supervisors, dean of students, and the administration. In addition to working closely with department chairs, the administration also works with the faculty leadership team. This image shows the 2016–2017 administration of Torrance High School. From left to right are (first row) assistant principals Cheryl Daugherty and Jeannie Kim; (second row) principal Karim Girgis and assistant principal Eric Spotts. (Courtesy of Lori Spradlin.)

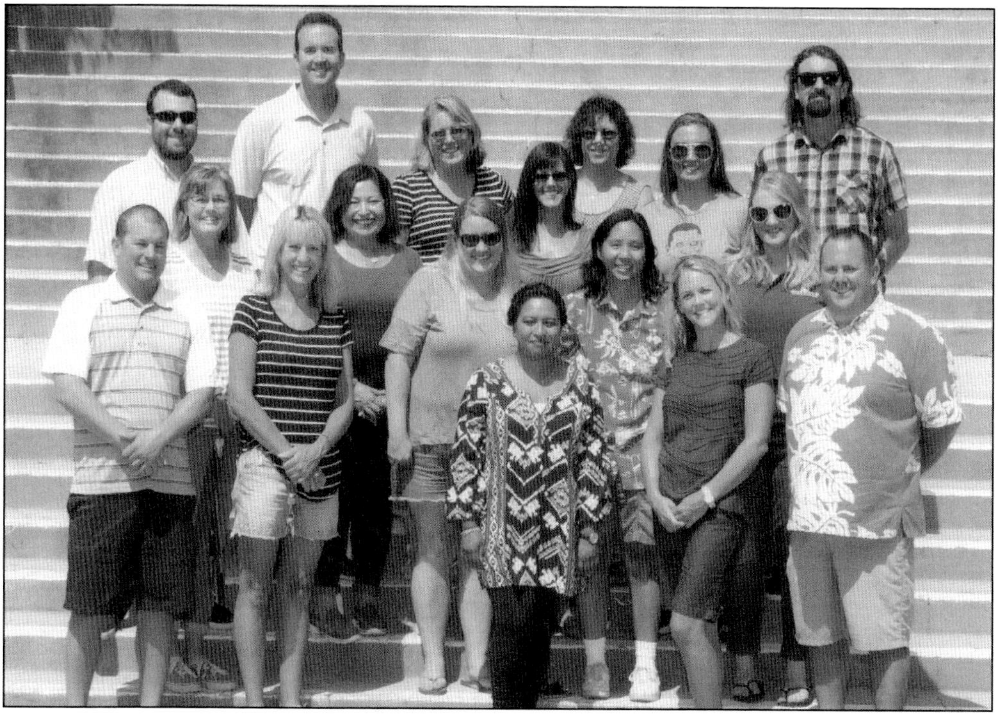

Many Tartars come back to teach at their alma mater. The first known graduate who took a teaching position at Torrance High was Pete Zamperini, brother of Louis. Over the years, many others have returned. From walk-on coaches to clerical staff to classroom teachers, as of 2016, there are just over 20 graduates who work in some capacity on the campus of Torrance High. (Courtesy of LifeTouch.)

Three

Sealed by Friendship's Ties

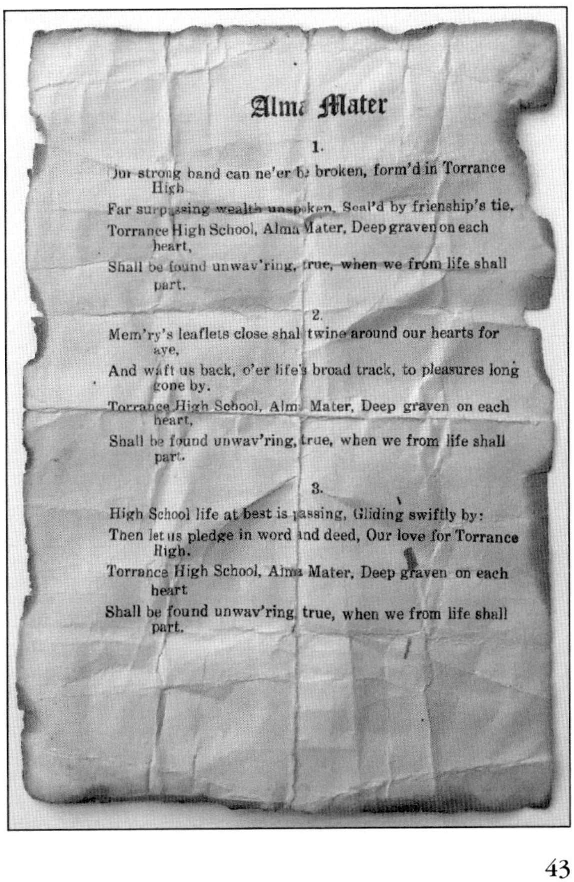

Alma Mater

1.

Our strong band can ne'er be broken, form'd in Torrance High
Far surpassing wealth unspoken, Seal'd by friendship's tie.
Torrance High School, Alma Mater, Deep graven on each heart,
Shall be found unwav'ring, true, when we from life shall part.

2.

Mem'ry's leaflets close shall twine around our hearts for aye,
And waft us back, o'er life's broad track, to pleasures long gone by.
Torrance High School, Alma Mater, Deep graven on each heart,
Shall be found unwav'ring, true, when we from life shall part.

3.

High School life at best is passing, Gliding swiftly by:
Then let us pledge in word and deed, Our love for Torrance High.
Torrance High School, Alma Mater, Deep graven on each heart
Shall be found unwav'ring, true, when we from life shall part.

The alma mater of Torrance High helps define the bond that is forged by Tartars. Only the first stanza is sung at pep rallies and athletic contests. Though there may be friendly rivalries between classes, especially at class competition rallies, when the student body joins together to perform the alma mater, those rivalries no longer exist. (Courtesy of the Torrance High School Alumni Association.)

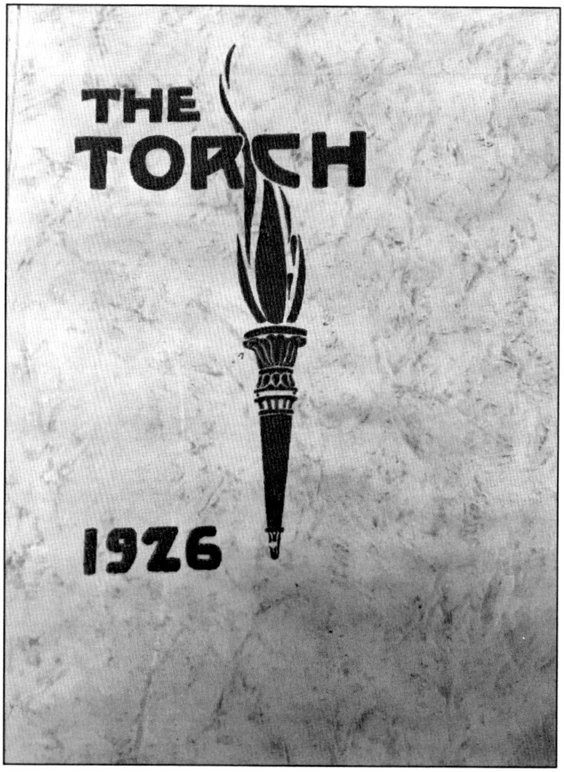

In 1926, Torrance High published its first yearbook. Called *The Torch*, the annual has been published every year since then. During the years of World War II, the yearbooks were significantly smaller. Covers were simply paper, and there were fewer pages. Much of this was a means to save money, as the print shop on campus published the book. While the first several editions did not indicate a theme on the outside cover, the cover page on the inside usually did. In the image to the left, the cover of the 1926 yearbook is shown. The cover was gray with maroon writing. The title was chosen perhaps because one of the school's mottos is "Let there be light." The second image shows the cover page of that yearbook—an ink drawing giving readers an indication of a nautical theme. (Both, courtesy of Torrance Historical Society.)

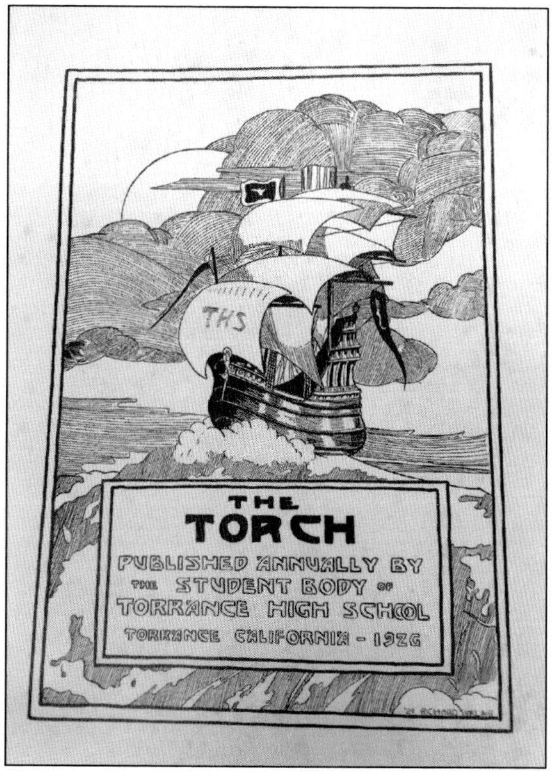

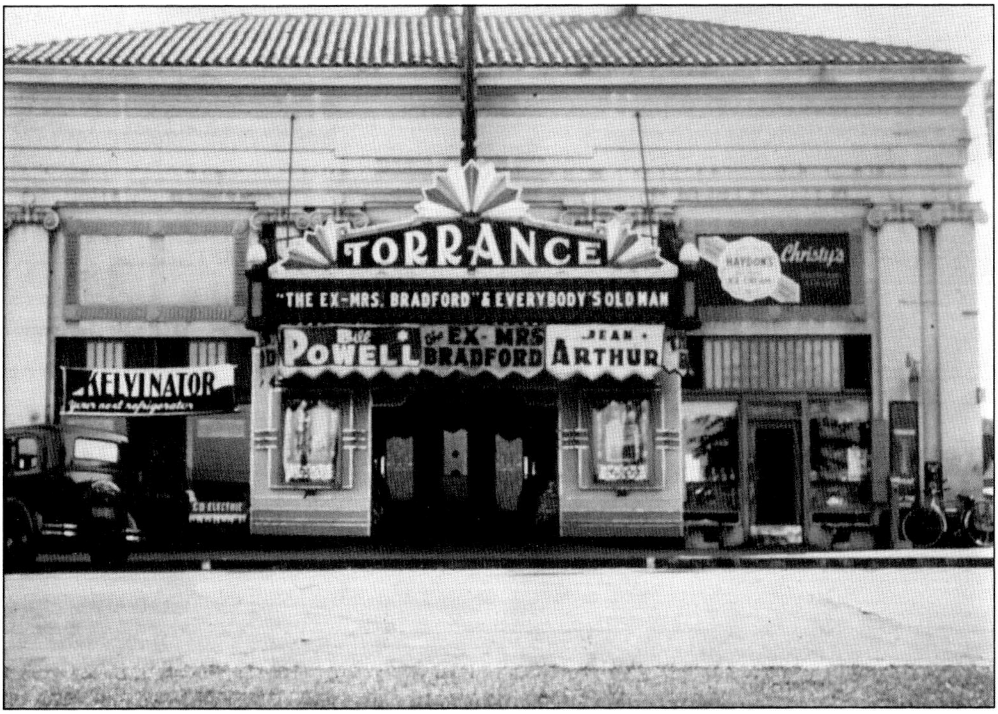

Until the Del Amo Mall opened, most Torrance High students spent some of their free time in the downtown part of Torrance. The Torrance Theater on Sartori Avenue was a popular place to find Tartars hanging out well into the 1950s, until it closed. Next to the theater was Christy's, a sandwich and ice-cream shop, another favorite spot for Torrance High students. (Courtesy of the Torrance Historical Society.)

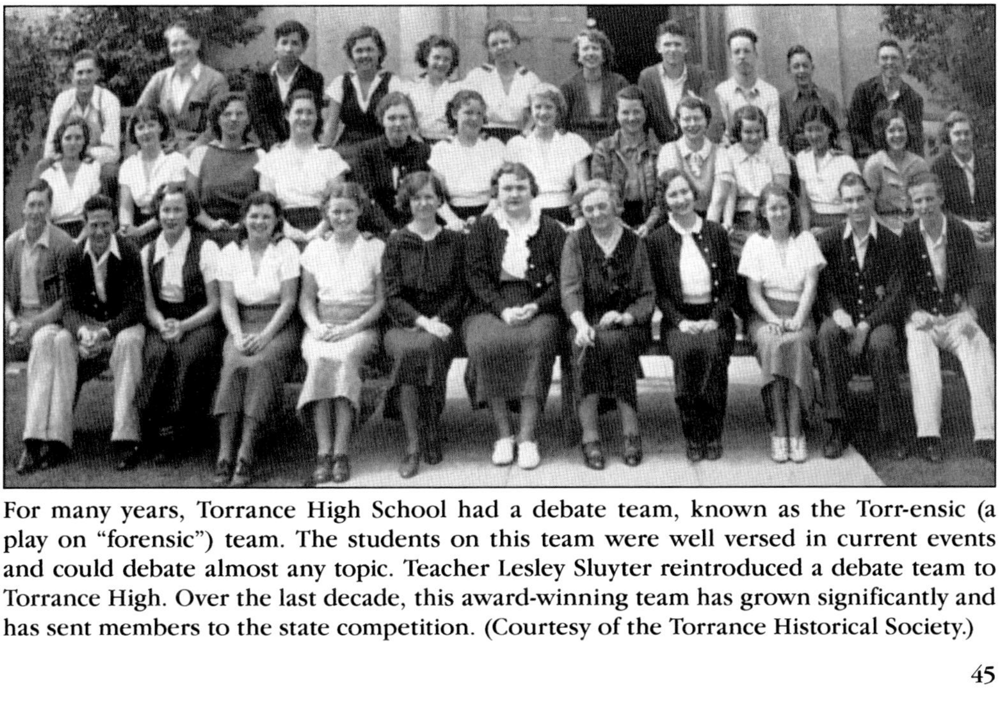

For many years, Torrance High School had a debate team, known as the Torr-ensic (a play on "forensic") team. The students on this team were well versed in current events and could debate almost any topic. Teacher Lesley Sluyter reintroduced a debate team to Torrance High. Over the last decade, this award-winning team has grown significantly and has sent members to the state competition. (Courtesy of the Torrance Historical Society.)

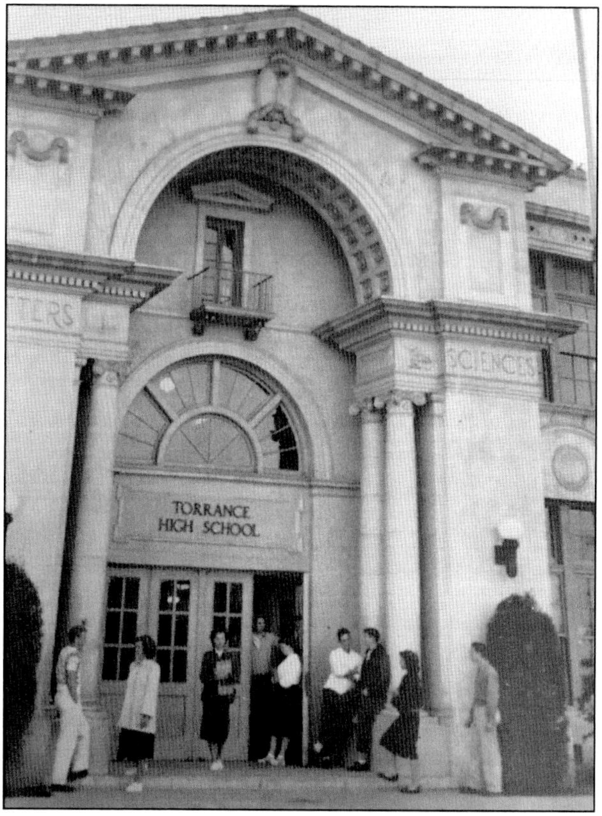

This 1950s photograph shows several students in front of the main building. The columns on either side of the door are merely for decorative purpose and serve no supportive function. Torrance High now has a closed campus, so students are unable to take advantage of the beauty of the exterior main building between classes. (Courtesy of the Torrance Historical Society.)

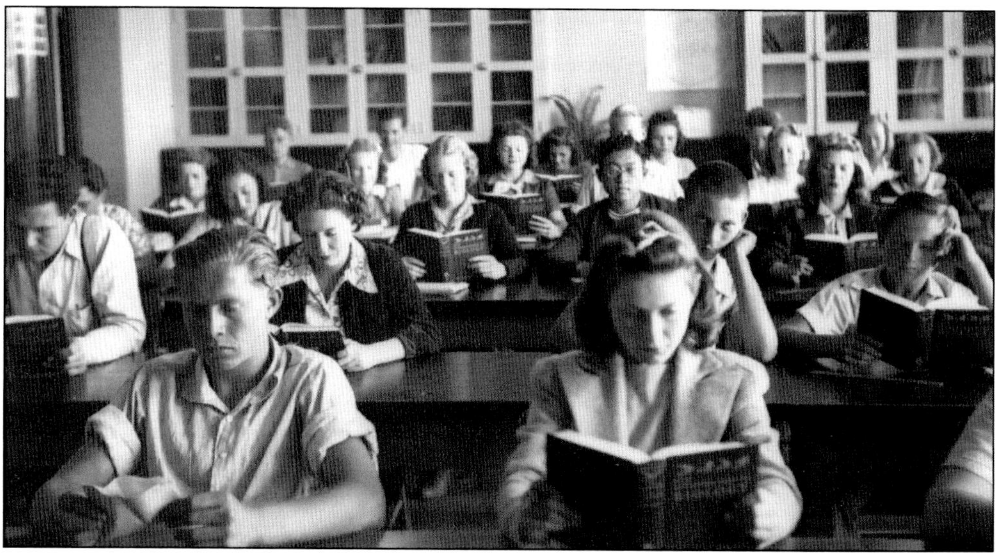

Curriculum has changed dramatically since the opening of the school. While students still learn core curriculum, like these sophomore biology students, there are many more options. Torrance High has kept up with societal and global changes as to what is important to teach our children. Advanced Placement courses allow students to challenge themselves with college-level courses while still in high school. (Courtesy of Torrance Historical Society.)

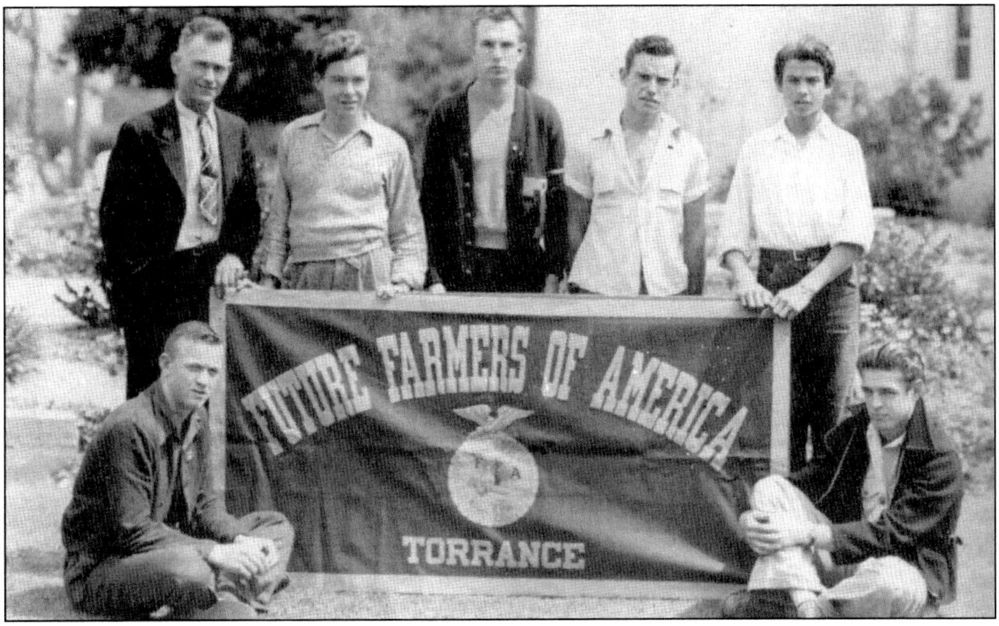

Clubs have long been a source of friendship and camaraderie for students. One of the most important student organizations of the 1930s and 1940s was the Future Farmers of America. These unidentified students in 1942 grew fruits and vegetables on campus, raised pigs and chickens, and won numerous awards in local competitions. Much of the land they used is near where the classroom bungalows currently sit, near the home economics building. (Courtesy of Torrance Alumni Association.)

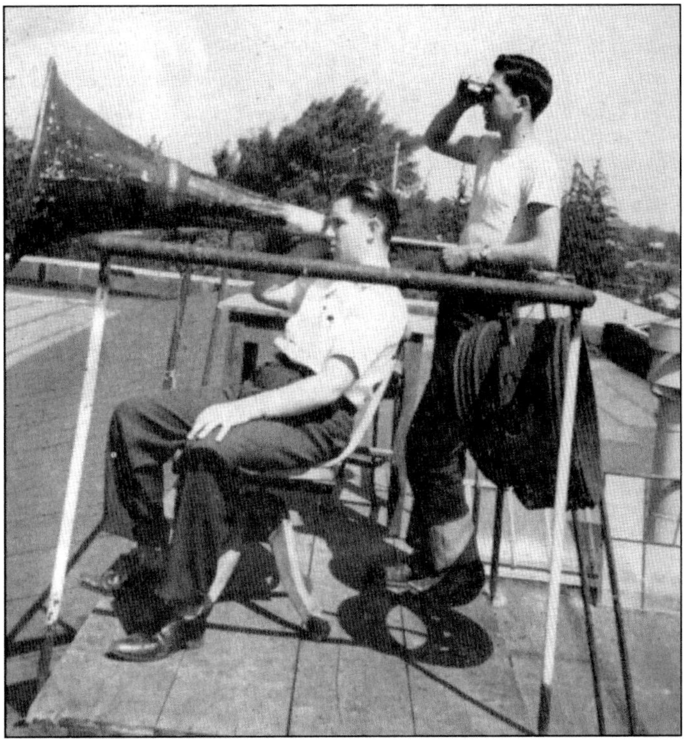

The day after the United States declared war in 1941, the Air Wardens were commissioned. Pictured here are Ed McCall and Elmer Vandergrift, whose function was to "observe airplanes and listen for any warning or message." Within three months of the Air Wardens being formed, many of the Japanese students at Torrance High were no longer enrolled, due to Executive Order 9066. (Courtesy of Torrance Alumni Association.)

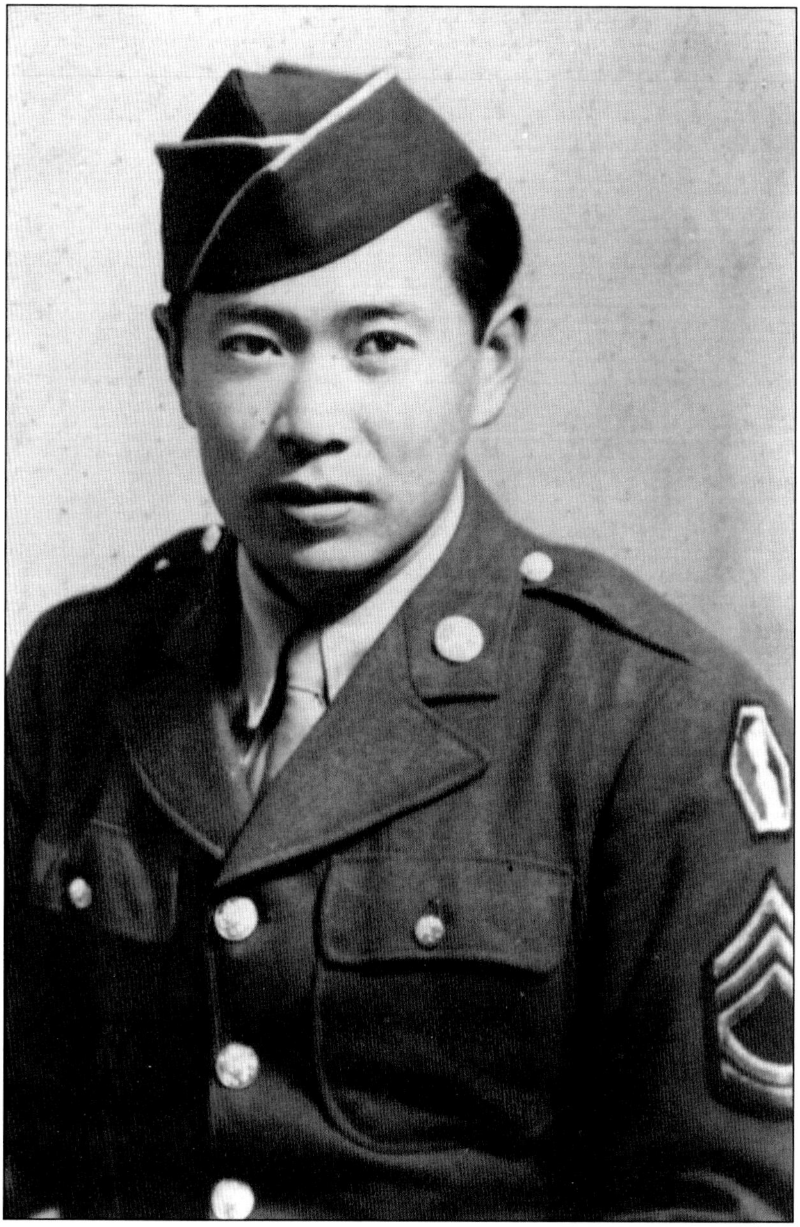

When the United States joined World War II in 1941, many Americans joined the military. When President Roosevelt issued Executive Order 9066, calling for the internment of all Japanese, Ted Tanouye's family was relocated to Arkansas. Tanouye, who graduated from Torrance High School in 1938, was a soldier in the 442nd Regimental Combat Team, US Army. His unit was sent to Italy. In July 1944, he was moving ahead of his unit, facing intense enemy fire but determined to secure a defensive position. Tanouye was severely wounded but continued to fight and refused to evacuate. Two months later, Tanouye returned to the front lines. He was once again wounded, this time fatally, and died of his wounds on September 6, 1944. He was posthumously awarded the Congressional Medal of Honor, which was presented to his surviving family in 2000. (Courtesy of Torrance Historical Society.)

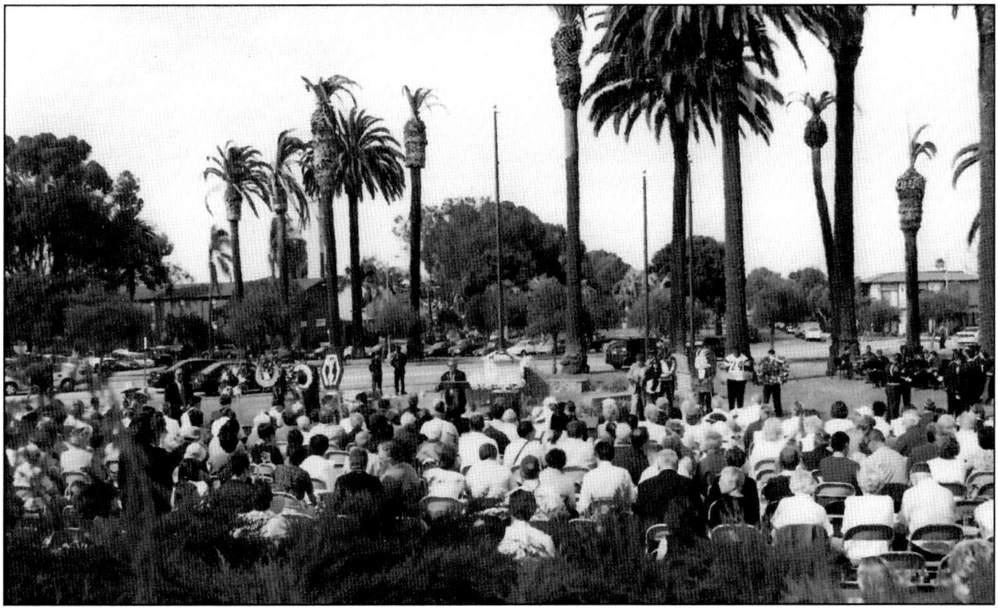

On July 7, 2004, the Ted Tanouye Memorial was dedicated in his honor. The Alumni Association led the efforts to have a memorial to honor the war hero and Congressional Medal of Honor recipient. The memorial sits across from the main building on what is known as the Triangle. (Courtesy of Torrance High School Alumni Association.)

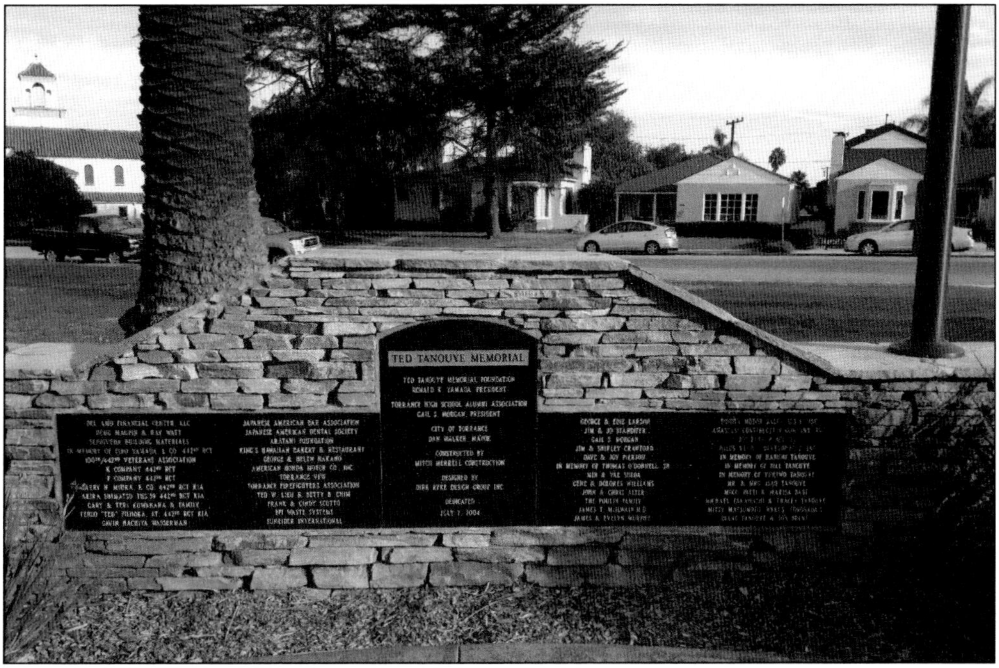

The Ted Tanouye Memorial was designed by Dirk Ryke Design Group, Inc. and constructed by Mitch Merrell Construction. Several low brick structures, like the one seen in this photograph, surround a small patio. The pieces of the memorial share Tanouye's story and feature a replica of the commendation given by Pres. Bill Clinton upon Tanouye being declared a Congressional Medal winner. (Courtesy of Jay Spradlin.)

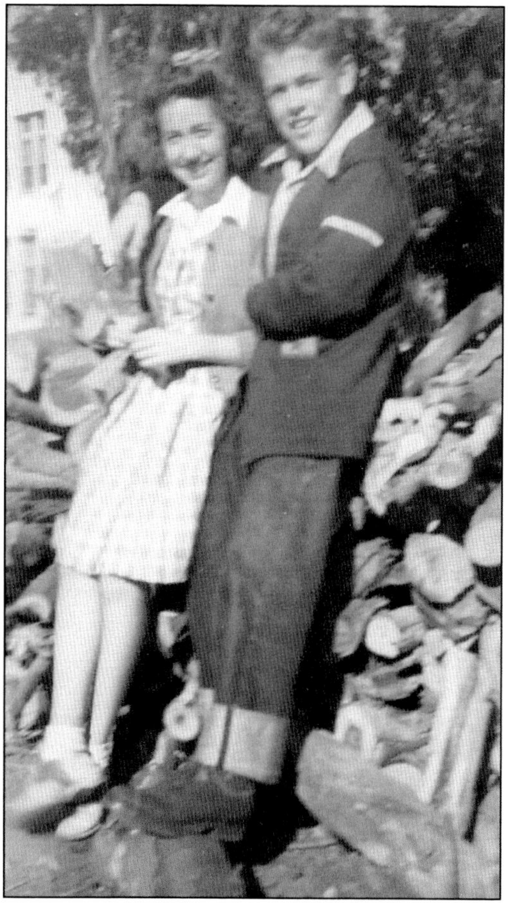

Torrance High's alma mater emphasizes the friendships that are formed while at Torrance High. In this 1945 image, Bill Floyd and "Bunky" Quaggin, from the class of 1949, are leaning against the remains of a tree that was removed, perhaps on the junior patio. Floyd is wearing a Torrance High sweater. (Courtesy of Janis Gragg.)

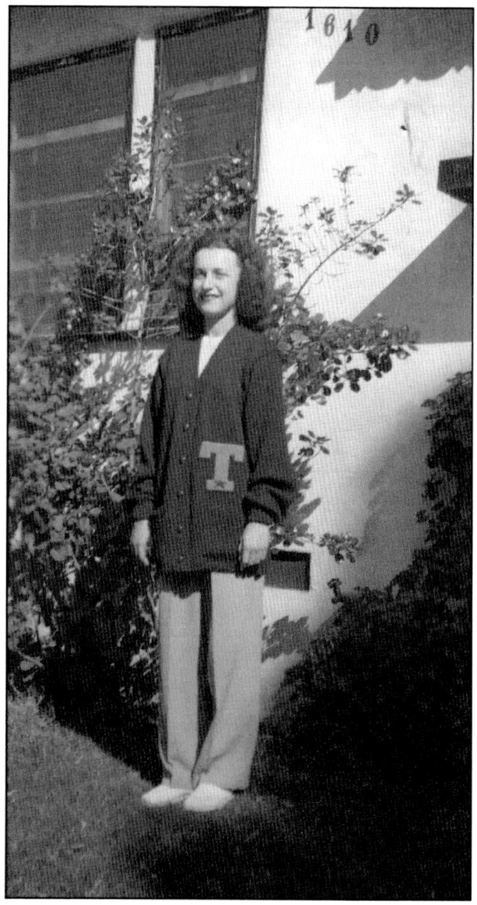

Anna Jane Kelley (left) graduated in 1949. She married her high school sweetheart, Milo Goettsch, and her two children, Janis and Gordon, both graduated from Torrance High. This photograph, taken in Anna Jane's freshman year shows of the Torrance High sweater. Anna Jane was on the yearbook and *News Torch* staff and was active in the Tri-Y club. (Courtesy of Janis Gragg.)

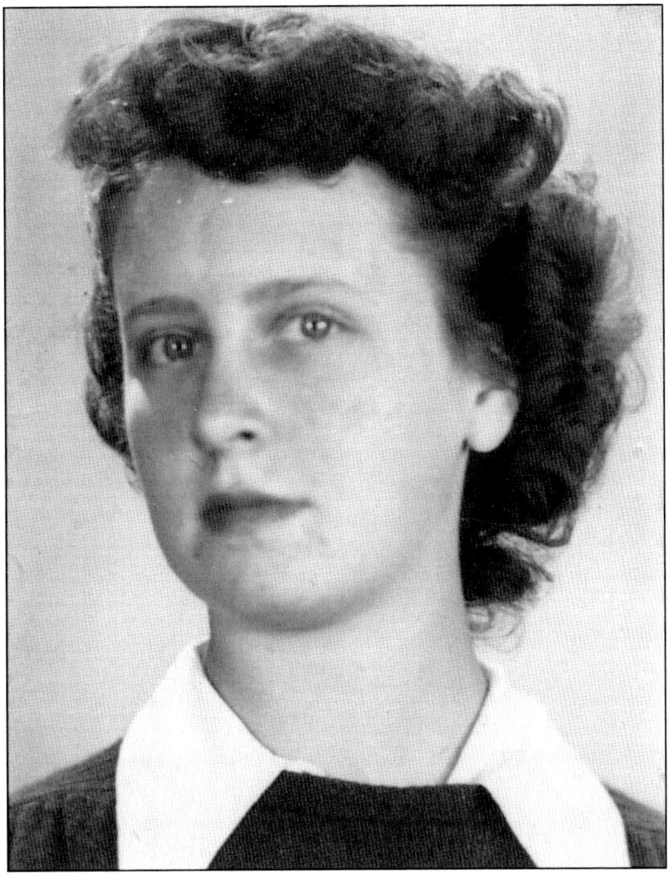

Mary Kathryn Kelley graduated from Torrance High in 1941. Active in many student organizations, such as Girls' League and Tri-Hi-Y, she is seen here participating in the school radio show *Teen and Twenty Time*. (Both, Courtesy of Janis Gragg.)

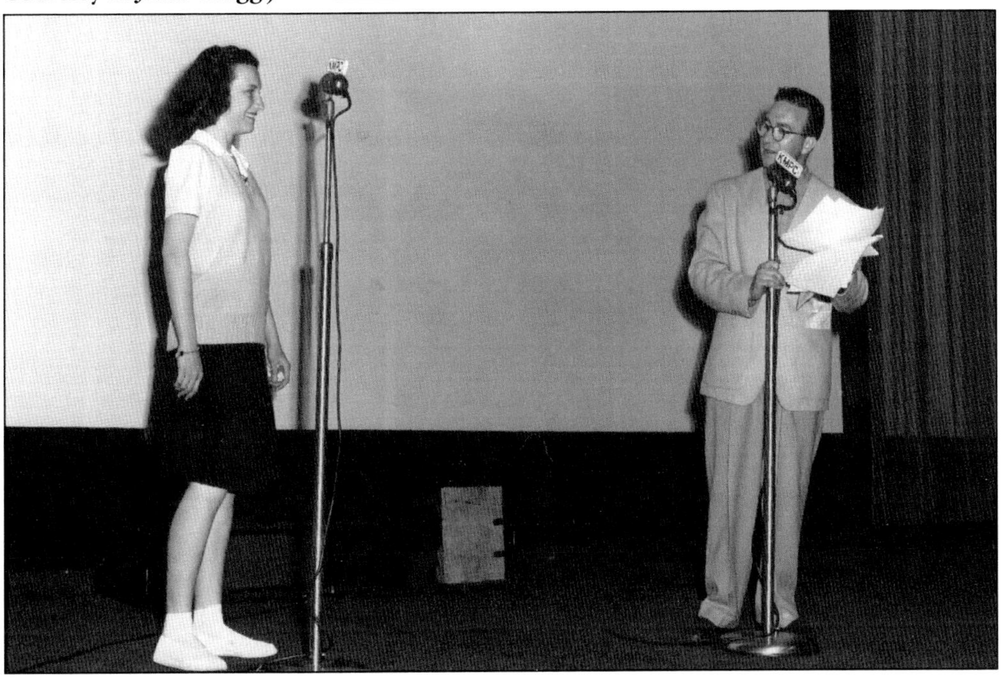

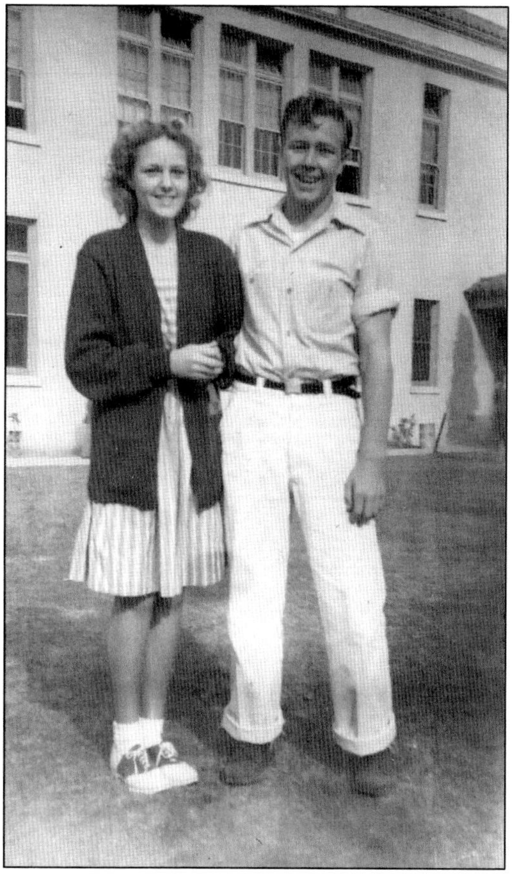

Eddie Fortin and an unidentified female companion pose on the junior patio in this photograph from the 1940s. The junior patio sits between the main building and the home economics building. During some class competitions like Red Ribbon Week, this area will be decorated by the junior class council. (Courtesy of Janis Gragg.)

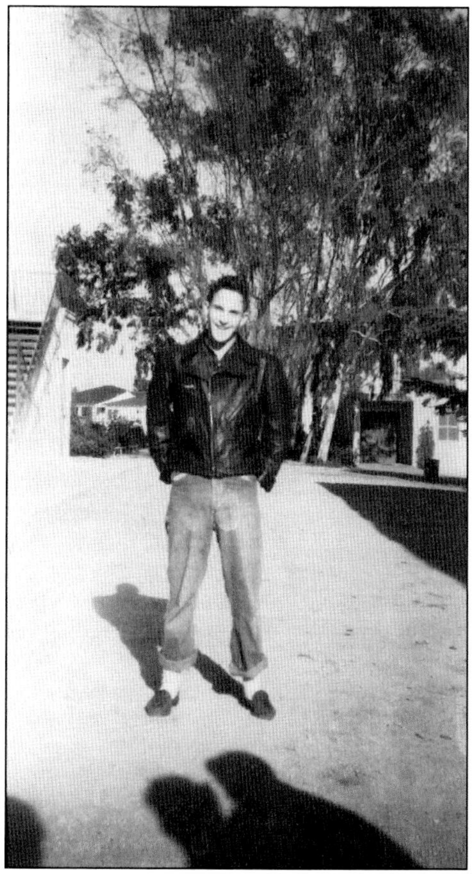

In the 1949 yearbook, most of the seniors have nicknames added to their photographs. Frank Farren, seen here in the late 1940s, sported the nickname "Stein." He was on the football and track teams. He is seen here wearing fashion typical of the era: rolled jeans and leather jacket. (Courtesy of Janis Gragg.)

This 1945 image shows Ralph George and Georgia Ramer of the class of 1949. They are by the home economics building on the junior patio. According to the yearbook, Georgia was part of the Tri-Y, a faith-based student organization, the Girls' Athletic Association, and a staff member of the *News Torch*. (Courtesy of Janis Gragg.)

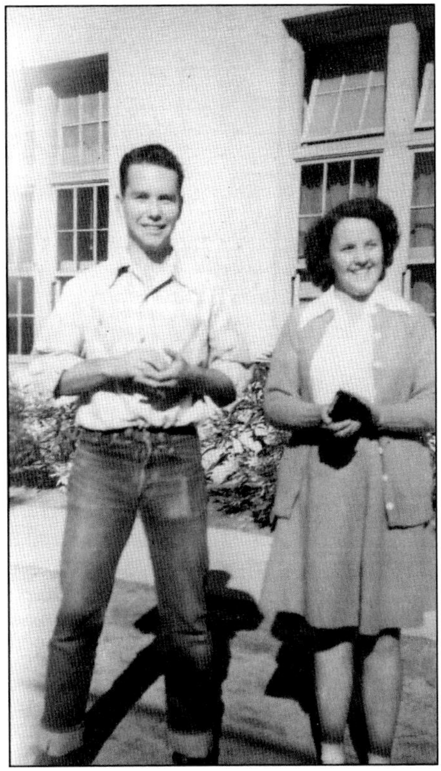

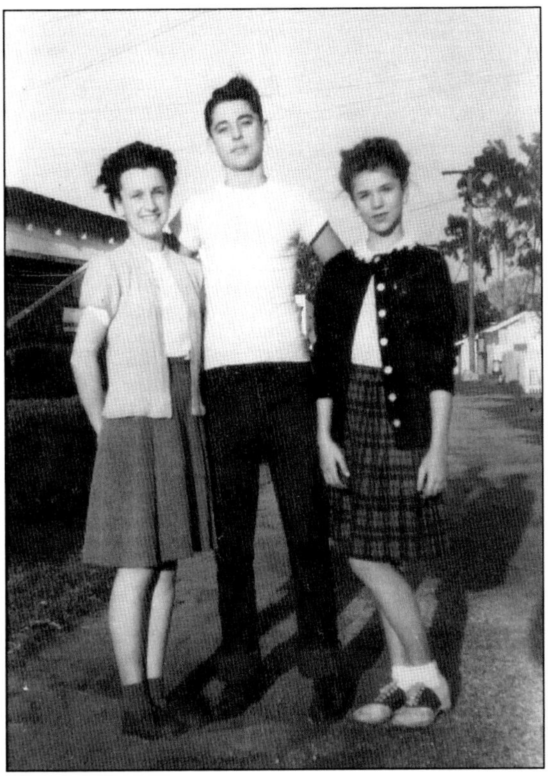

Anna Jane Kelly (left) is pictured with Robert Bowers and an unidentified friend. The trio appears to be standing in an alleyway between homes in the historic part of Torrance. Much of the residential district of Old Torrance is connected via these alleys. This neighborhood is across the street from the front of the main building. (Courtesy of Janis Gragg.)

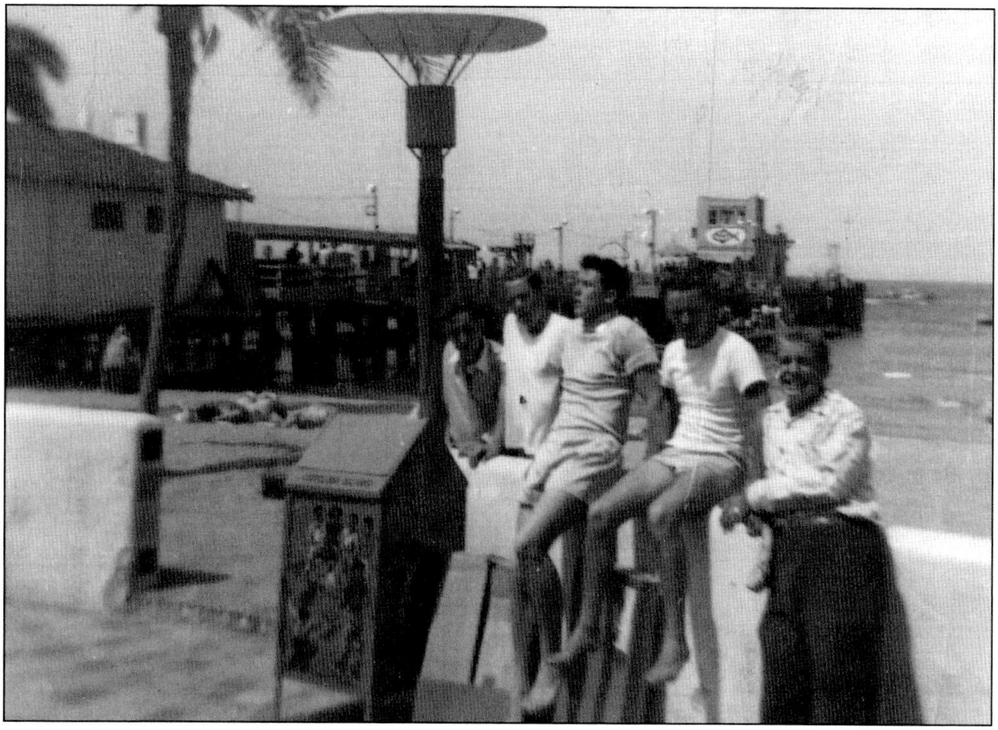

In 1953, the seniors took a trip to Catalina Island. In the above image from 1953, Jerry Johnson (far right) and four friends are relaxing by a patio. In the below image, students are sunbathing on the beach near Avalon. Senior trips were an important part of high school. School officials and class officers planned the excursions, which were financed through class fundraisers. School-sanctioned senior trips were halted around 1956, reportedly after an incident in which several students put their peers in a potentially dangerous situation. By the 1960s, rather than a senior trip, many seniors participated in Senior Ditch Day, which was unofficially scheduled around prom time. (Both, courtesy of Jerry Johnson.)

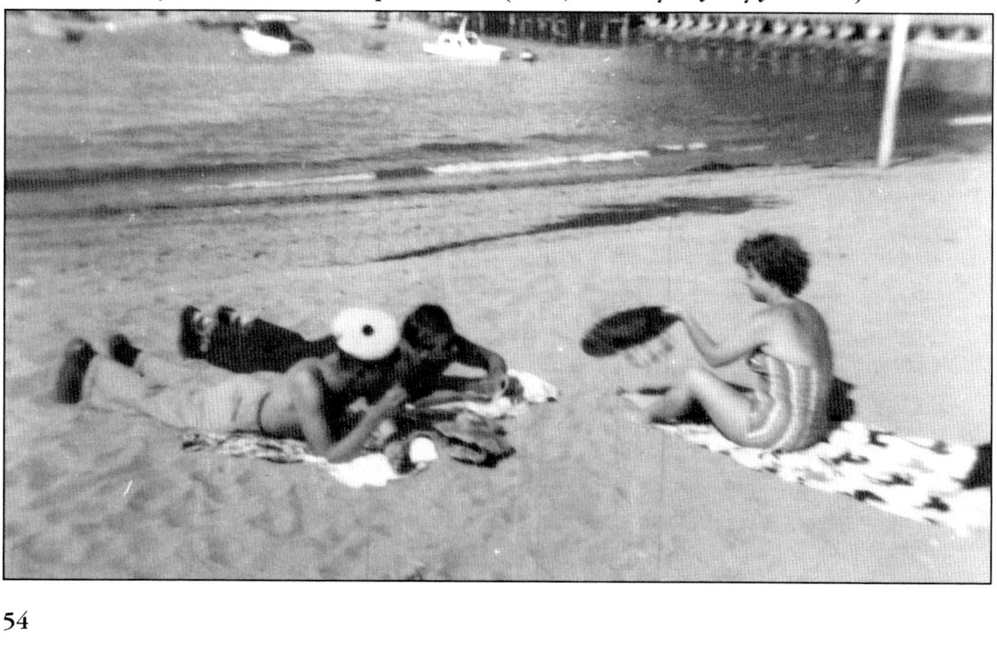

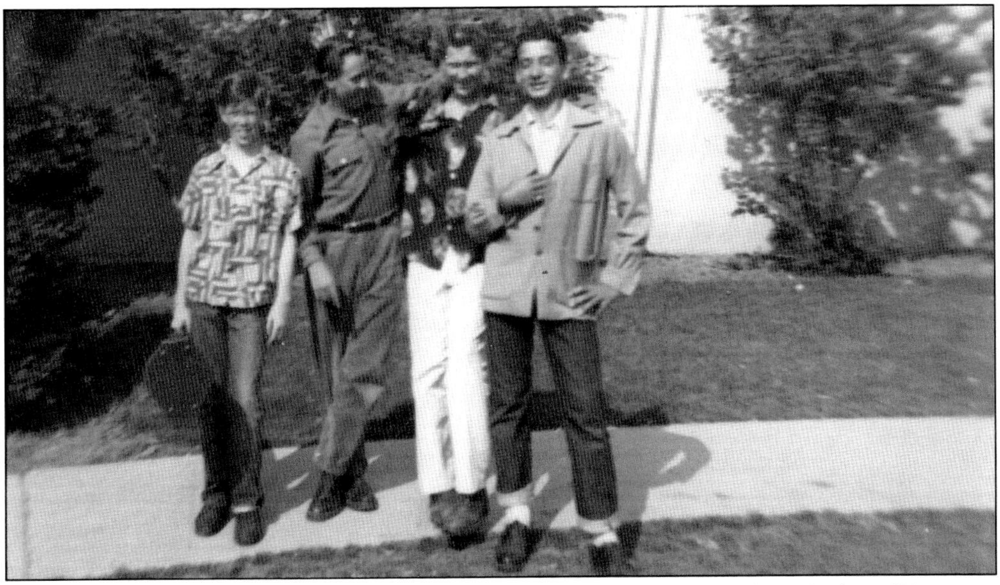

The 1967 yearbook celebrated Torrance High's 50th anniversary and shared a list of Torrance High "firsts." According to that list, the first marching band was introduced in 1941 and has since been a Tartar tradition. However, earlier yearbooks indicate that a band was part of Torrance High in through the late 1930s and was reintroduced in 1941. These unidentified students were part of the band around 1953. (Courtesy of Jerry Johnson.)

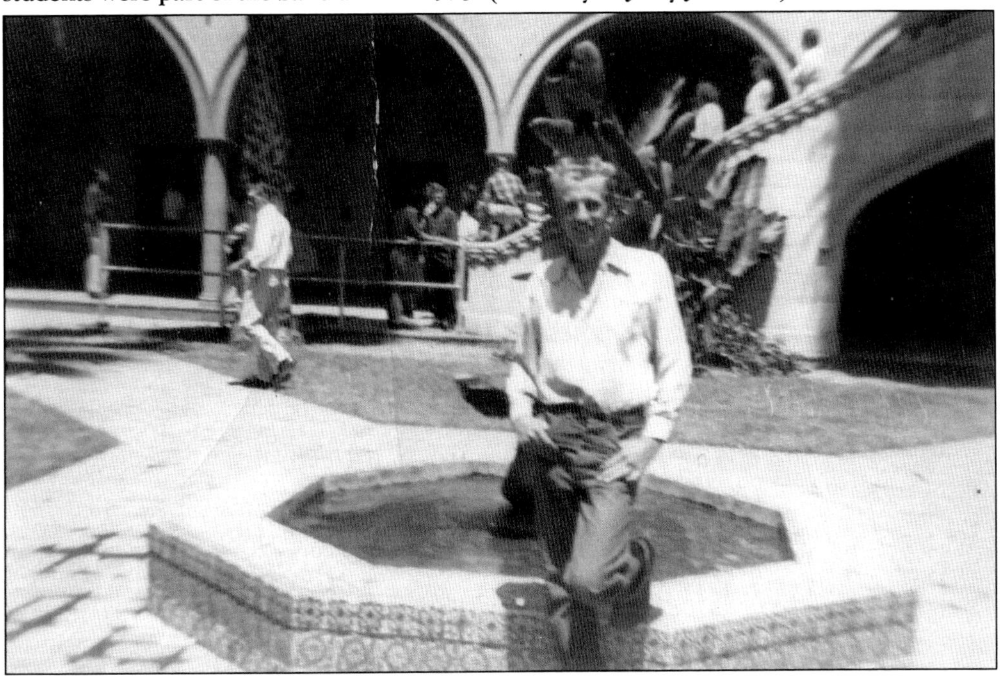

Senior Jerry Johnson stands by the fountain on the senior patio in this 1953 image. The fountain sits on the patio behind the main building. Many people affectionately refer to the fountain as the senior pond. In this photograph, the bowl of the fountain has been painted brown, a change from the original lighter color when the fountain was first installed. (Courtesy of Jerry Johnson.)

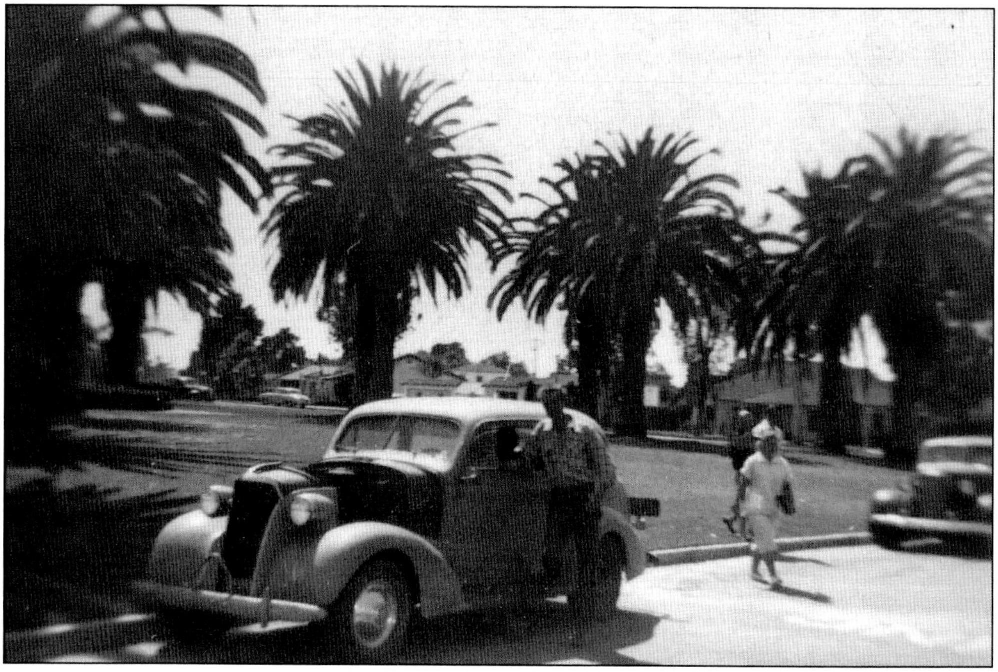

Having a car while in high school is an important rite of passage for any teenager, regardless of the era. In this early 1950s image, Jerry Johnson proudly shows off his 1938 Chevy. His car is parked across from the main building. By the late 1960s, students had their own parking lot near the Annex. (Courtesy of Jerry Johnson.)

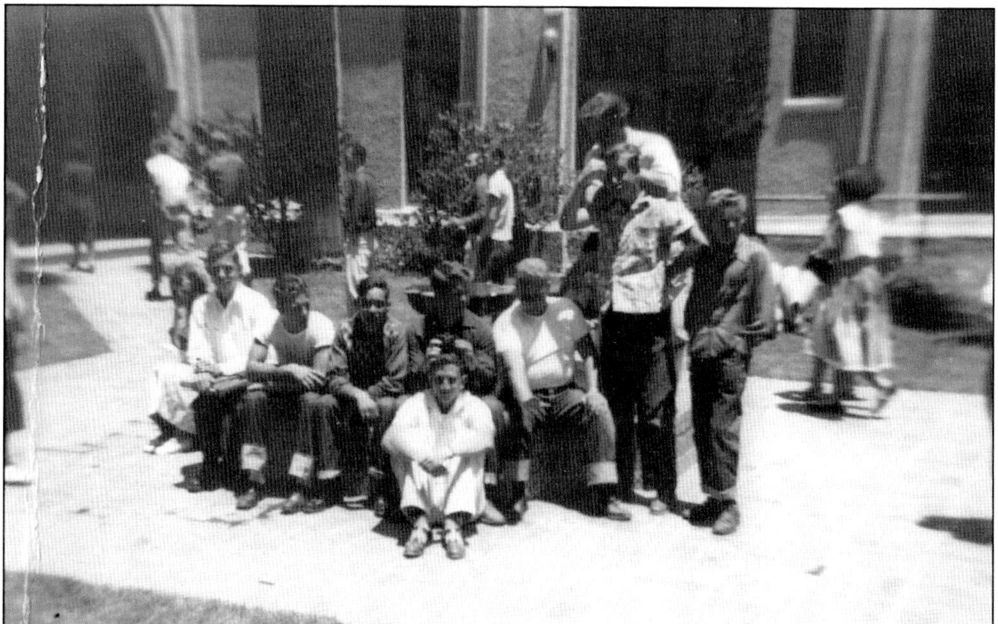

For many years, it was understood that the senior patio was off limits to any underclassmen. Non-seniors were not to cross the patio, nor were they to stop and enjoy the fountain. Jerry Johnson and his friends are dutifully watching for trespassers. (Courtesy of Jerry Johnson.)

From pep rallies to football games, Tartars have shown their spirit. By the 1970s, spirit weeks were organized by the Associated Student Body (or ASB). Spirit weeks typically include dress-up days, like this 1954 photograph demonstrates. These unidentified students are showing their aloha spirit. Modern spirit weeks always include a Class Color Day, and of course, Maroon and Gray Day. (Courtesy of Joan Paour.)

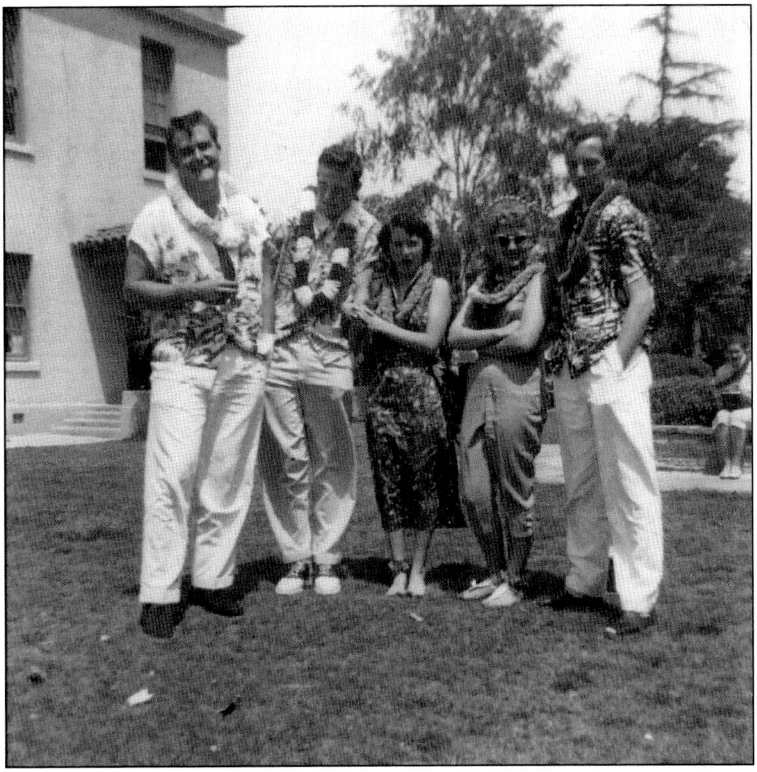

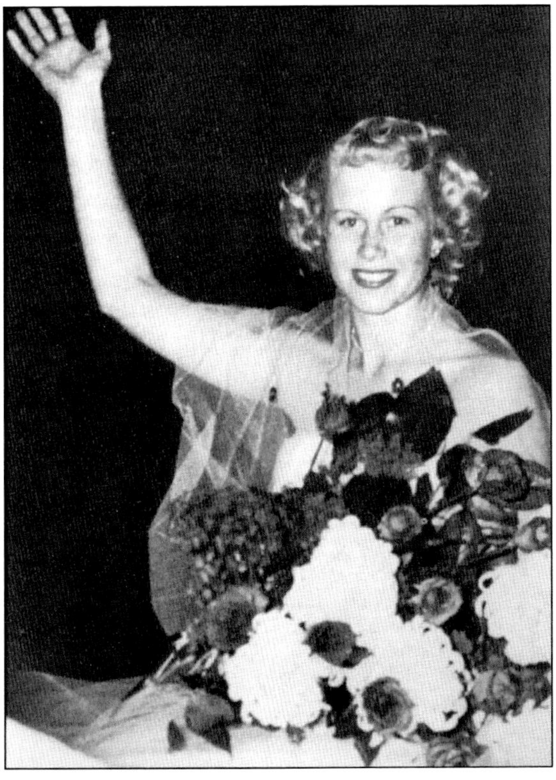

One of the most beloved traditions at Torrance High is our homecoming celebration. Initially, 15 girls were chosen, and one of these would become the homecoming queen. Torrance High's first homecoming queen was Shirley York in 1952. The crown she received was handmade by some of her fellow students. (Courtesy of Torrance High Alumni Association.)

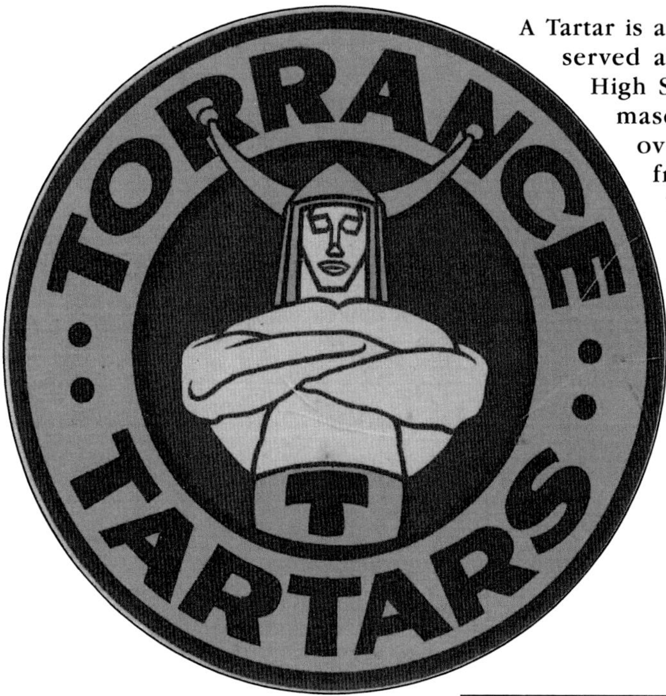

A Tartar is a Mongolian warrior and has served as the mascot for Torrance High School since 1923. Like any mascot, the Tartar has evolved over the years. This sticker from the 1960s depicts the Tartar with more Caucasian features. The Tartar mascot continued to change during the 1970s, and through the last two decades, he has been consistent with his nearly floor-length robes and sword. (Courtesy of Torrance High Alumni Association.)

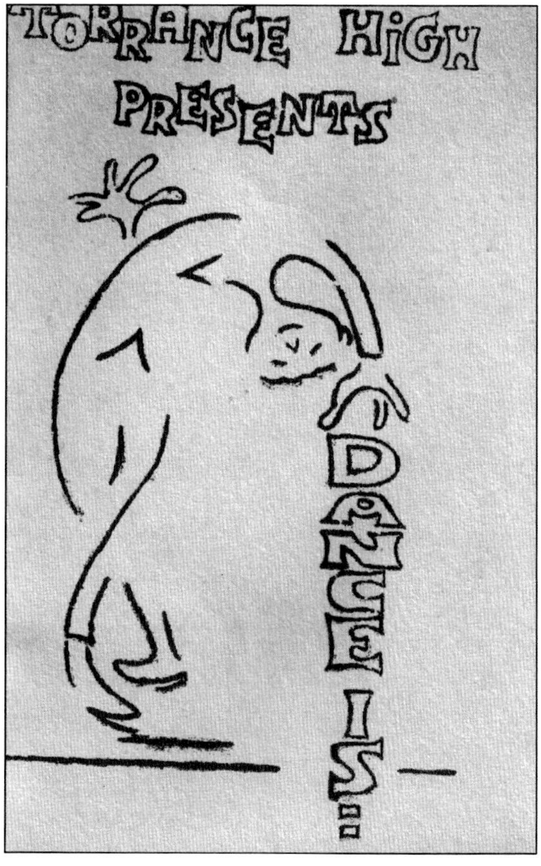

The modern dance program started during the 1966–1967 school year. During the first year, Lee Warner taught the class as a seventh-period PE elective. The following year, Jessica Hollowell assumed leadership, and the program put on a two performances a year. A dance team continued to perform into the 1980s. (Courtesy of Karen McKim Gebhard.)

For many years, Torrance High received an exchange student from American Field Service. In return, a Tartar would spend time in a different country. From June to September 1969, Karen McKim represented Torrance High in Brazil. In this article from the *News Torch*, Karen commented about how beautiful the country is and how friendly the people were. (Courtesy of Karen McKim Gebhard.)

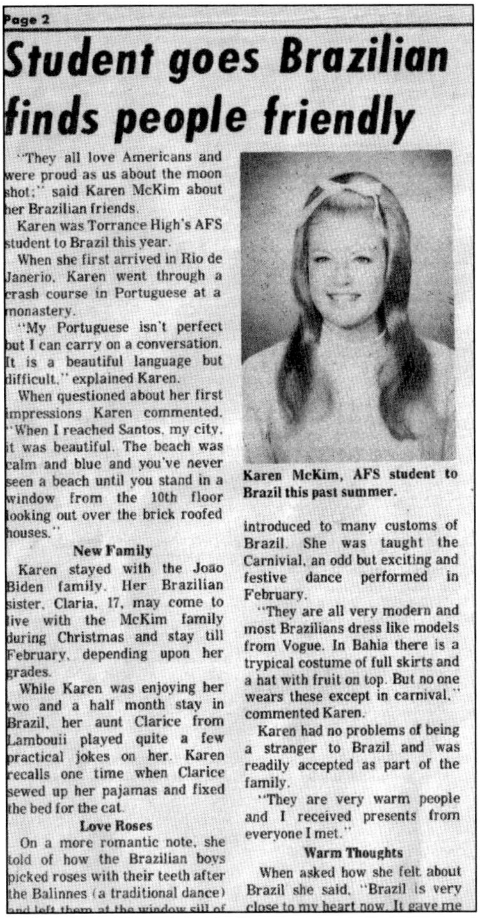

Page 2

Student goes Brazilian finds people friendly

"They all love Americans and were proud as us about the moon shot;" said Karen McKim about her Brazilian friends.

Karen was Torrance High's AFS student to Brazil this year.

When she first arrived in Rio de Janerio, Karen went through a crash course in Portuguese at a monastery.

"My Portuguese isn't perfect but I can carry on a conversation. It is a beautiful language but difficult," explained Karen.

When questioned about her first impressions Karen commented, "When I reached Santos, my city, it was beautiful. The beach was calm and blue and you've never seen a beach until you stand in a window from the 10th floor looking out over the brick roofed houses."

New Family

Karen stayed with the Joao Biden family. Her Brazilian sister, Claria, 17, may come to live with the McKim family during Christmas and stay till February, depending upon her grades.

While Karen was enjoying her two and a half month stay in Brazil, her aunt Clarice from Lambouii played quite a few practical jokes on her. Karen recalls one time when Clarice sewed up her pajamas and fixed the bed for the cat.

Love Roses

On a more romantic note, she told of how the Brazilian boys picked roses with their teeth after the Balinnes (a traditional dance)

Karen McKim, AFS student to Brazil this past summer.

introduced to many customs of Brazil. She was taught the Carnivial, an odd but exciting and festive dance performed in February.

"They are all very modern and most Brazilians dress like models from Vogue. In Bahia there is a trypical costume of full skirts and a hat with fruit on top. But no one wears these except in carnival," commented Karen.

Karen had no problems of being a stranger to Brazil and was readily accepted as part of the family.

"They are very warm people and I received presents from everyone I met."

Warm Thoughts

When asked how she felt about Brazil she said, "Brazil is very

During the 2016–2017 school year, Torrance High hosted 14 international students. They represent countries from all over the world, such as Italy, Norway, Brazil, Poland, Denmark, Czech Republic, and China. Several of these students had a choice as to which American high school they wished to attend and chose Torrance High because they had seen the school in movies. (Courtesy of Torrance High School Associated Student Body.)

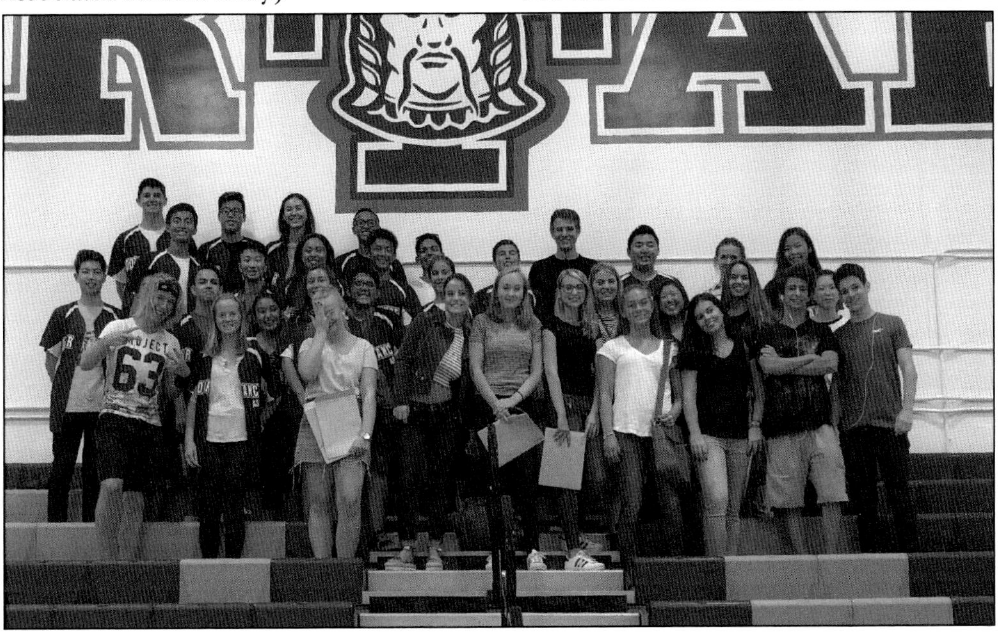

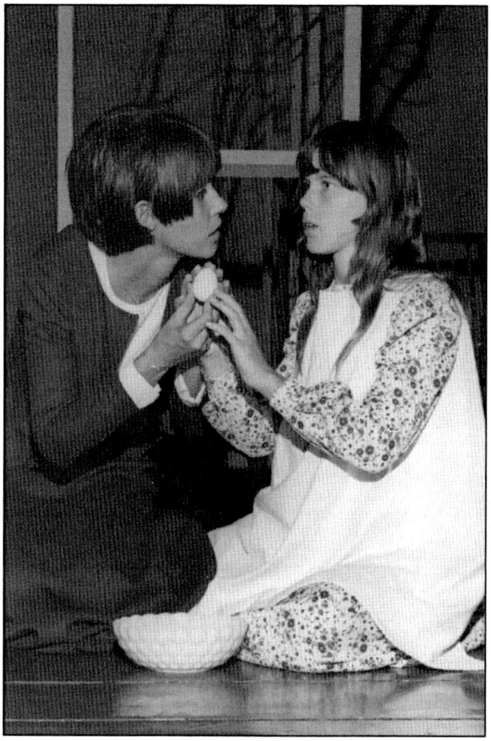

The earliest senior classes at Torrance High staged play productions throughout the school year. Eventually, the junior class also put on plays. By the 1950s, a solid drama department was producing plays. In 1962, Charles Slater joined the Tartar faculty. His productions were always well executed. In the 1965 image at left, Kathy Lynch (left) and Mary Walls portray Anne Sullivan and Helen Keller in *The Miracle Worker.* Slater often took still shots of the performers. During the 1968 school year, he produced *Arms and the Man* (below). Slater's daughter Casie was hired in 1993 following his retirement, and she has continued the tradition of excellence in staging productions. Both father and daughter chose productions well suited to their talented students and often incorporated faculty members. (Both, courtesy of Charles Slater.)

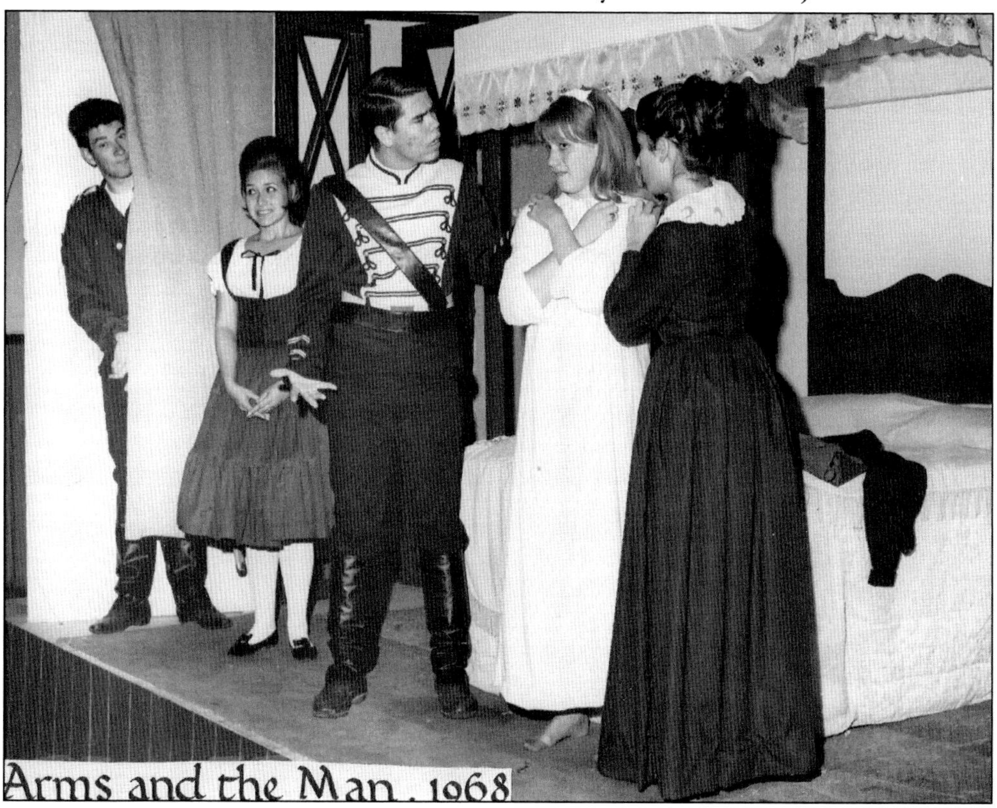

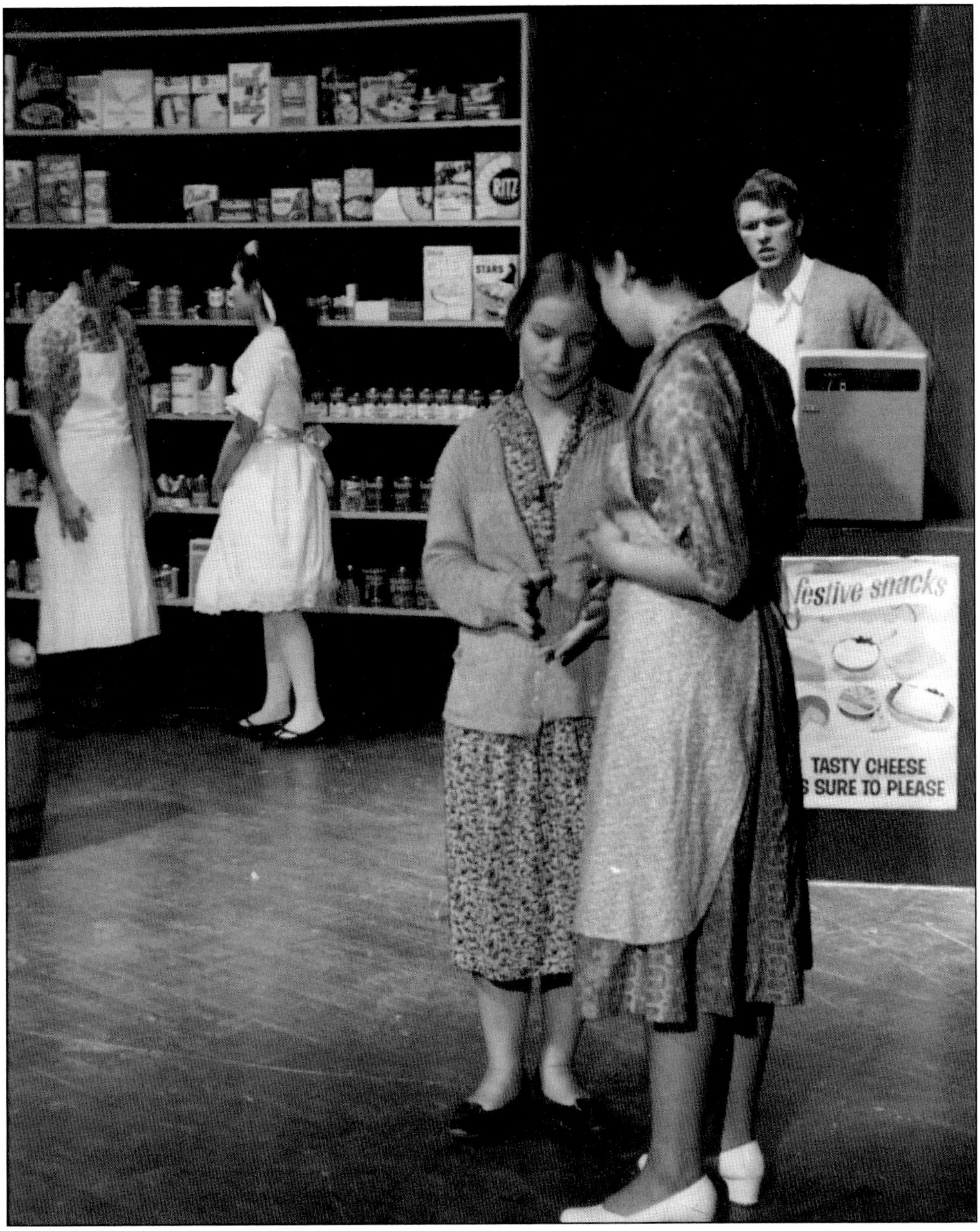

To encourage would-be playwrights, the drama department puts on the Festival of One-Acts. This yearly activity began in the 1950s, when local actress Rosemary DeCamp sponsored a playwriting contest. Students were encouraged to write a one-act play. Students wrote, cast, and directed their own plays. Rosemary DeCamp would review the submission and select three plays to be performed for an audience and produced by the Torrance High drama department. The three wining playwrights received trophies. The productions were open to the public for two performances, and a panel of experts, including actress Ann B. Davis (Alice from *The Brady Bunch*) and Dwayne Hickman (television's Dobie Gillis), critiqued the overall performance and scripts. (Courtesy of Charles Slater.)

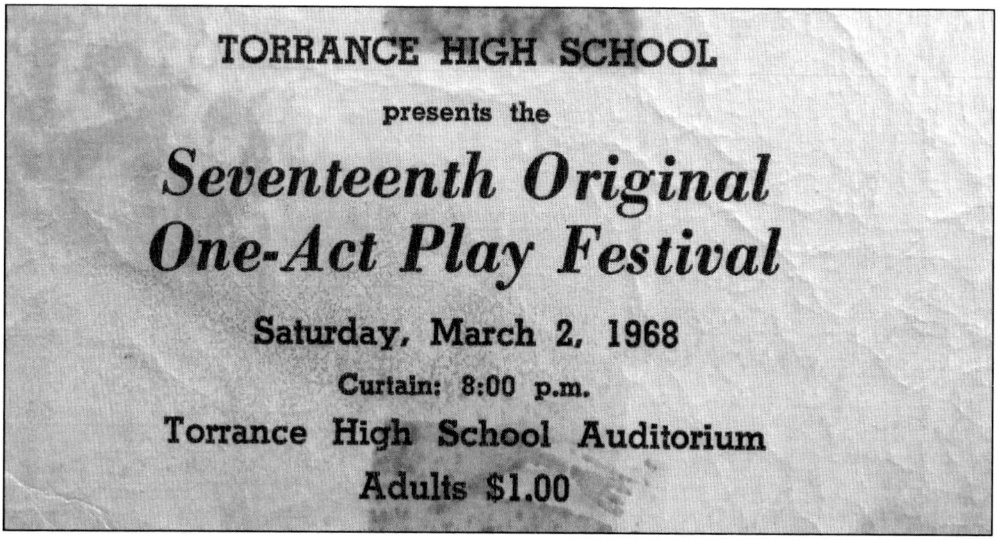

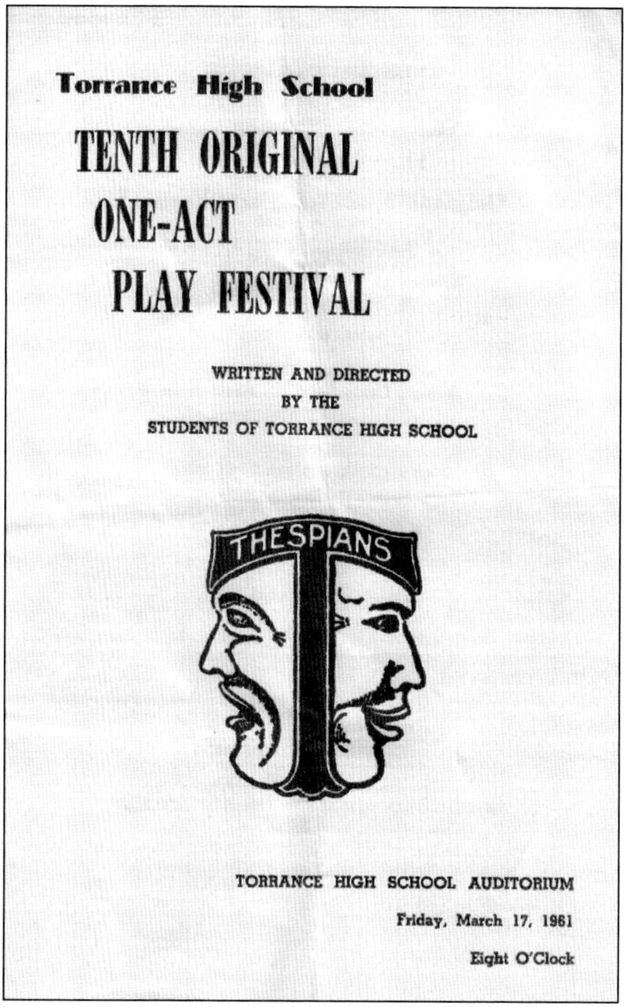

Though the Festival of One Acts continues to take the stage, it has changed over the years. Where the contest was originally open to all grade levels, it is now the advanced theater students who write, cast, and direct their peers in the class. There is no longer a panel of judges to critique the scenes, but they are still open to the public for viewing. (Courtesy of Karen McKim Gebhard.)

This program is from the Festival of One Acts in 1961. For many of the fine arts performances on campus, from stage productions to band and choir concerts, students design the programs handed out to guests. Often, they reflect the theme of the performance and highlight one more way in which Tartars are talented. (Courtesy of Torrance High School Alumni Association.)

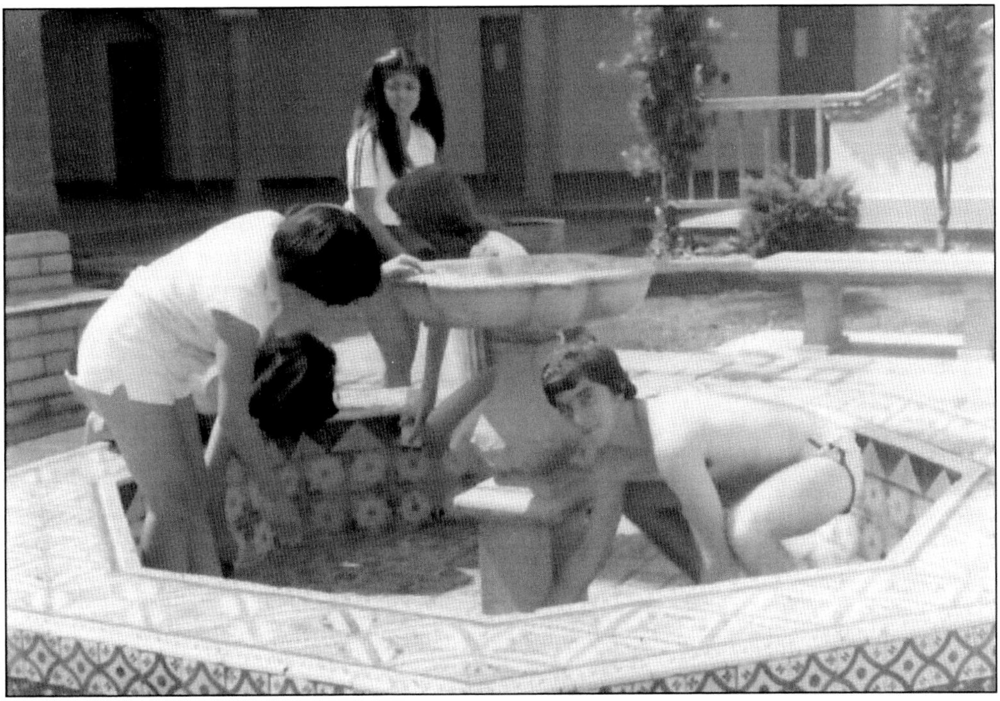

The senior patio and fountain (pond) are a source of amusement for these unidentified seniors, as they play in the water. Until the 1990s, though it was not common, underclassmen who walked across the patio could be picked up by seniors and dumped into the fountain. Students are no longer allowed to do this, mostly for safety reasons. (Courtesy of Torrance High Associated Student Body.)

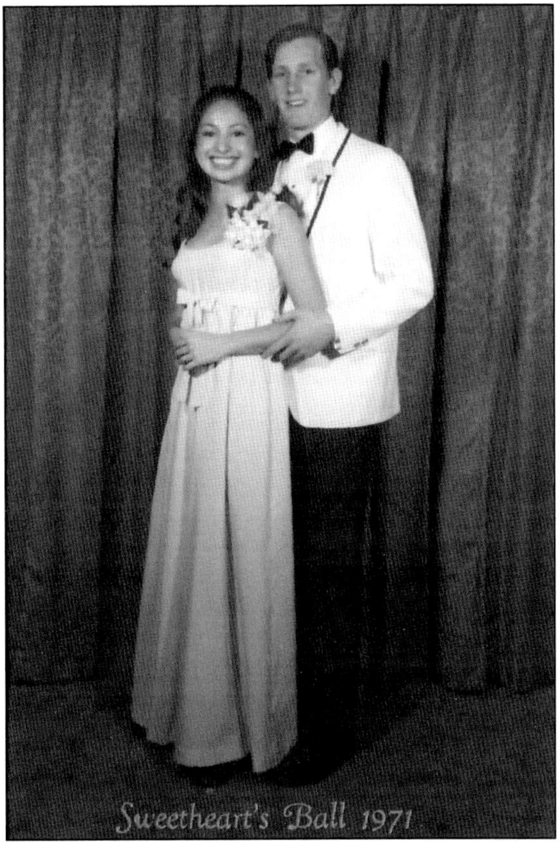

In this photograph from 1971, Theresa Fagan and her friend Bob Fitzgerald pose at the Sweetheart's Ball. Starting in 1967, this dance used to be held annually in February. A formal dance, it was often held off-site. By the early 2000s, student attendance had decreased, and rather than hold the dance on site, the annual winter formal, or "Sweethearts," was permanently cancelled. (Courtesy of Theresa Fagan Hollis.)

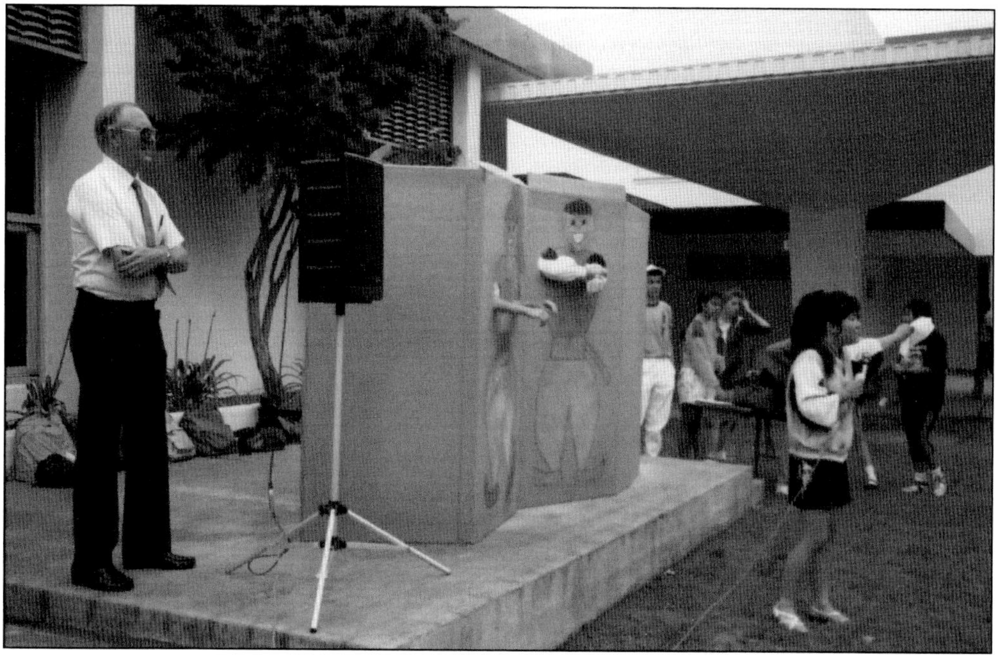

The area in front of the main gym, formerly the boys' gym, was often used for pep rallies. Through the 1970s, assemblies and rallies were referred to as Aud Calls. By the 1980s, most rallies took place at snack time, as students could leave campus at lunch. In this image from the late 1980s, John Radcliffe, the student activities director, overseas the activity led by ASB. (Courtesy of Torrance High Associated Student Body.)

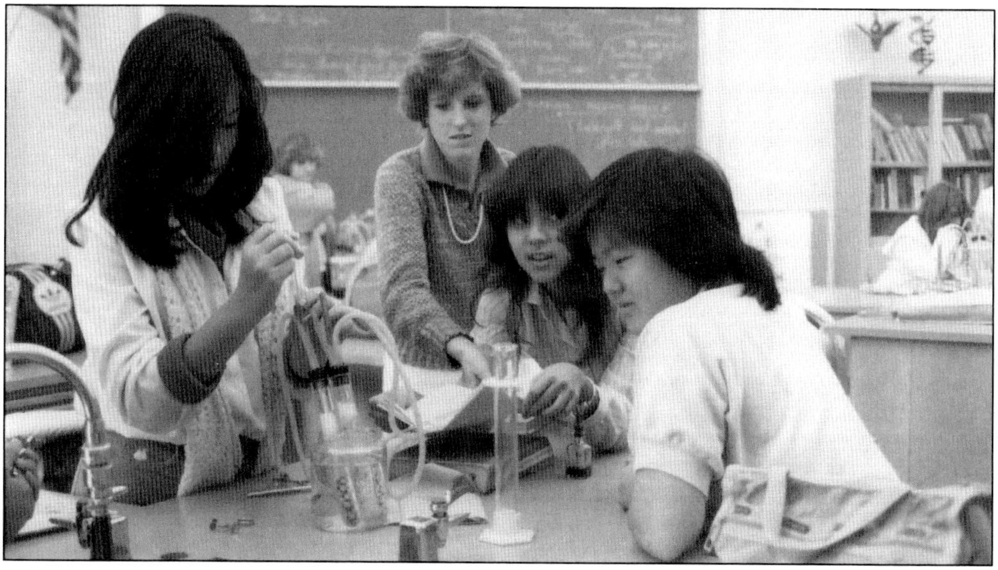

While Tartars enjoy their activities, they are also serious about academics. Students are encouraged to challenge themselves academically. In this c. 1983 photograph, from left to right, Alice Sun, Karen Hahn, Sherry Jang, and Colleen Kozawa are taking the experiment in Frank Simon's biology 2 class seriously. Torrance High curriculum allows students to explore multiple sciences and mathematics, leading students to focus on STEM (science, technology, engineering, and mathematics)-related majors. (Courtesy of Alice Sun Davis.)

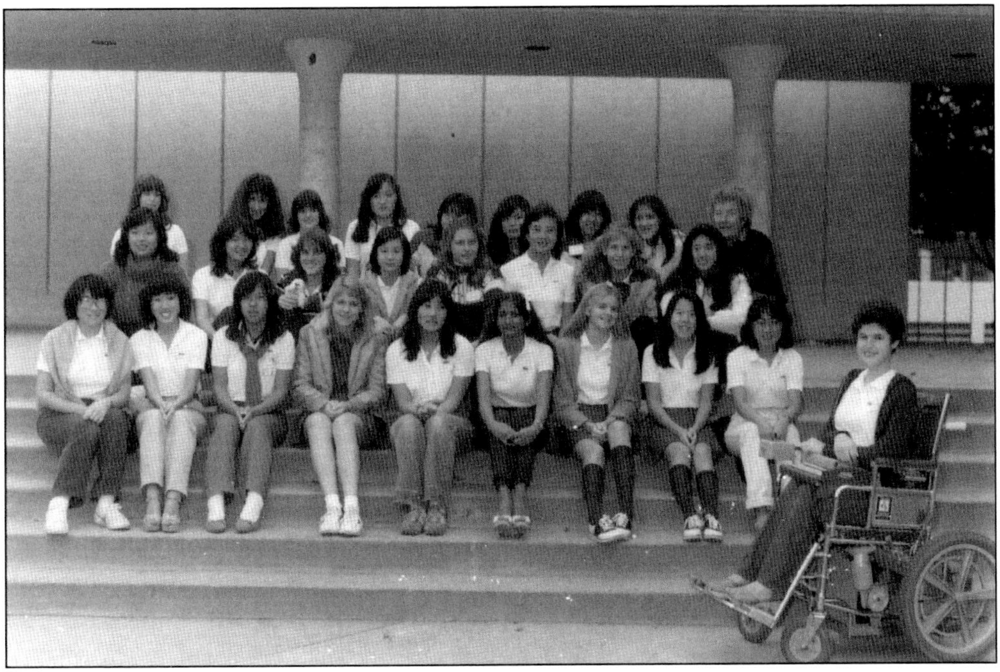

One of the most prominent student organizations on campus is the Tartar Ladies, or "TLs." Tartar Ladies began in 1943 as a female counterpart to the existing Tartar Knights. Now, Tartar Ladies provide help with campus events and are also active in the community. This 1984 photograph is of the Tartar Ladies. Their longtime sponsor, Pat Wright, is in the back row on the right. (Courtesy of Alice Sun Davis.)

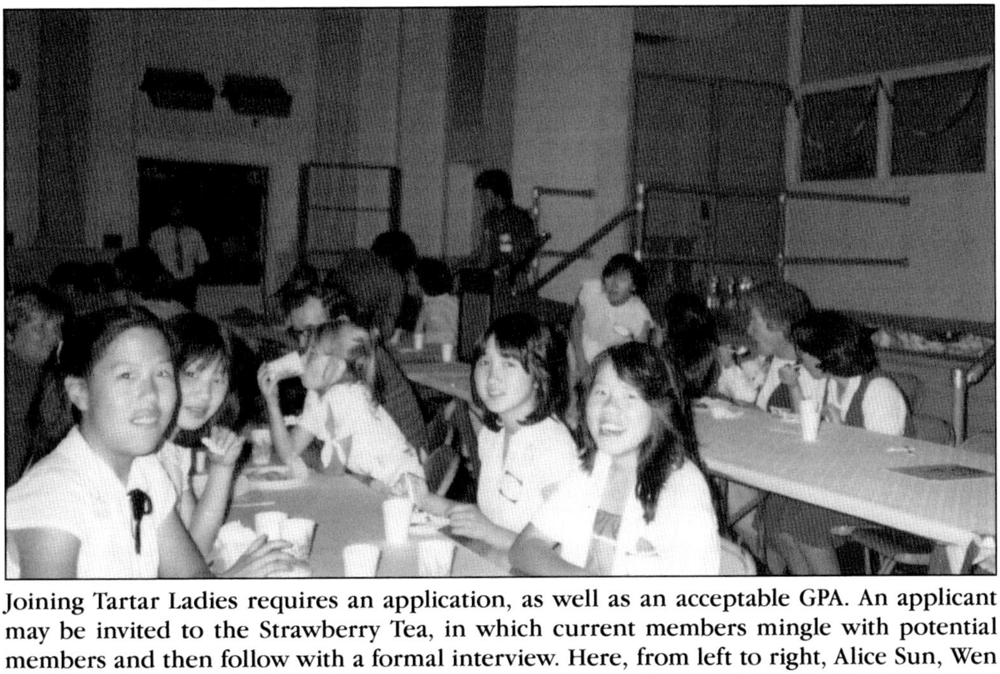

Joining Tartar Ladies requires an application, as well as an acceptable GPA. An applicant may be invited to the Strawberry Tea, in which current members mingle with potential members and then follow with a formal interview. Here, from left to right, Alice Sun, Wen Hsin, an unidentified student, and Yoshiun Kuo enjoy the strawberry tea. (Courtesy of Alice Sun Davis.)

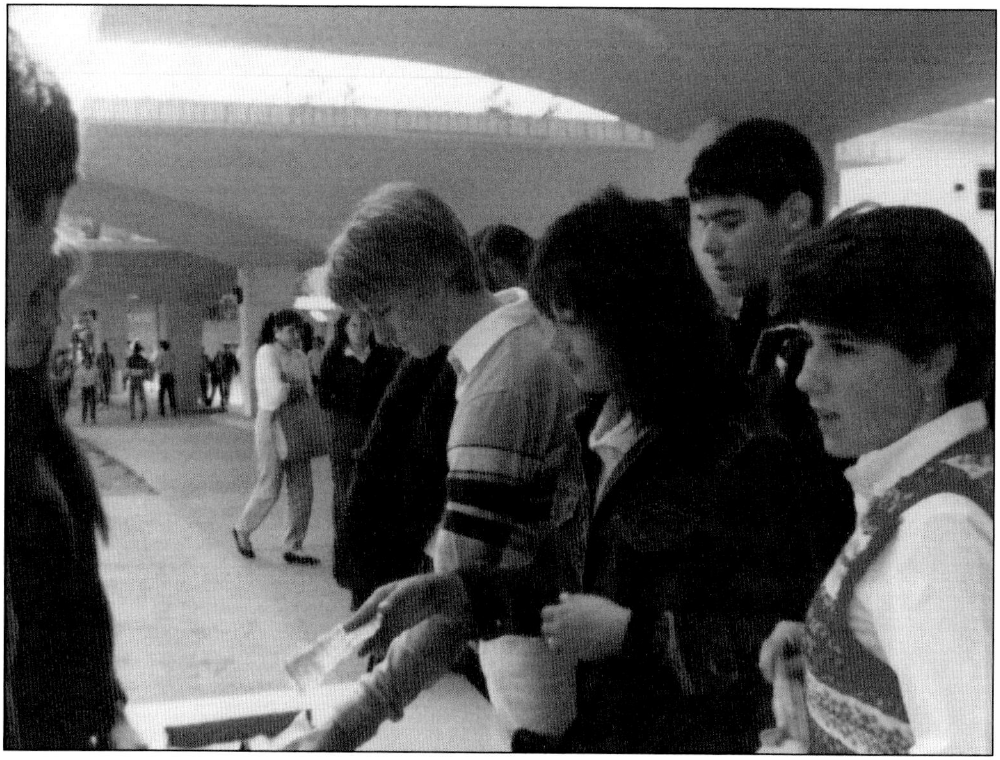

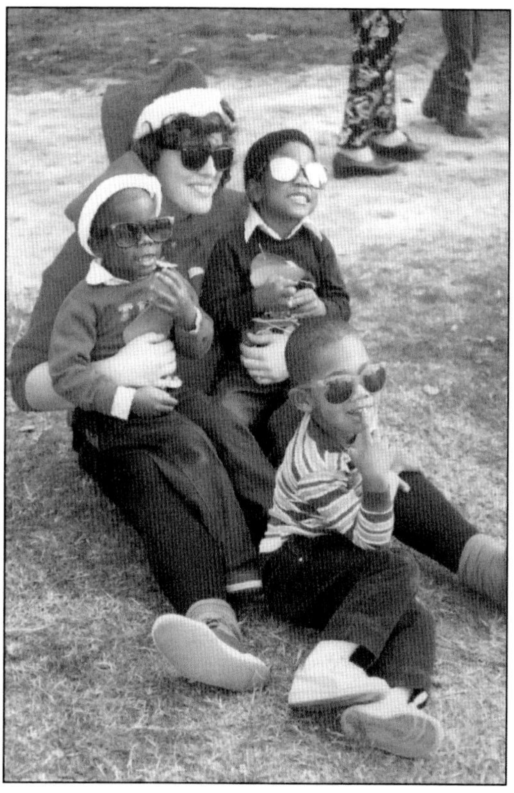

During the 1980s and 1990s, snack time often became a feeding frenzy as students rushed from their second period class to get to the doughnut carts. While the sales were mostly conducted by the ASB, other clubs would be allowed the opportunity to sell glazed, apple fritters, and chocolate bars for 50¢ each. The students in this image are along the breezeway, by the science building. (Courtesy of Torrance High Associated Student Body.)

Twice a year, Tartars used to participate in Head Start. Students would be given the chance to play with underprivileged children at Wilson Park for several hours. During the Christmas Head Start, the children were given small gifts, such as coloring books, purchased by ASB, before they left. One student recalls, "If you wanted to participate, you had to get in line by 6:45 in the morning!" (Courtesy of Torrance High Associated Student Body.)

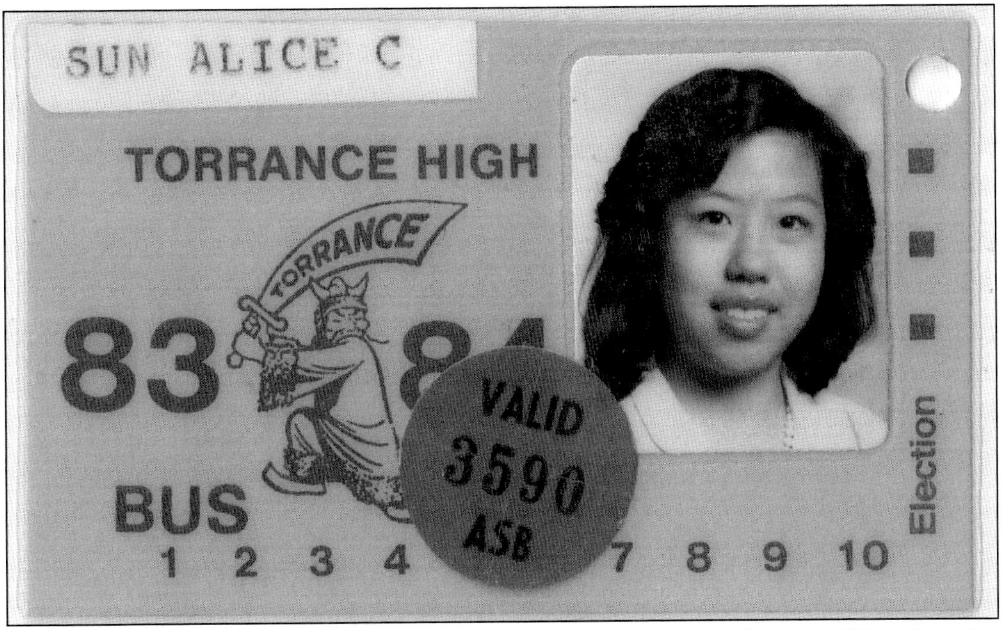

Students are encouraged to purchase the ASB unified dues. In the 1980s and 1990s, the price was around $65. By 2016, the cost had increased to $90. Included in the purchase of these dues is the yearbook, entrance to football and basketball games, and discounts on dance tickets. On Alice Sun's ID card, the ASB sticker is clearly visible. (Courtesy of Alice Sun Davis.)

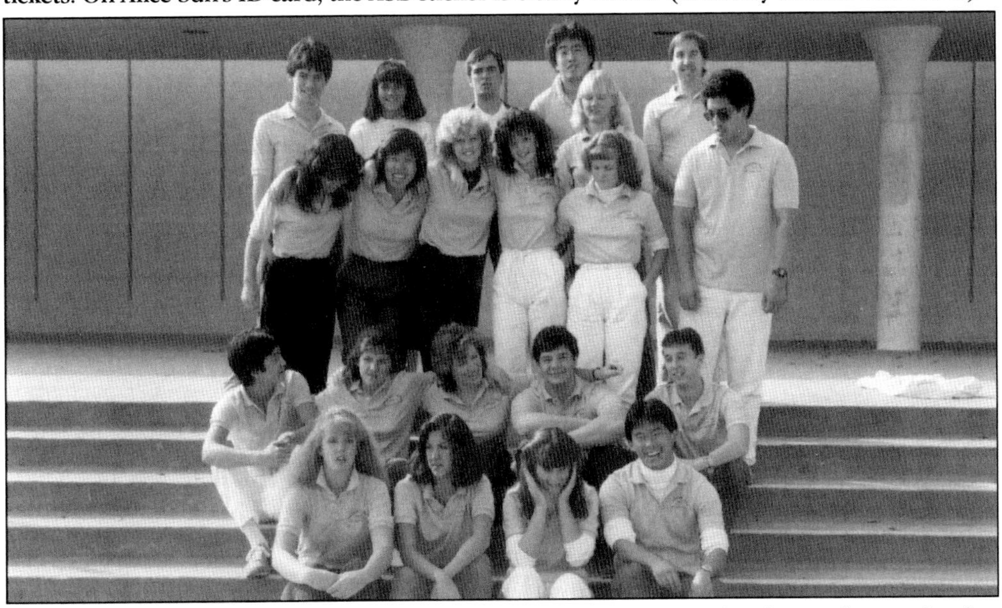

The Associated Student Body dates back to the 1920s, with a school president and a few other officers. This photograph shows the 1984 ASB. From left to right are (first row) Lisa St. Amand, Amanda Watase, Kelly Tynan, and Alan Matsumoto; (second row) Keith Kato, Debbie Miller, Marie Garvey, Steve Silbiger, and Scott Zatan; (third row) June Kikuchi, Alice Sun, Kathy Middleton, Regina Talmo, Rikki Rauhala, Lisa Provost, and Frank Marumoto; (fourth row) Craig Burgner, Julie Jamile, Dean Spizziri, Jay Chong, and advisor John O'Brien. (Courtesy of Alice Sun Davis.)

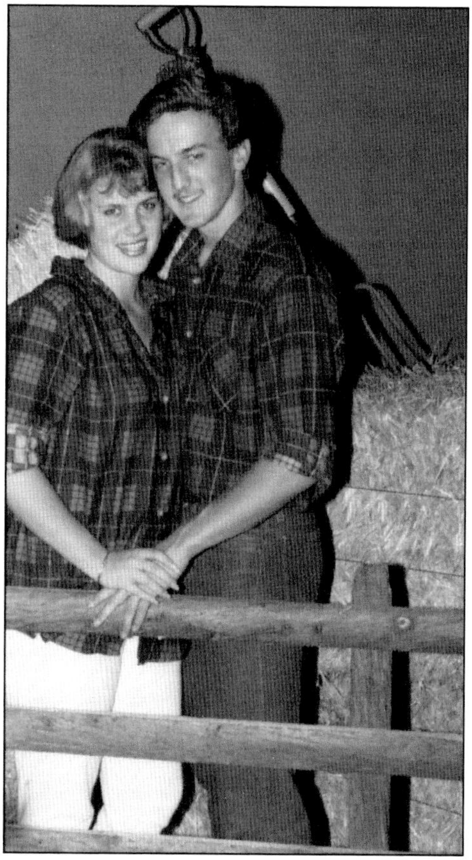

One of the most popular traditions at Torrance High is the Sadie Hawkins Dance. Started by the Girls' Athletic Association, the first dance was held November 15, 1944, during fourth period. The cost of admission was 30¢. In keeping with the origins of Sadie Hawkins, the girls ask the boys to the dance. By the 1980s, the junior class sponsored the dance as a fundraiser. Typically, boys and girls wore matching flannel shirts and jeans, as shown by Lori Sibley and her date, Scott Rye, in 1987 (left). Dances in the 1980s also featured local disc jockeys, such as Jed the Fish, from KROQ, seen below with Yoshiun Kuo (left) and Alice Sun. By 2001, the Western theme was seen as no longer relevant and was replaced by new themes like "Shipwrecked Sadies" and "Super Hero Sadies." (Left, courtesy of Torrance High Associated Student Body; below, courtesy of Alice Sun Davis.)

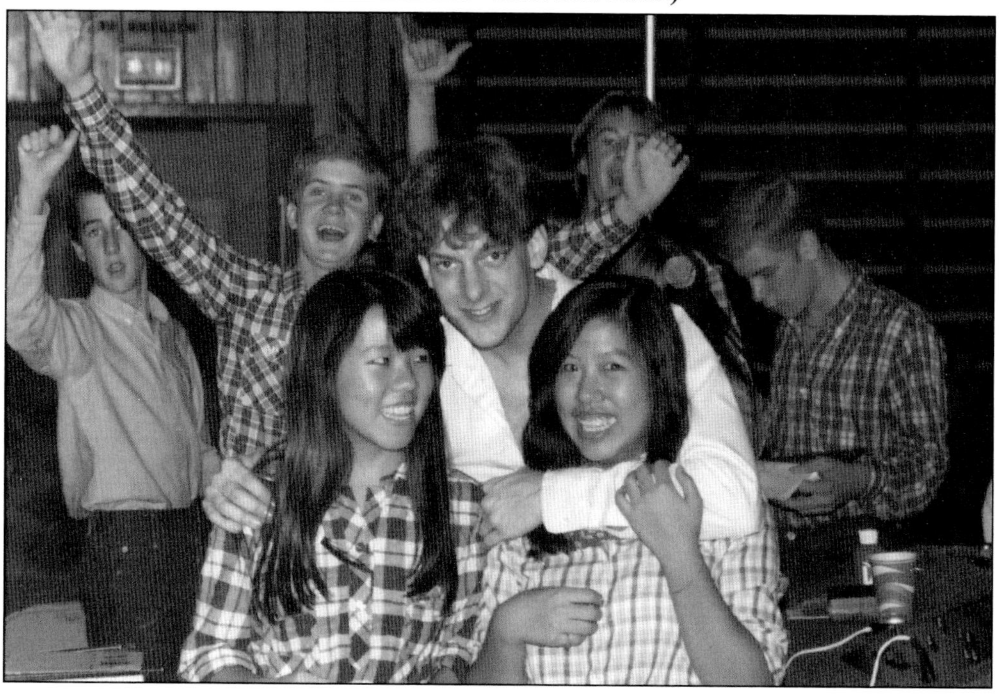

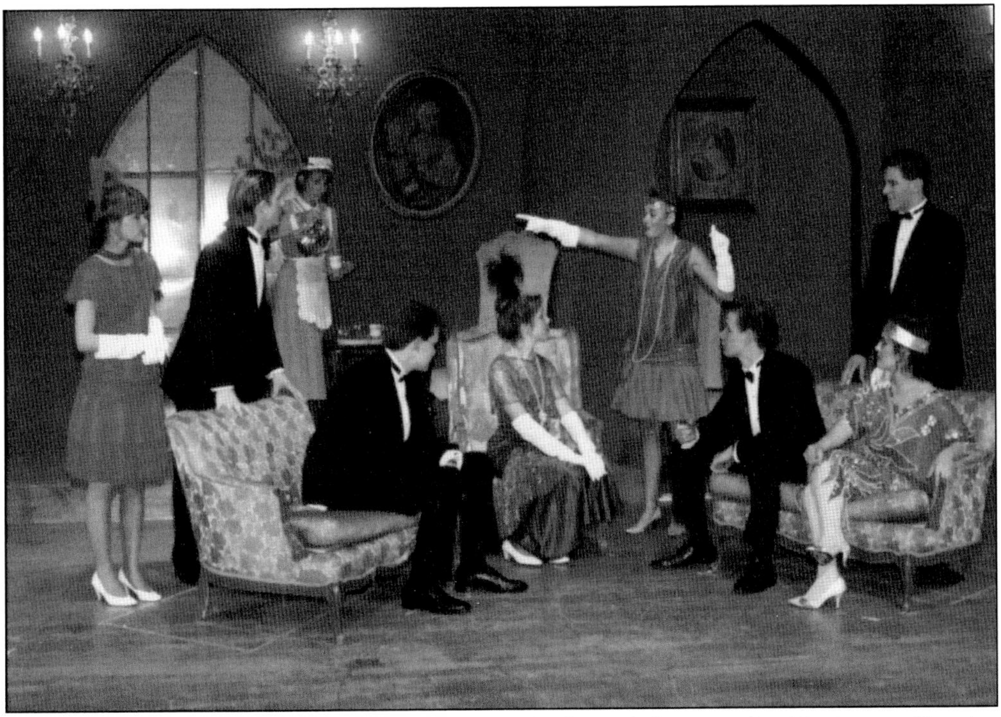

The 1989 production of *Hay Fever* featured, from left to right, Tanimara Martin, Christopher Allen, Christy Kerkvoorde, Curtis Rice, Rebecca Mar, Jan Clark, Andrew Lawrence, Valerie Mares, and Mark Austin. Each play staged at Torrance High is selected to showcase the talents of aspiring thespians. Typically, the spring production, every other year, is a musical. (Courtesy of Torrance High Associated Student Body.)

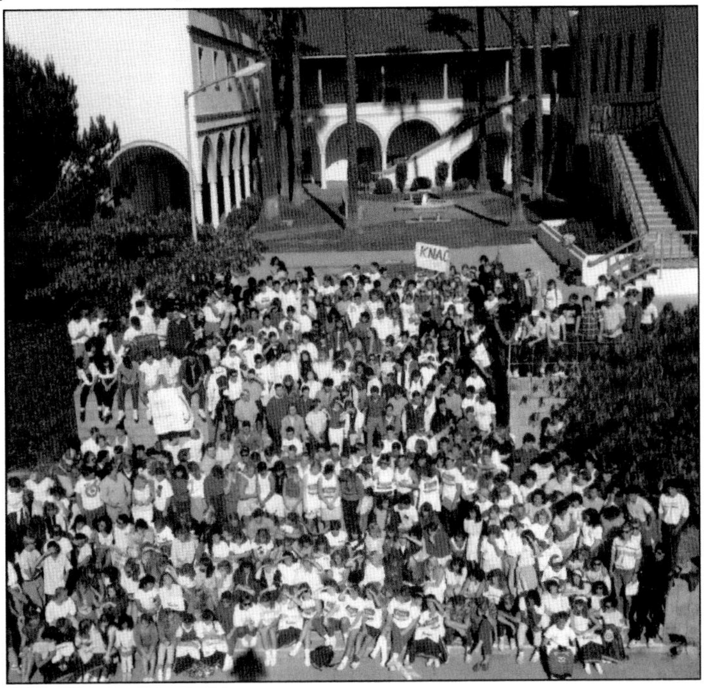

The senior panoramic photograph is one of the highlights of the yearbook. The entire senior class gathers on the stairs by the administration building. In this 1987 image, students are displaying signs. Students are no longer able to display signs, but the class slogan is spelled out on T-shirts worn by the class council. Students not on class council traditionally wear their class shirt. (Courtesy of Torrance High Associated Student Body.)

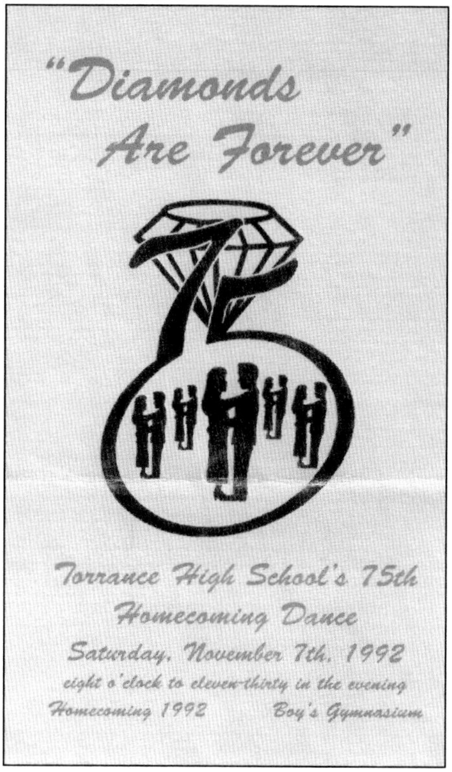
"Diamonds Are Forever"

Torrance High School's 75th Homecoming Dance

Saturday, November 7th, 1992

eight o'clock to eleven-thirty in the evening

Homecoming 1992 Boy's Gymnasium

This homecoming invitation from November 1992 inaccurately proclaims the dance as the "75th Homecoming Dance." The homecoming traditions did not begin until 1952, with the first queen being announced at the football game. The number of students attending the dance is usually quite high, as all grade levels are welcome to attend the dance. In earlier decades, all graduates were welcome to attend the dance with the current student body. (Courtesy of Lori Spradlin.)

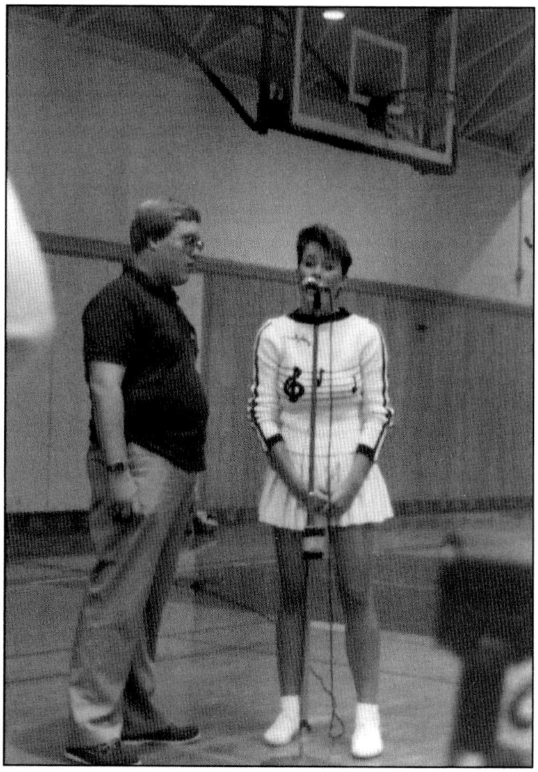

Students used to sing the theme song for the various dances. In this 1983 photograph, Jay Spradlin and Jennifer Carslon sing "Never Gonna Let You Go" by Sergio Mendes. During the 1983–1984 school year, a film crew captured a year in the life of an exchange student, Rikki Rauhala, at an American school. Titled *All-American High*, the documentary received renewed attention in the last two years. (Courtesy of Torrance High Associated Student Body.)

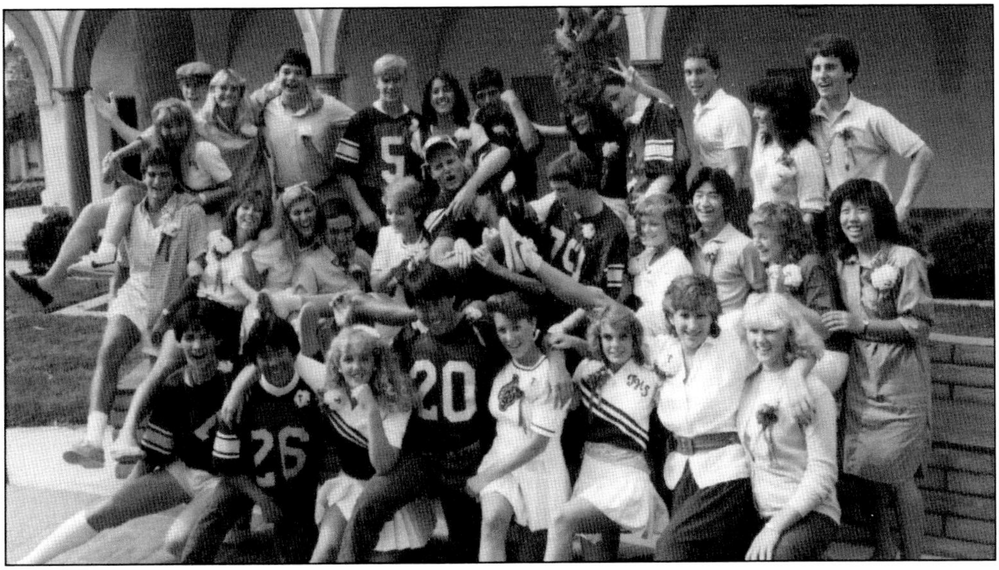

Another aspect of Torrance High's homecoming celebration is the selection of the Top 30. Initially, this was the Top 15, as only girls were included. Following the passage of Title IX, in the 1970s, a Top 15 boys were added. Students are chosen by their peers in the senior class. This photograph shows the Top 30 seniors from the class of 1984. (Courtesy of Alice Sun Davis.)

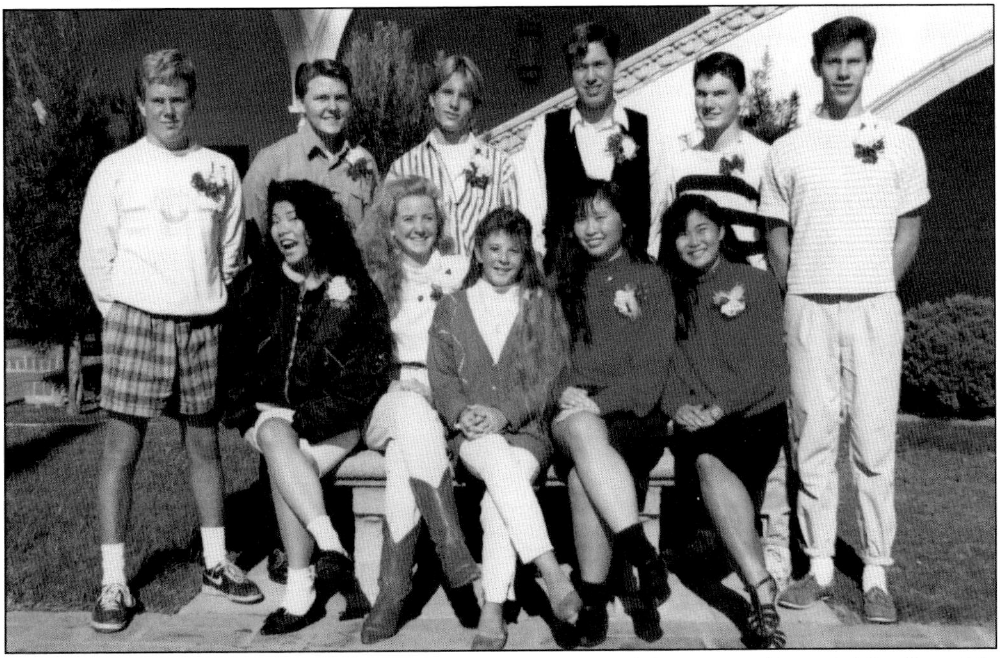

Once the Top 30 have been selected, the list is narrowed down to a Top 10. The five girls and five boys become the homecoming court, and from this group a king and queen are named. In 1989, the Top 10 included, from left to right, (first row) Gina Uehara, Michelle Webber, Tanya Bynum, Linda Ng, and Julie Ohara; (second row) Nathan Jones, Curtis Rice, Jorn Schultz, Jon Connett, David Snow, and Keith Herbers. (Courtesy of Torrance High Associated Student Body.)

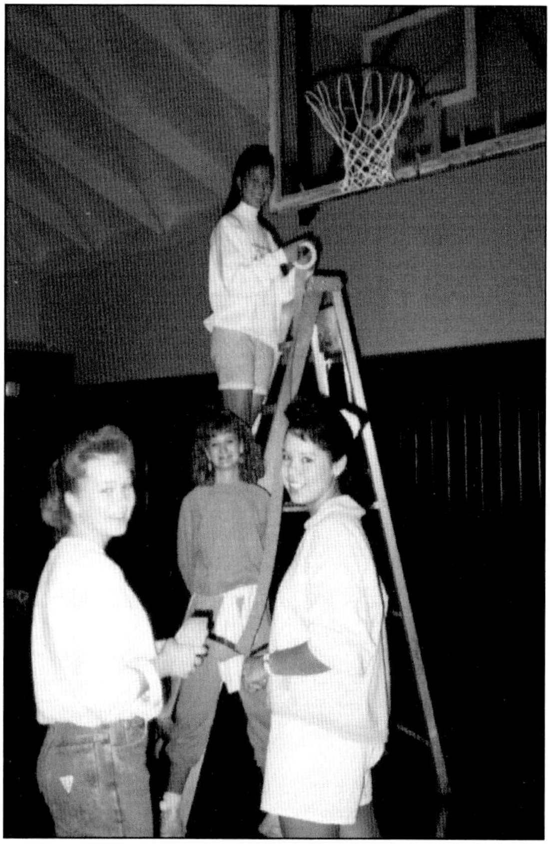

For many years, the Girls' League helped plan the homecoming festivities. Now, Service League plans a dinner for the Top 30 and organizes the decorations for the dance. Early traditions included the Top 15 girls sharing a tea with their mothers. When the boys were added, a pizza party was planned for them. By 2010, the entire Top 30 celebrated together, with their parents, at a catered dinner. Butcher paper, streamers, balloons, and twinkle lights are used to transform the gym into something less like a gym (left). Below, students celebrate the homecoming dance. It was not uncommon through the 1980s to have a band play at school dances, but by the 1990s, a DJ was hired. (Both, courtesy of Torrance High Associated Student Body.)

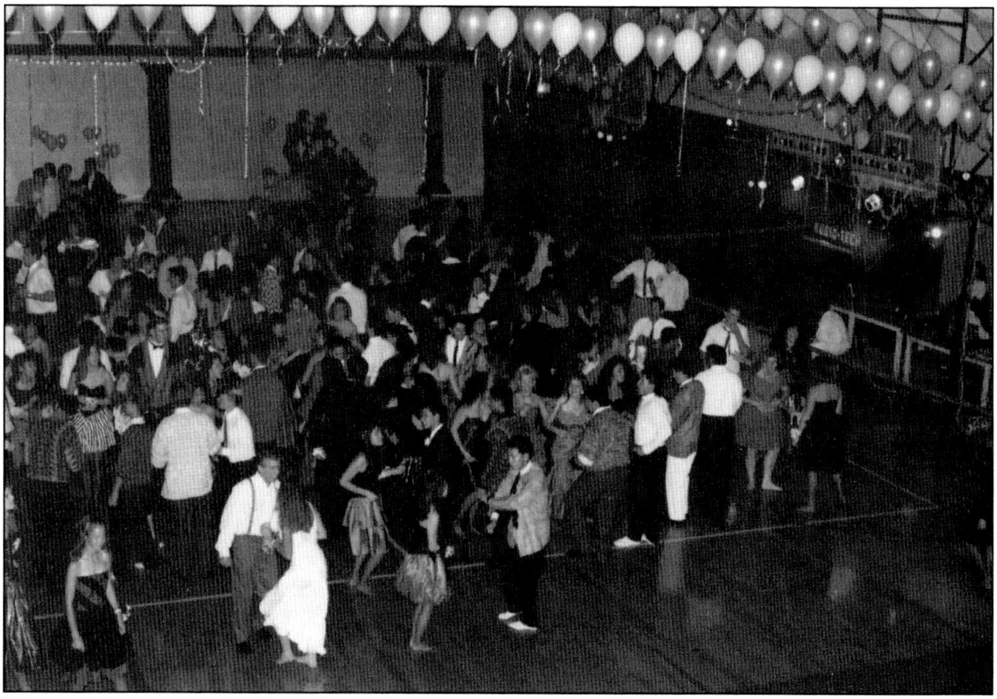

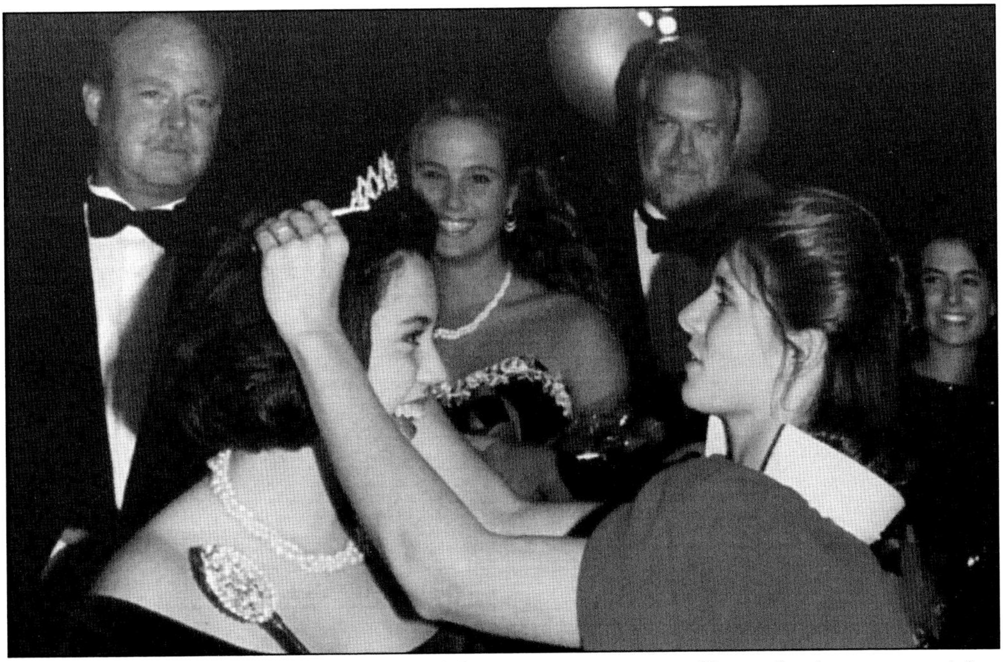

In 1992, Christine Connett was named homecoming queen. Here, she is seen receiving her crown from the previous queen, Wendy McCamish. In the 1950s, the captain of the football team would present the queen with an autographed football. In a slight departure from that tradition, the queen and four princesses each receive a football signed by the seniors on the football team. (Courtesy of Torrance High Associated Student Body.)

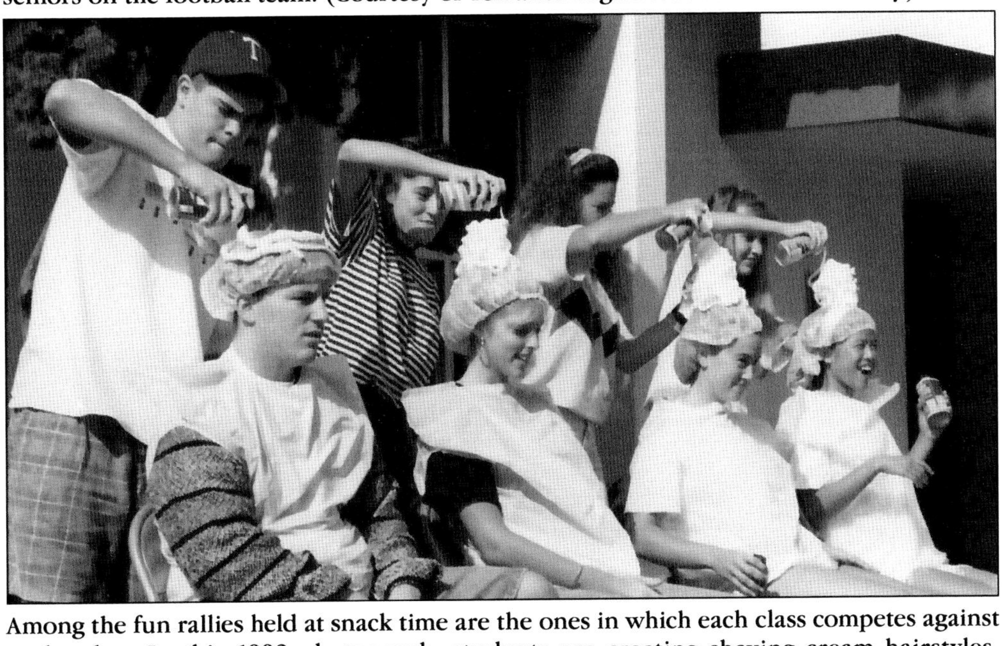

Among the fun rallies held at snack time are the ones in which each class competes against each other. In this 1992 photograph, students are creating shaving cream hairstyles, similar to Marge Simpson. It appears that the freshman and sophomore teams to the far right are leading, while the seniors on the left are struggling. (Courtesy of Torrance High Associated Student Body.)

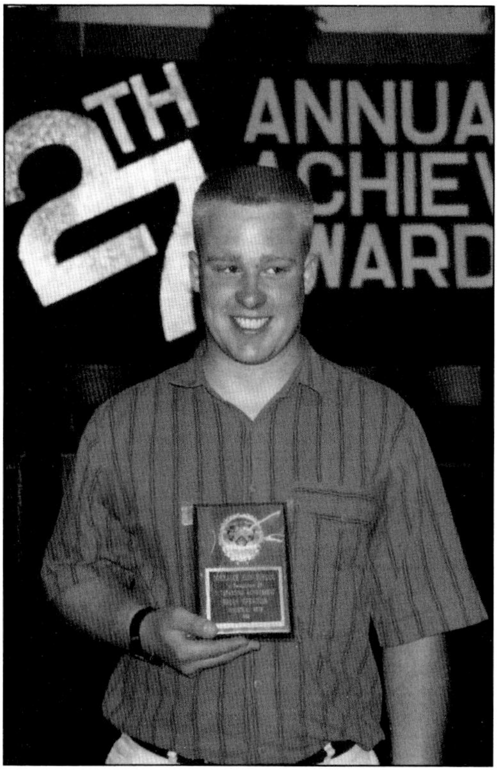

For over 50 years, the school has held its achievement awards ceremony. Torrance High School honors students in all the curricular areas, as well as other categories, like athletics and service to school. Teachers nominate students in their discipline. All nominees receive a certificate, but one student receives a plaque, like Brian Spradlin did for industrial arts in 1992 (left). In addition to honoring students in all grade levels, the achievement awards highlight seniors receiving scholarships. The program for this event, like the one seen below, list each category and each student's name. All seniors receiving scholarships are listed as well. (Left, courtesy of Charlene Spradlin; below, courtesy of Karen McKim Gebhard.)

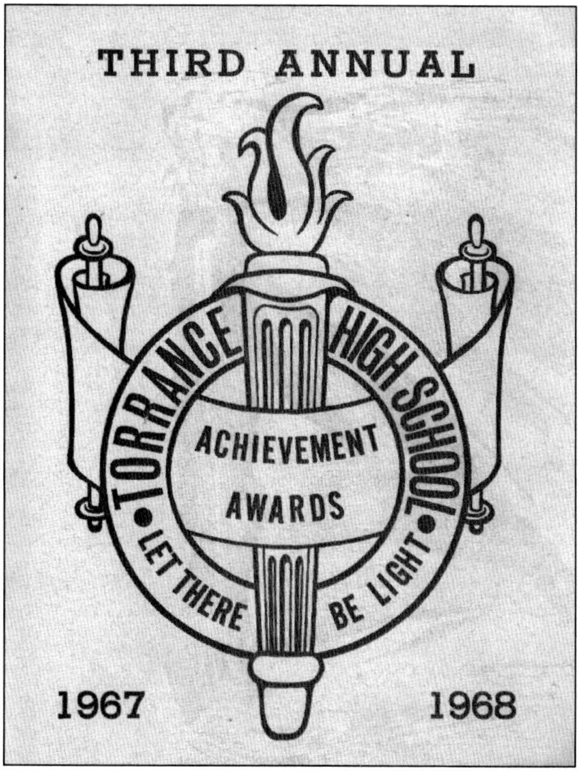

It was not uncommon to see multiple dances a year, almost one a month. The Howdy Dance was always held in September at the end of the first spirit week. Groups of friends organized whatever theme they wanted for the Howdy Dance. Chris Campbell (right) displays his disco finery, while Derek Bonnet (left) dons a more relaxed style. (Courtesy of Torrance High School Associated Student Body.)

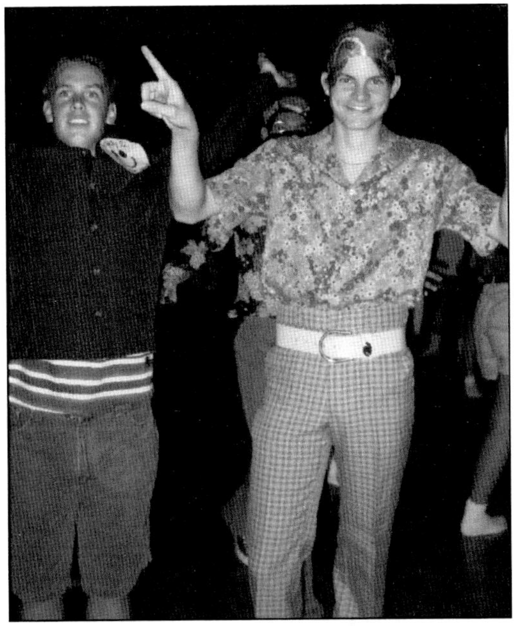

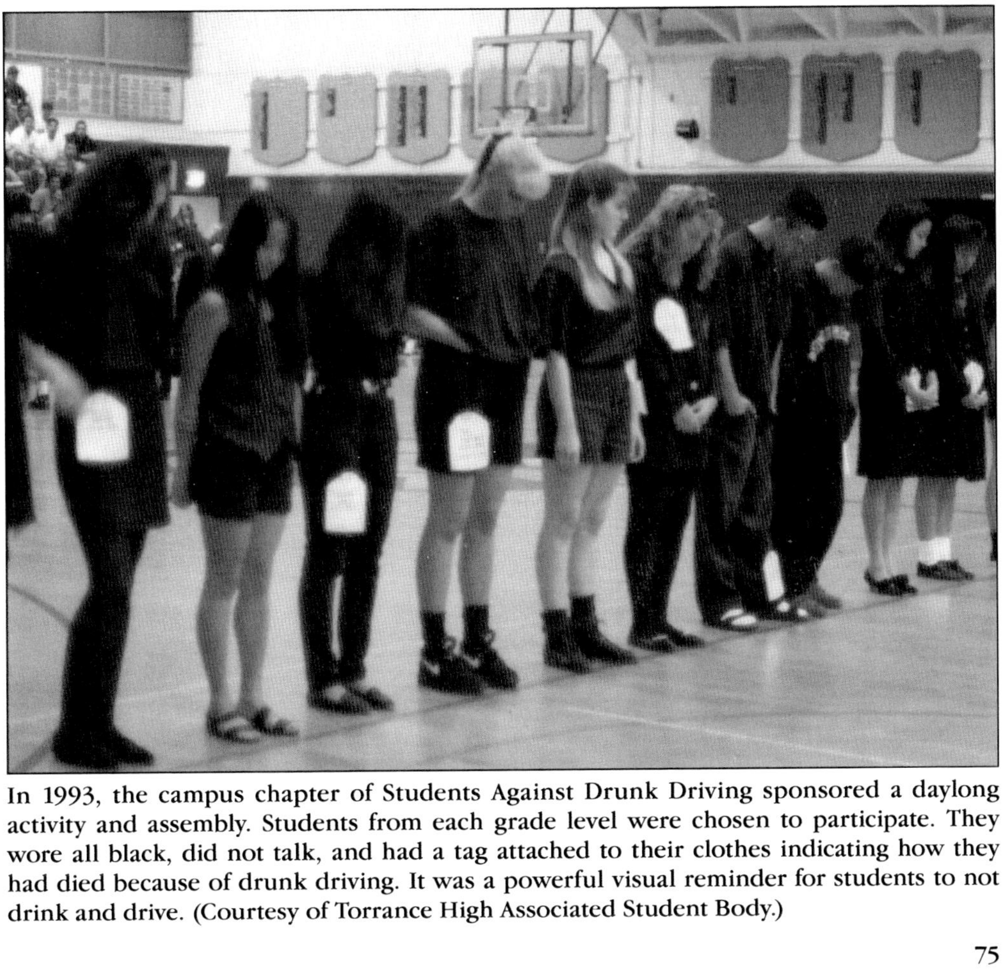

In 1993, the campus chapter of Students Against Drunk Driving sponsored a daylong activity and assembly. Students from each grade level were chosen to participate. They wore all black, did not talk, and had a tag attached to their clothes indicating how they had died because of drunk driving. It was a powerful visual reminder for students to not drink and drive. (Courtesy of Torrance High Associated Student Body.)

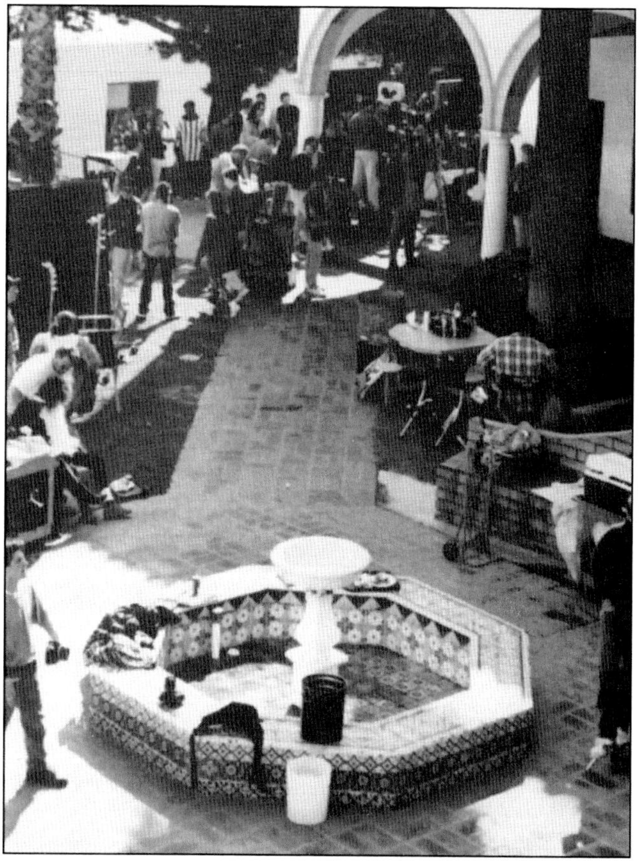

In the spring of 1990, Aaron Spelling Productions began filming *Beverly Hills, 90210* on campus. For several weeks that spring, the campus was filled with cameras, lights, and props. Periodically over the next three years, crews would return for several days at a time to film more exterior shots. While it caused some chaos on campus, it led to other productions using Torrance High. In the image to the left, crews are filming a scene on the senior patio. Below, Torrance High freshman Bryan Truchin is with Shannen Doherty, who played Brenda Walsh. In 1997, the pivotal series *Buffy the Vampire Slayer* used the campus. In 1999, the movie *She's All That* with Freddie Prinze Jr. and Paul Walker shot at Torrance High. (Left, courtesy of Torrance High Associated Student Body; below, courtesy of Lori Spradlin.)

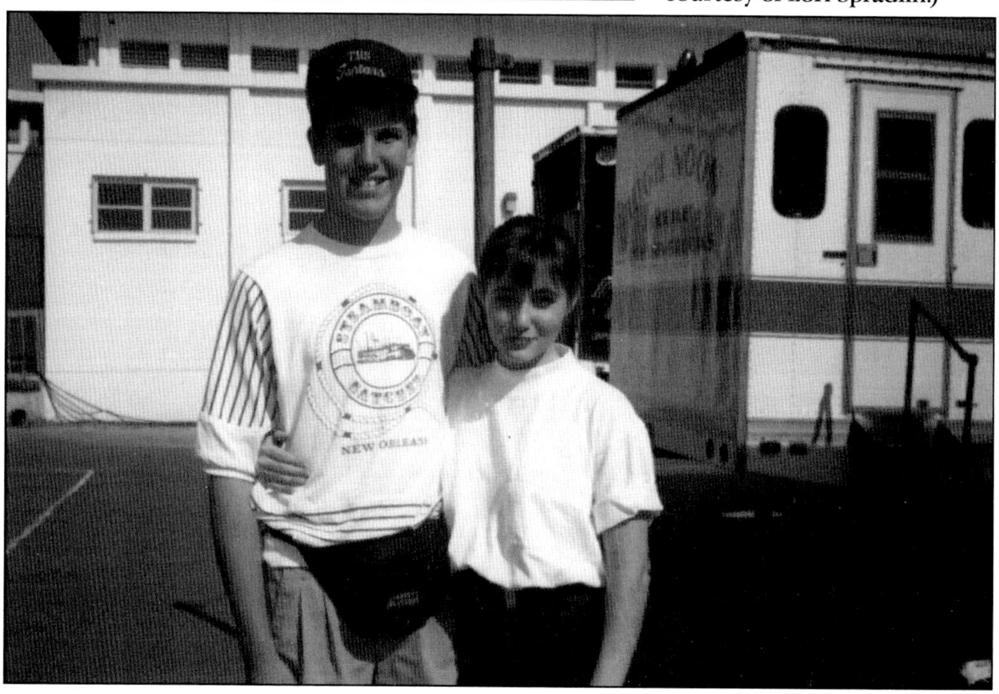

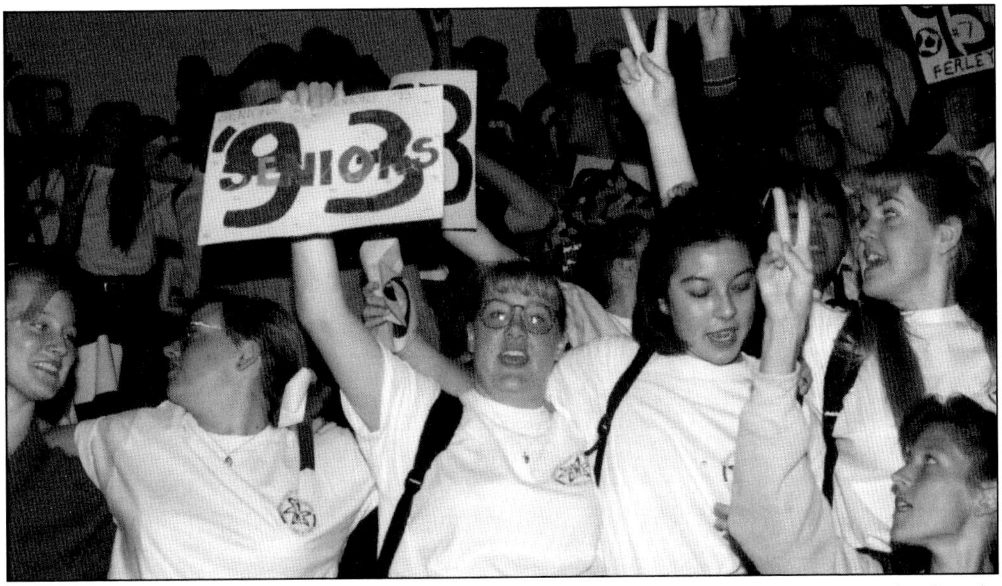

Rallies were held at snack time because students were able to leave campus for lunch. These rallies typically included a quick game and announcements. They were still a way for classes to earn spirit points and the coveted spirit stick. In this photograph from 1993, senior girls cheer their class on. From left to right are Kelci Gilley, Cynthia Donald, Lori Spradlin, Angelique Teerawatananont, Trisha Jensen, and Shelene Dale. (Courtesy of Torrance High Associated Student Body.)

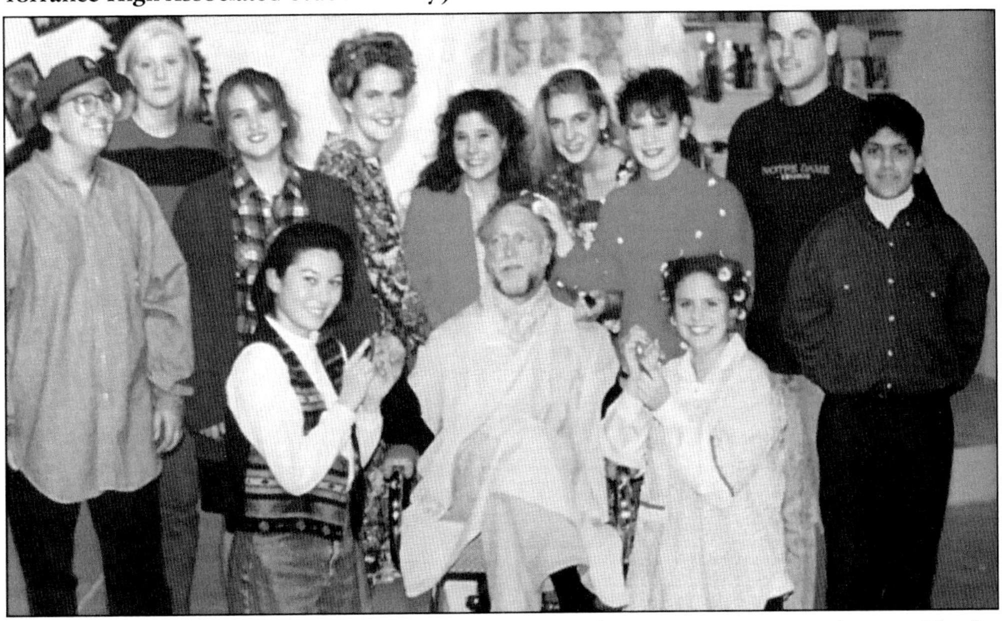

As the play producer, Chuck Slater would invite classes in to see previews, with the idea of piquing their interest to see the whole production. This 1992 production of *Steel Magnolias* featured a cast and crew of, from left to right, (first row) Angelique Teerawatananont, Slater, and Becky Sweet; (second row) Laura Corzine, Kelci Gilley, Crystal Ackman, Trisha Jensen, Dani Mador-Linnetz, Katherine Miller, Elizabeth Valleni, Chris Shea, and Minaz Ahamed. (Courtesy of Torrance High Associated Student Body.)

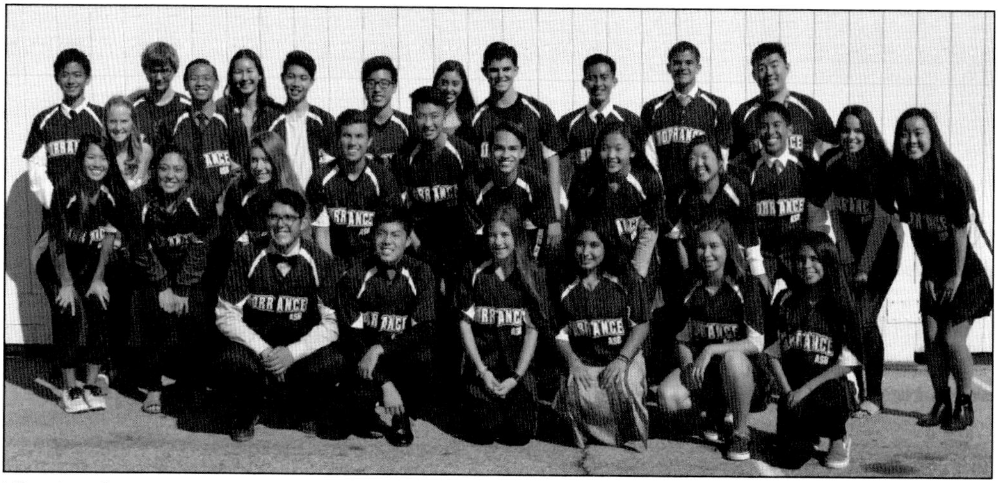

The 2016–2017 THS Associated Student Body included, from left to right, (first row) Andrew Santamaria, Chris Eguchi, Sarah Simpson, Samanta Montano, Katie Mendoza, and Daniela Sanchez; (second row): Kelly Chow, Amber Sylvester, Britny Jumalon, Ian Lutap, Jewel Mollet, Sam Gallegos, Torrey Park, Blake Porter, Subin Cho, Sara Sasaki, John Garcia, Samantha Pollock, and Macy Ishida; (third row) Jerry Chen, Ian Sloan, Ashley Sasaki, Joseph Chang, James Lee, Beth Trueman, Ryan Kirkwood, David Alejandrino, John Harvey, and Jacob Cho. (Courtesy of Torrance High School Associated Student Body.)

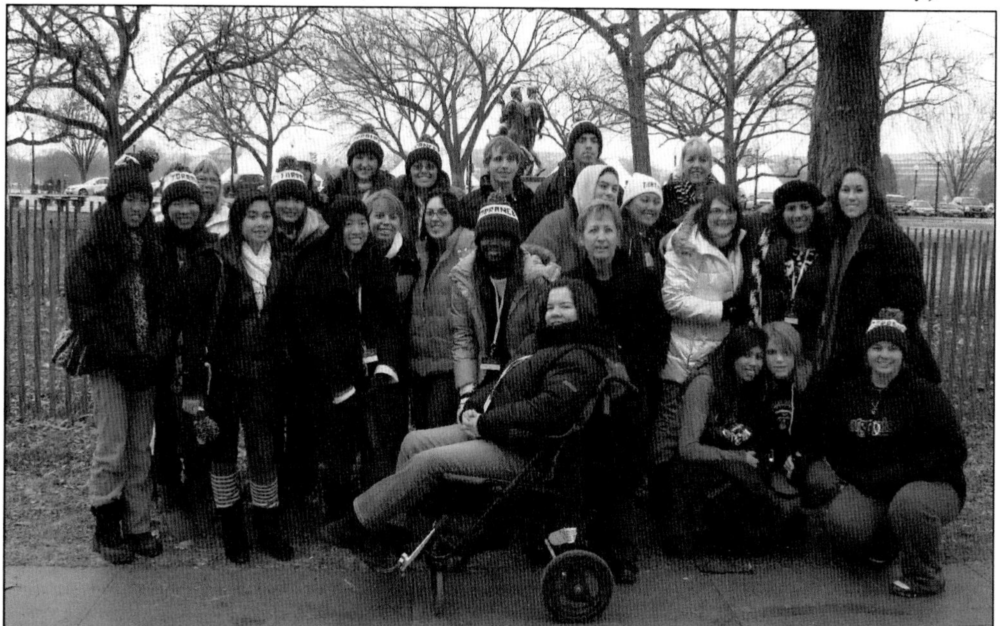

In January 2009, Torrance High teachers took a group of students to Washington, DC, to witness the inauguration of Barack Obama. While in the nation's capital, students also toured historic landmarks and visited museums. Some of the students identified in this photograph are Liz, Beyukian, Sammi Burd, Hailee Castro, Tanner, Castro, John Galyardt, Lucy Gerdes, Rochelle Gonzalez, Jennifer Hill, Heather Knudson, Zuleyma Trujillo, and Kimberly Uy; the teachers are Debbie Galyardt and Traci Castro. (Courtesy of Traci Liston Castro.)

Four

Our Strong Band

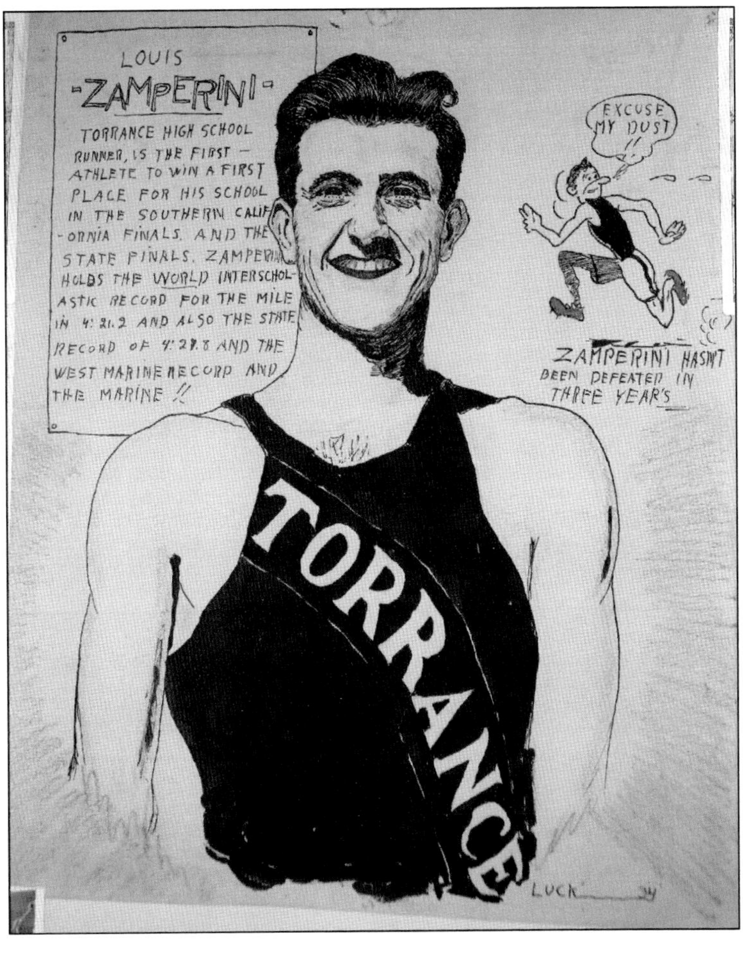

Louis Zamperini was a track star at Torrance High School in the 1930s. This drawing, done by Luck in 1934, hails Louis's achievements. Louis was the first in the region to win first place. He held the world record for the mile, a 4:21.2, along with other records. (Courtesy of Torrance Historical Society.)

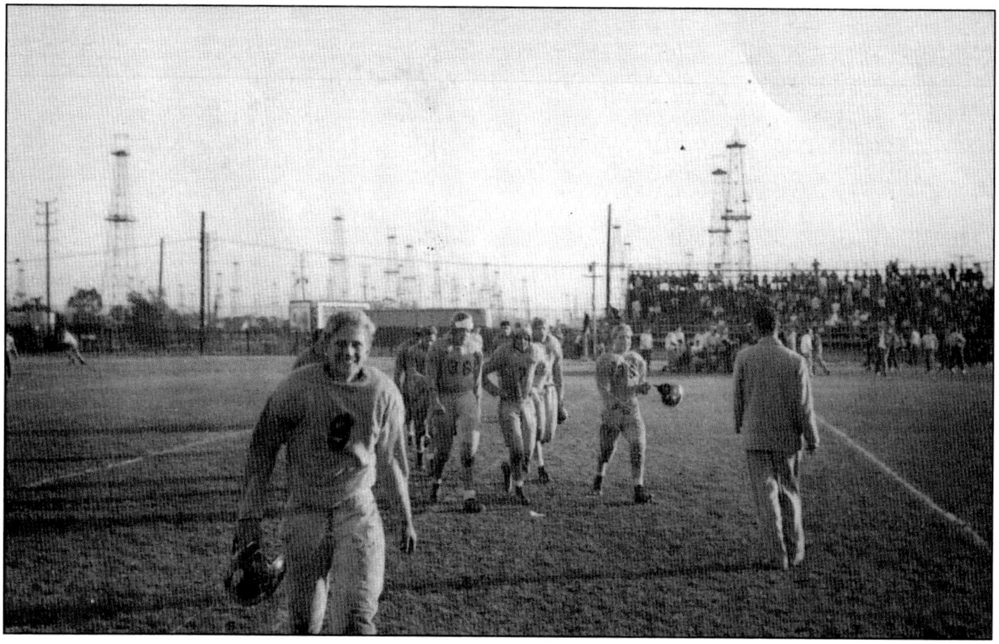

Football is one of the oldest sports played at Torrance High. In this image from around 1948, the Tartars are walking off the field in victory. Note the number of oil derricks in the background. Oil, like real estate and ranching, was an industry that really helped Southern California develop. (Courtesy of Janis Gragg.)

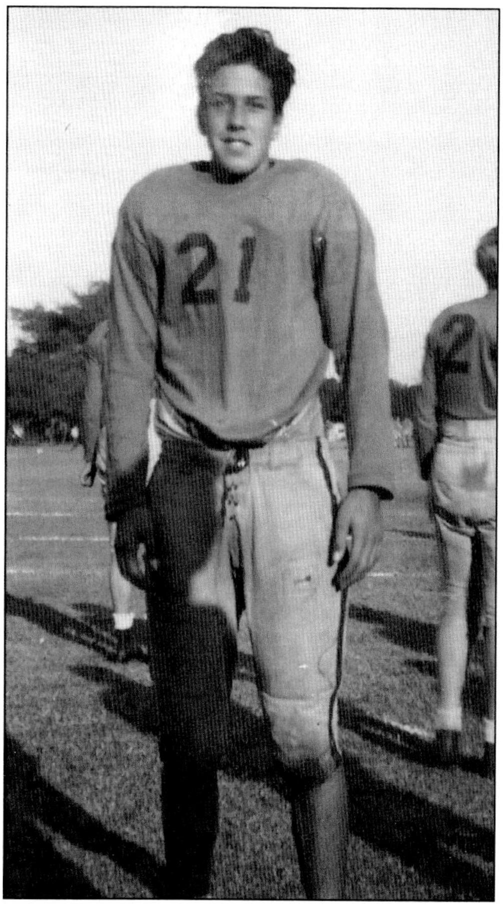

This 1948 image shows Dick Turner on the field. Turner was the cocaptain of the team, along with Milo Goettsch. During the 1948–1949 school year, Turner was the fall semester student body president. Turner was also a member of the Varsity Club and Tartar Knights. He later returned to Torrance High and served as a coach for football. (Courtesy of Janis Gragg.)

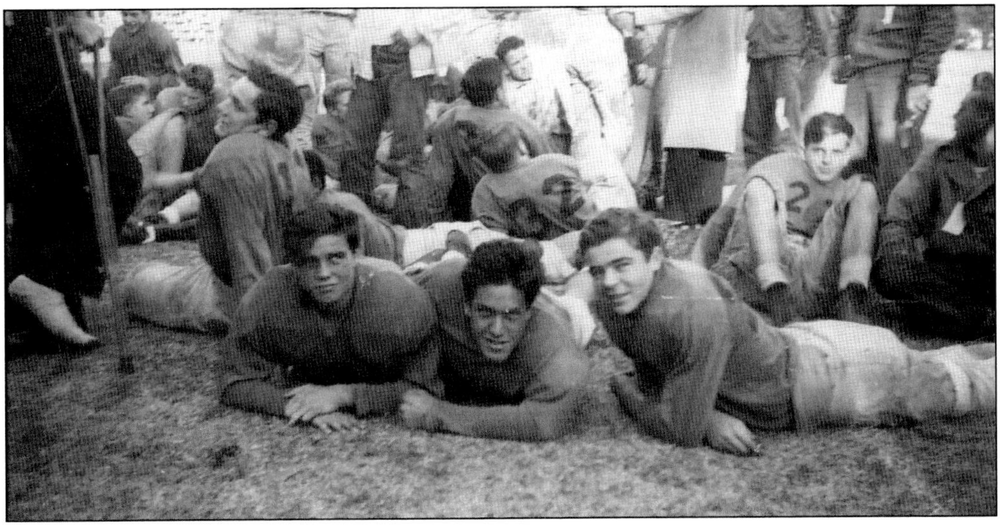

Football is one of the original sports played at Torrance High. Teams were formed as early as the 1920s to play other schools in the area. In the 1920s and 1930s, there were only a few schools near Torrance High, including Gardena and Leuzinger. As more high schools were opened in the South Bay, leagues were formed, and the California Interscholastic Federation, which was formed in 1914–1915, took oversight of many high school athletics. In the above photograph, from left to right, students only identified as Onal, Dick, and Bill rest after a successful game. The below photograph shows the varsity team from about 1948. (Both, courtesy of Janis Gragg.)

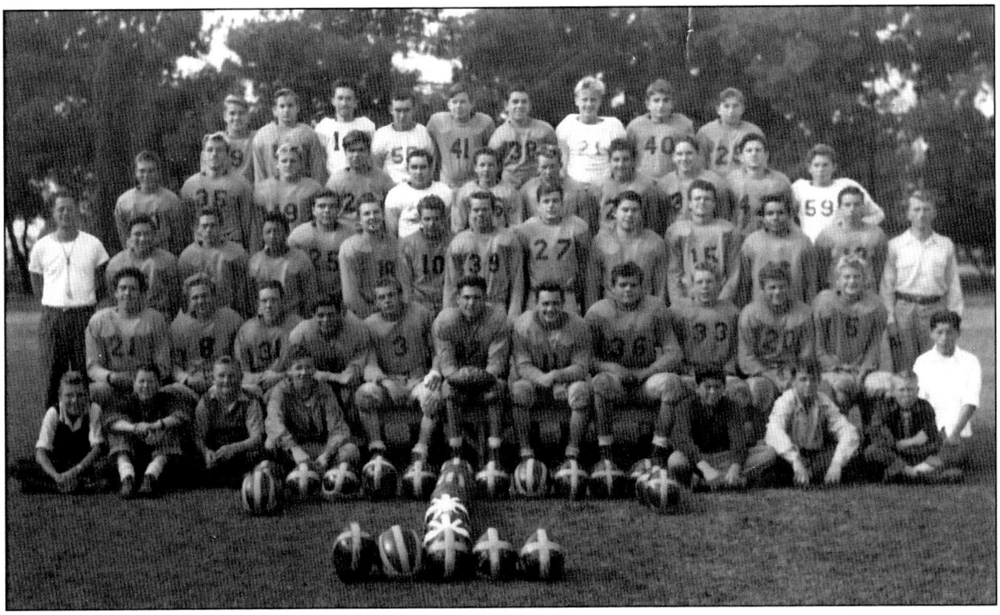

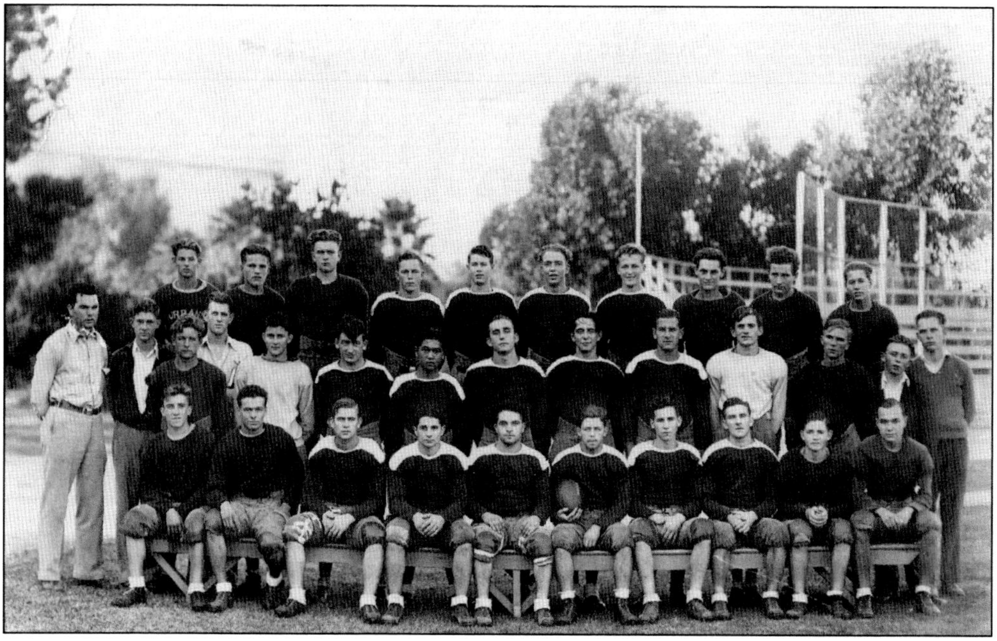

This photograph shows a football team with a date of 1932, though it does not match any from the yearbooks at that time. By the 1930s, athletic teams for football, track, baseball, basketball, and tennis had already created their strong foundations of student participation. (Courtesy of Torrance Historical Society.)

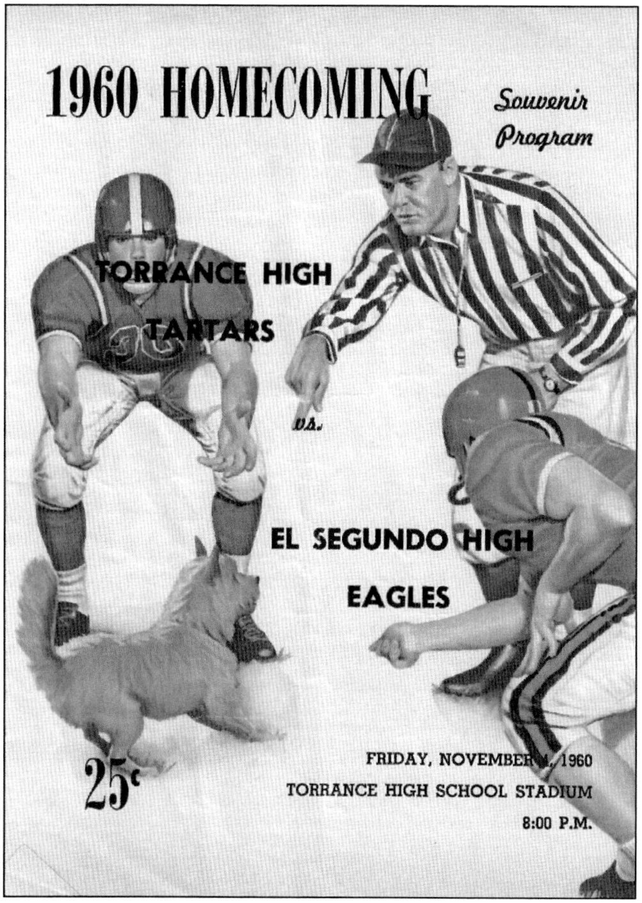

Souvenir programs were available at all football games. Inside is a list of players from each team, as well as the team's record. It is not uncommon to see diagrams of basic referee signals in these programs, so the novice viewers can understand the game. (Courtesy of the Torrance High Alumni Association.)

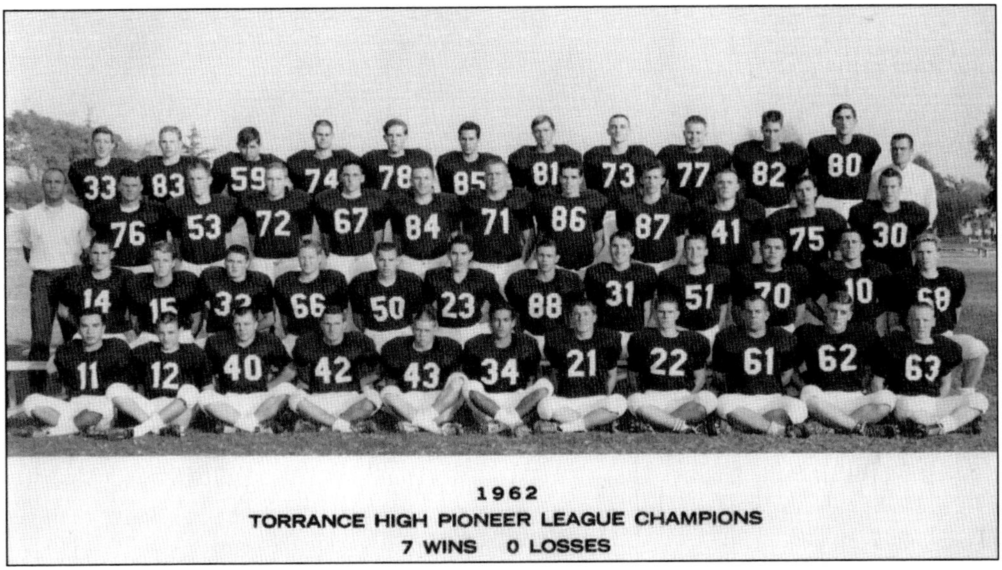

The 1962 Tartar football team went undefeated. They became the Pioneer League Champions with seven wins. Player No. 67 is Ed Foster, who, after his retirement from private industry, returned to Torrance High to work as a member of the security team. Ed retired in 2015 and moved to Tennessee to be near his son and his family. (Courtesy of the Kathy Novotny Nelson.)

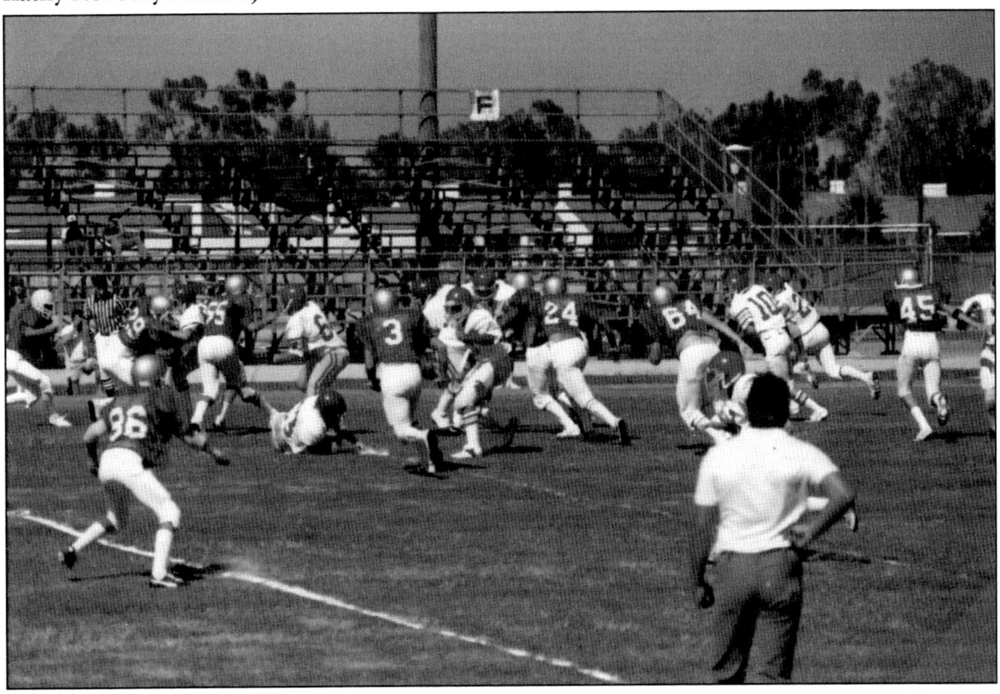

As pictured here in 1984, Torrance High fielded a freshman football team. For many decades, the lower division teams were called Bees and Cees. Today, the rough equivalent of those teams would be the junior varsity and frosh/soph levels. The lower division teams serve as strong training for the varsity level. Some lower division players may get promoted to varsity. (Courtesy of Torrance High Associated Student Body.)

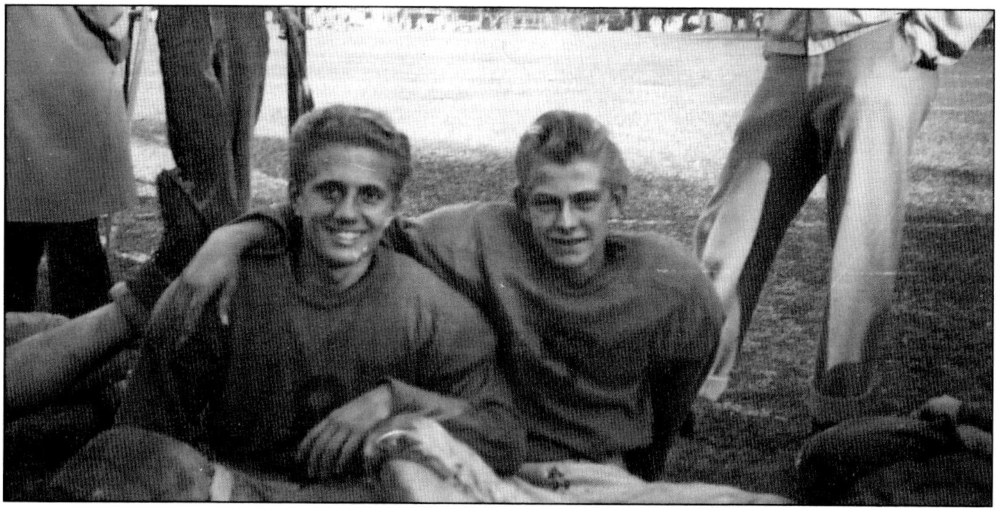

In this 1949 image, Frank Farren (left) and Milo Goettsch take a break from football. Friendships forged on the field add strength to the team. Tartar football is perhaps the most consistent athletic program. Dating to the 1920s, Torrance High has fielded a team every year. Like many programs, some years have more successful records, but each team always puts forth their best effort. (Courtesy of Janis Gragg.)

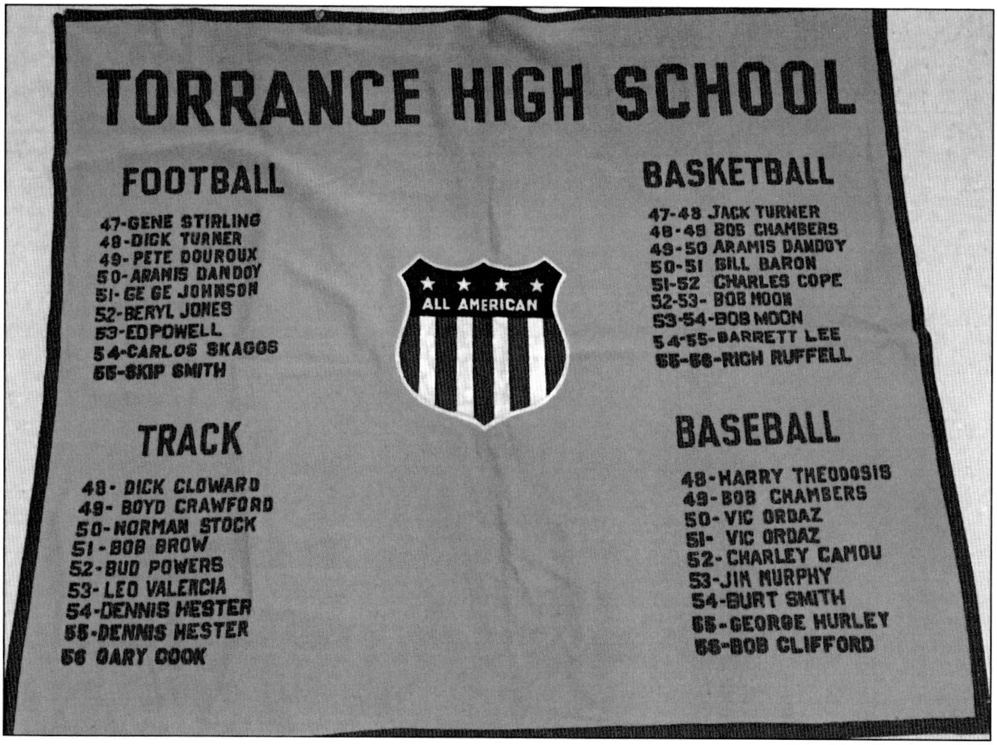

At the end of each season, one athlete's name was added to the Blanket Award. Originally, the names were sewn on an actual fabric wall hanging, as seen in this photograph. When some of the blankets started wearing thin and becoming damaged, the names were instead added to shields that hang in the main gym. (Courtesy of Torrance High Alumni Association.)

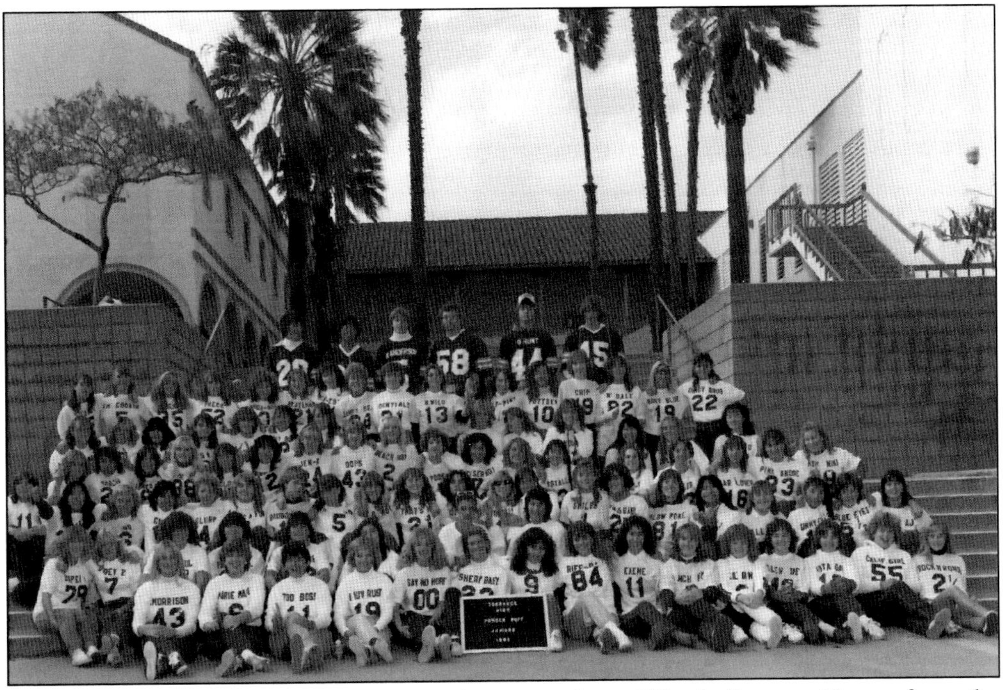

Each spring, senior girls can sign up to play a powderpuff football game. Players from the varsity football team sign up to coach the girls and there is a draft to determine which team the girls will join. Originally, the powderpuff games were played in the fall. As the game moved to the spring, it became a fundraiser for the PTSA. (Courtesy of Torrance High Associated Student Body.)

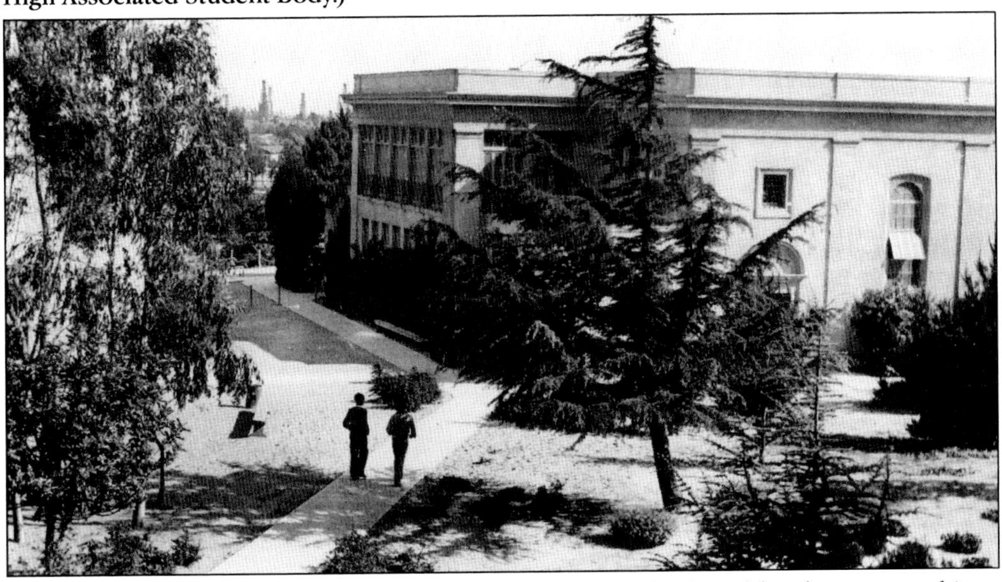

In 1936, a gymnasium was constructed on the campus. Designed by the same architect as the new auditorium, this photograph from the 1940s shows the boys' gym as being constructed in a similar design as the earlier buildings. The gym was renovated in 1965, the same time a separate gymnasium was built for girls. (Courtesy of Torrance Historical Society.)

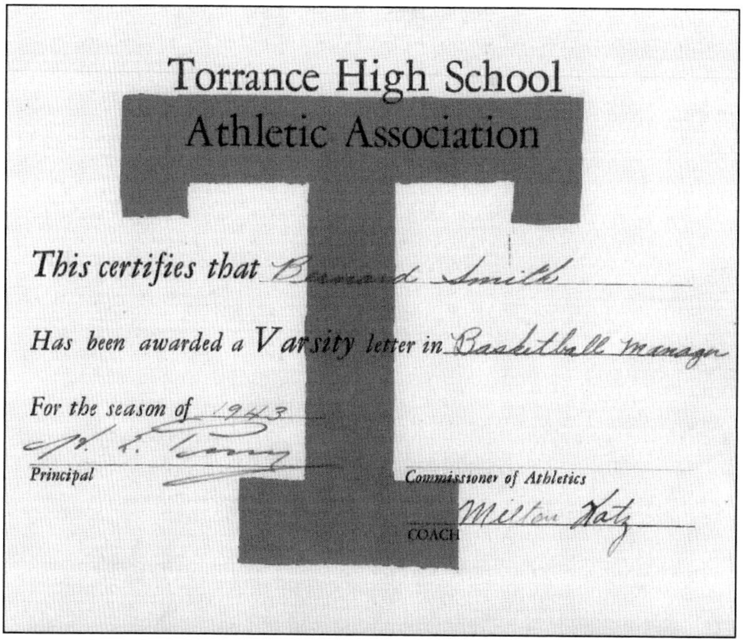
Torrance High School
Athletic Association

This certifies that Bernard Smith

Has been awarded a Varsity letter in Basketball manager

For the season of 1943

Principal

Commissioner of Athletics

Milton Katz
COACH

This 1943 athletic certificate was awarded to Bernard Smith, who earned his varsity letter for managing the basketball team. Like many students, Smith was a multisport athlete, playing football and participating on the track team in addition to basketball. Students who reach varsity level earn a letter. (Courtesy of Torrance High Alumni Association.)

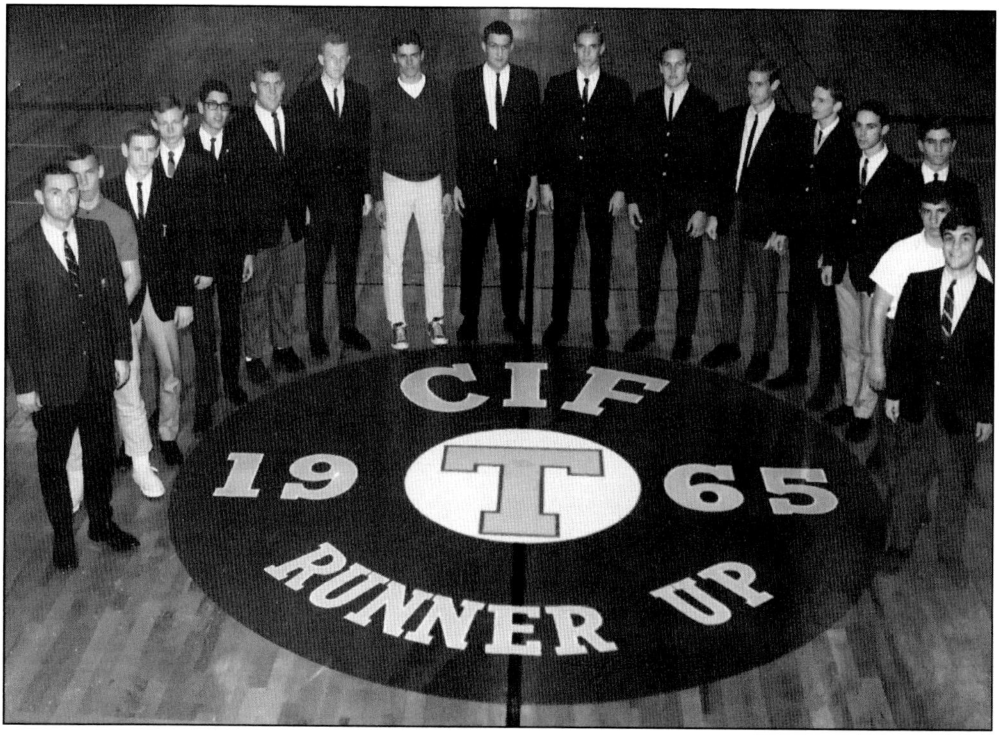

Coach Will Boerger took the 1965 basketball team to the CIF Championships. The team, known as "Boerger's Bombers," fell short of the title. Here, the team is circled around the mat honoring their achievement. Pictured here are Coach Boerger (far right) and (alphabetically) Bob Brennan, Jon Chayowski, Jim Crocket, Richard Davies, Robin Fischer, Walt Hale, Bart Johnson, Dick Kruel, Jim Oliver, John Osbourne, Mike Troup, Jack Tweedy, Louis Velarde, and Bob Whittney, (Courtesy of Torrance High School Alumni Association.)

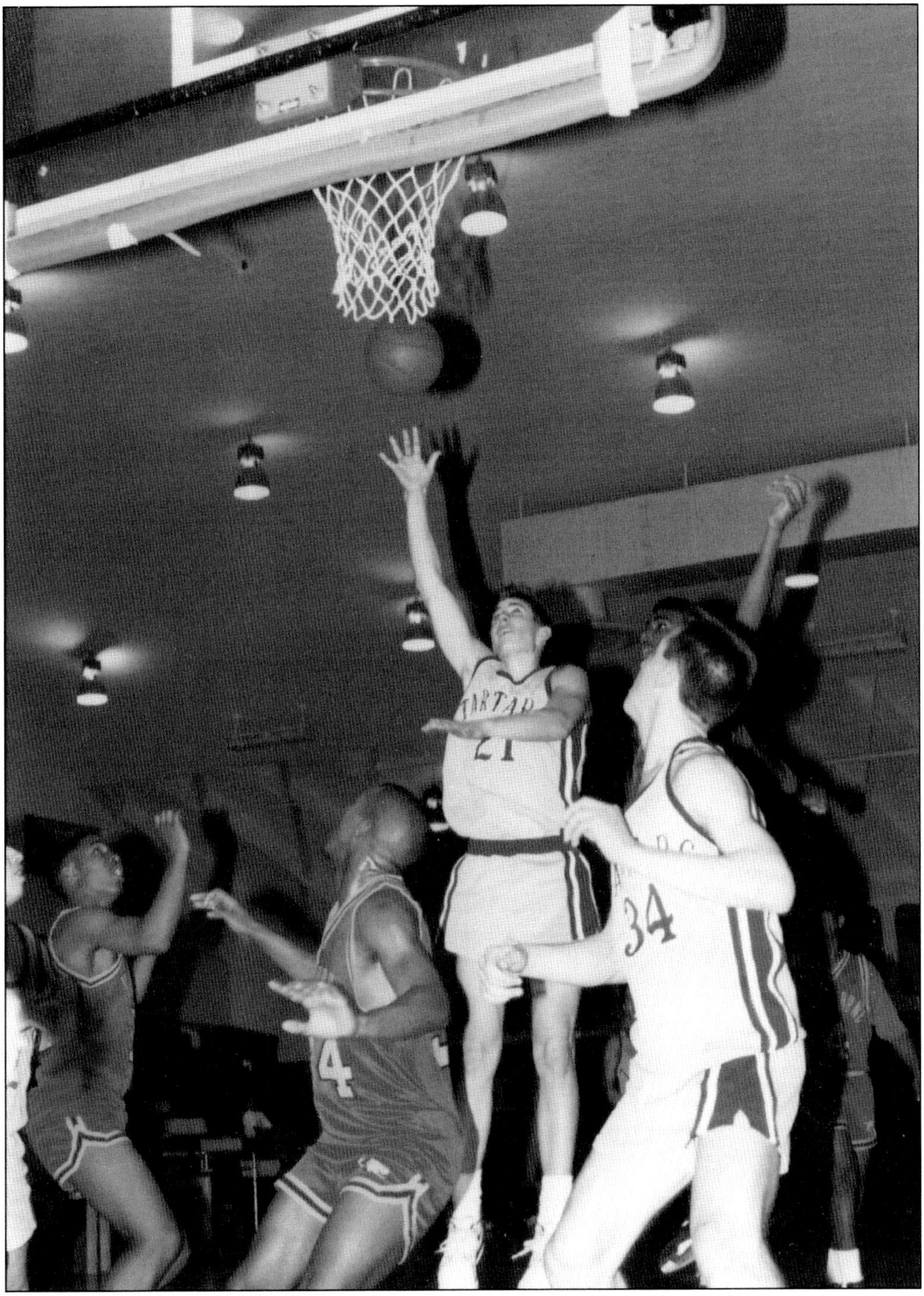

Like football, basketball at Torrance High dates back to the 1920s. In this photograph from 1990, junior Joe Zalatel protects senior Rick Robison as he makes a shot. The team ended that season with a 10-14 record, amid a challenging season with coaching changes that continued to just prior to the season starting. (Courtesy of Torrance High Associated Student Body.)

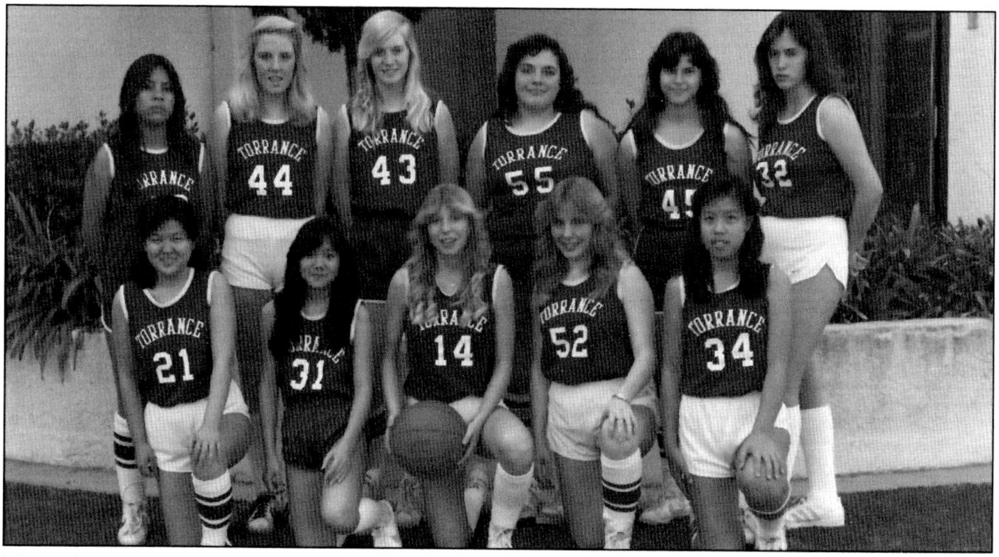

This photograph shows the 1982 junior varsity girls' basketball team. Pictured from left to right are (first row) Colleen Kozawa, Stacey Shimabukuro, Jill Kling, Sherri Blaurock, and Alice Sun; (second row) Virginia Alonzo, Christine Irvine, Crissa Brown, Liz Torres, Veronica Vigil, and Jamie Morris. (Courtesy of Alice Sun Davis.)

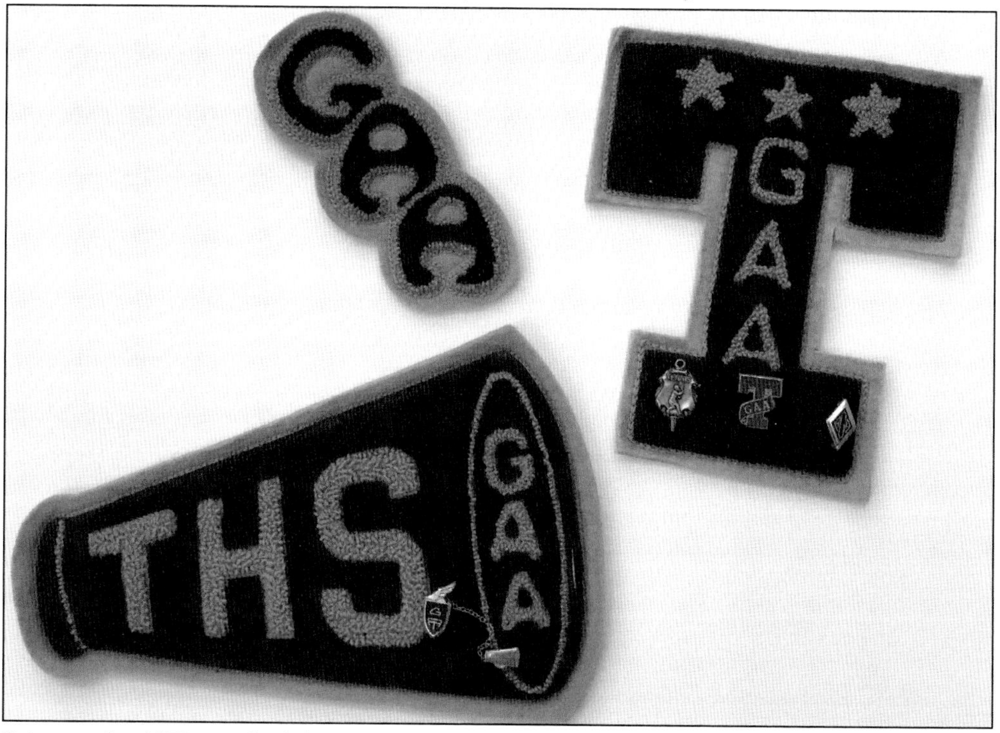

Prior to the 1970s, girls did not play sports in leagues aligned to the boys. Girls played competitively through the Girls' Athletic Association (GAA). This group organized athletic competitions for girls at neighboring schools. In 1972, the passage of Title IX prompted gender equity for all educational activities receiving federal funding. By the late 1970s, the GAA had disappeared, and girls enjoyed more sports. (Courtesy of Torrance High Alumni Association.)

In the late 1970s, Dale Liston helped organize a program for girls' soccer at Torrance High. In 1981, the team went to the California Interscholastic Federation final against Palos Verdes High School, as seen by the CIF program at right. Though they lost in that matchup, the Tartars finished the season with a record of 17-1. Pictured from left to right are (first row) Monique Marcoux, Lisa Santo, Beth Snodgrass, Norine Aoki, Yvonne Cucci, and Kathy Fitzgerald; (second row) Jolene Hansen, Katy Urwin, Colleen Kevanny, Traci Stevenson, and Traci Snodgrass; (third row) Patti Lobb, Conni Cowman, Lori Morris, Traci Liston, Carol Johnson, and coach Dale Liston. (Both, courtesy of Traci Liston Castro.)

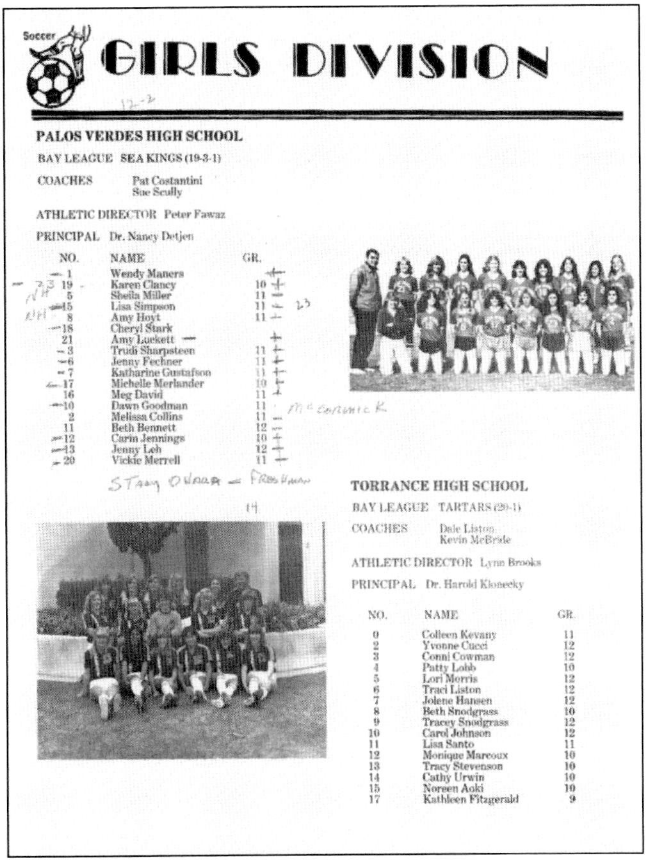

Soccer

GIRLS DIVISION

PALOS VERDES HIGH SCHOOL

BAY LEAGUE SEA KINGS (19-3-1)

COACHES Pat Costantini
Sue Scully

ATHLETIC DIRECTOR Peter Fawaz

PRINCIPAL Dr. Nancy Detjen

NO.	NAME	GR.
1	Wendy Maners	
19	Karen Clancy	10
5	Sheila Miller	11
15	Lisa Simpson	11
8	Amy Hoyt	11
18	Cheryl Stark	
21	Amy Luckett	
3	Trudi Sharpsteen	11
6	Jenny Fechner	11
7	Katharine Gustafson	11
17	Michelle Merlander	10
16	Meg David	11
10	Dawn Goodman	11
2	Melissa Collins	11
11	Beth Bennett	12
12	Carin Jennings	10
13	Jenny Leh	12
20	Vickie Merrell	11

TORRANCE HIGH SCHOOL

BAY LEAGUE TARTARS (20-1)

COACHES Dale Liston
Kevin McBride

ATHLETIC DIRECTOR Lynn Brooks

PRINCIPAL Dr. Harold Klonecky

NO.	NAME	GR.
0	Colleen Kevany	11
2	Yvonne Cucci	12
3	Conni Cowman	12
4	Patty Lobb	10
5	Lori Morris	12
6	Traci Liston	12
7	Jolene Hansen	12
8	Beth Snodgrass	10
9	Tracey Snodgrass	12
10	Carol Johnson	12
11	Lisa Santo	11
12	Monique Marcoux	10
13	Tracy Stevenson	10
14	Cathy Urwin	10
15	Noreen Aoki	10
17	Kathleen Fitzgerald	9

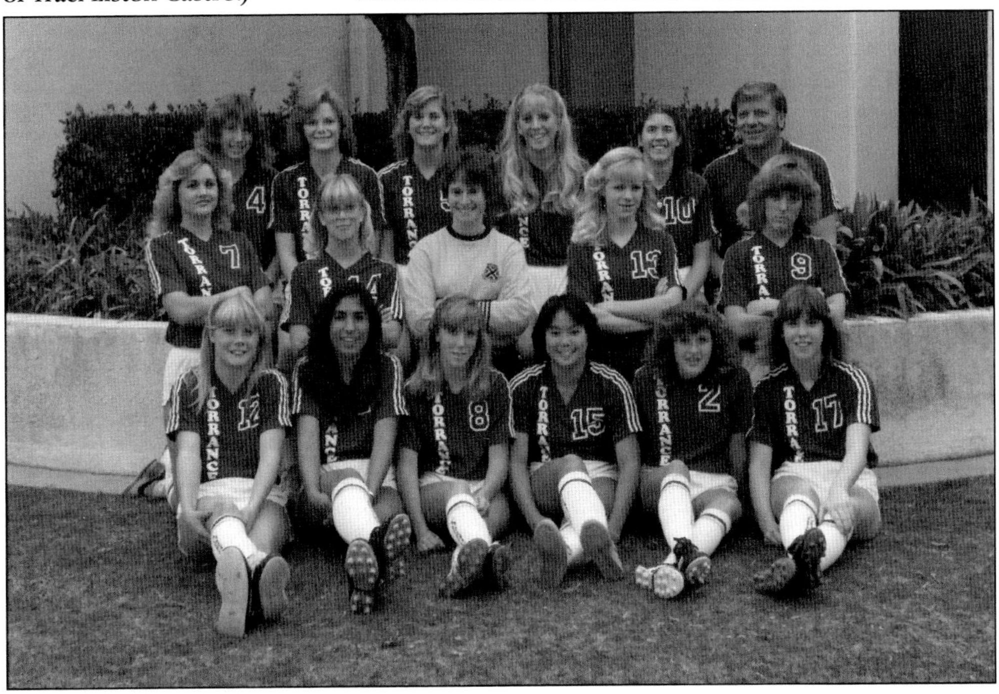

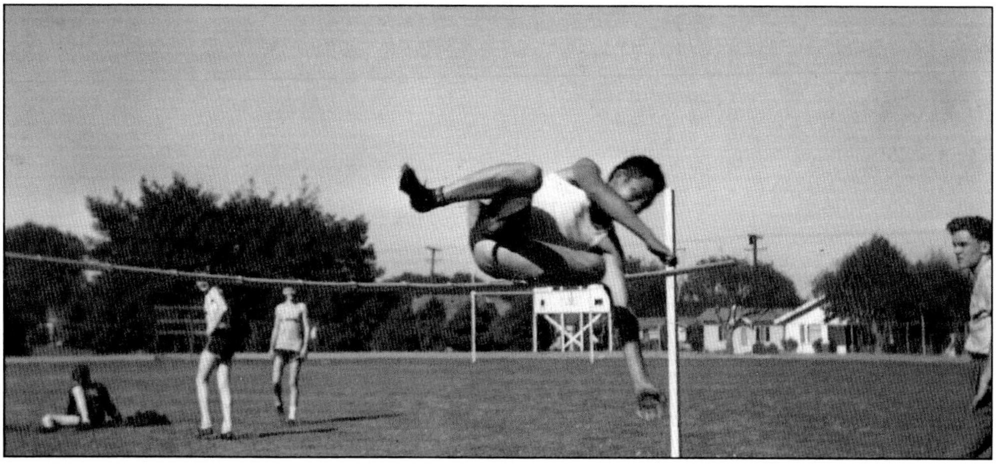

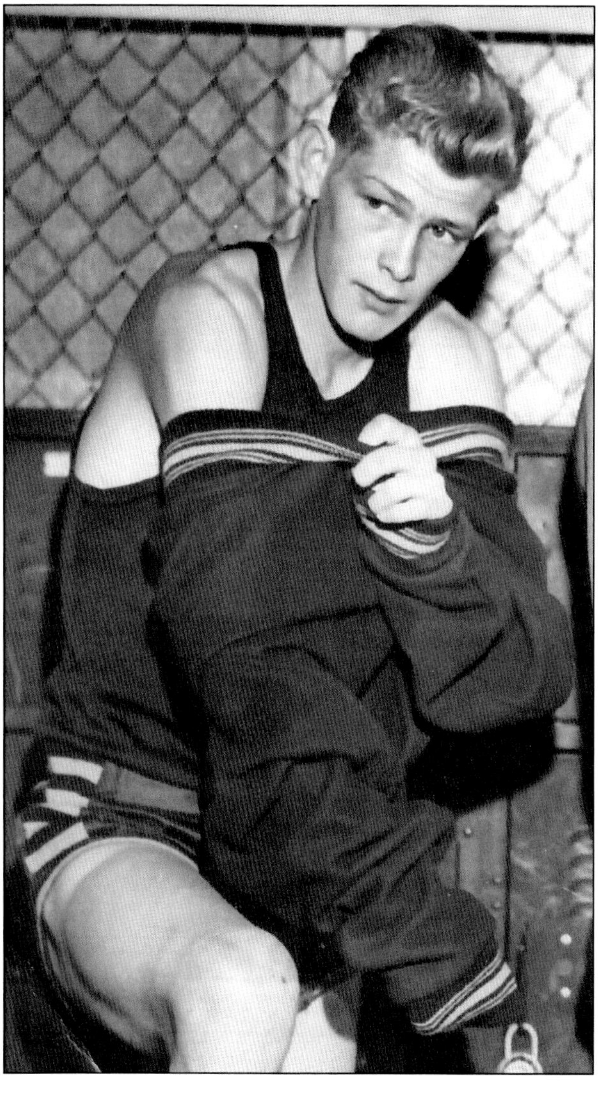

An unnamed high jumper clears the bar in this image from the 1930s. Track and field events have been a significant part of the Torrance High athletic program. By the 2000s, it was not uncommon to find 100 students on the roster for track. Because of the many events, it is appealing to many different athletes, even from other sports. (Courtesy of the Torrance Historical Society.)

Milo Goettsch was a premier athlete in 1949. He lettered in track, basketball, and football. Until sometime in the 1970s, he held the school record for the high hurdles. Goettsch was scouted by Stanford and ready to play football at the collegiate level, but he put his collegiate athletics on hold by getting married to Anna Jane Kelley. (Courtesy of Janis Gragg.)

Long before he was known to the world as a hero, Louis Zamperini was a track star at Torrance High. In 1934, he broke the high school mile record with a time of 4:21.2. Louis ran in the 1936 Olympics in Berlin, Germany, but he did not medal. (Courtesy of Torrance High School.)

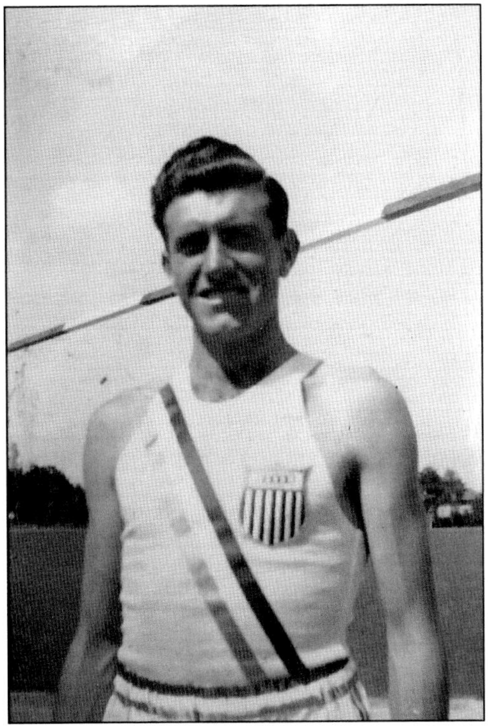

Over the years, Louis Zamperini would return to Torrance High to visit with the students and share his remarkable story. On March 31, 2011, which was declared Louis Zamperini Day, Louis made his last visit to Torrance High School. ASB president Danish Akmal presented Zamperini with the No. 1 Tartar Award. In this photograph, Akmal is seen shaking Zamperini's hand, while Torrance High Alumni Association president Gail Morgan looks on. (Courtesy of Danish Akmal.)

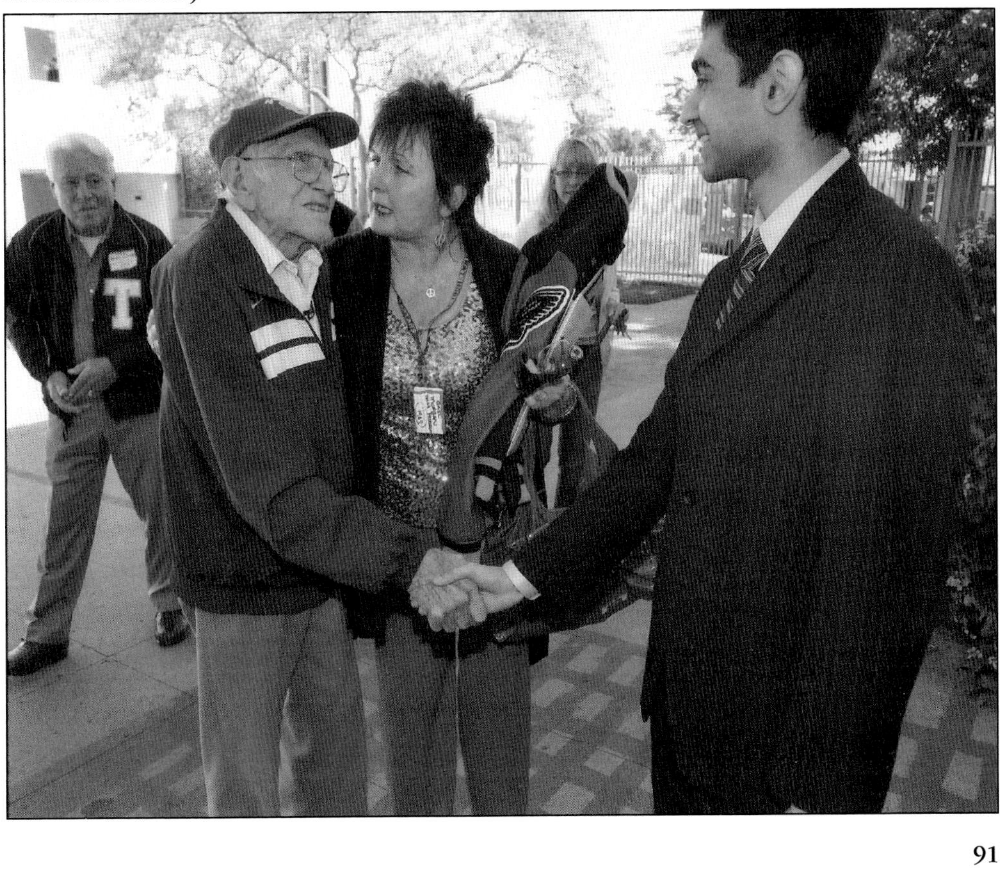

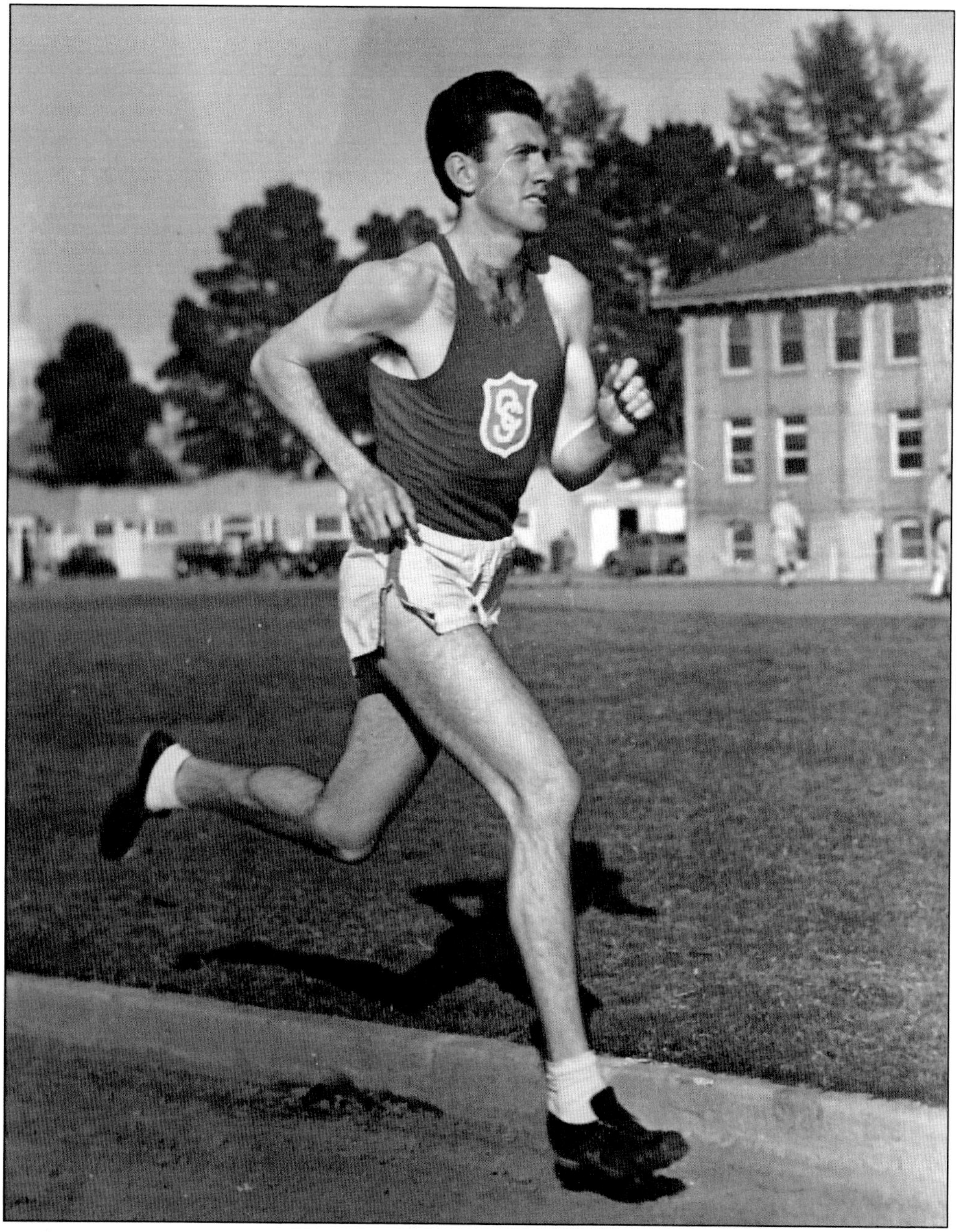

By the time Louis Zamperini was in his early teens, the police chief in the city of Torrance knew him well, as he had been caught stealing more than once. Running track became a way out of his troubled lifestyle. With the help of his brother Pete, Louis had a renewed focus that led him to break several track records. Louis ran in the 1936 Olympics in Berlin. When he returned, he attended University of Southern California. He joined the Army Air Corps during World War II and was stationed in Hawaii as a bombardier. During a flying mission, Louis's plane was shot down. He and two others survived the crash and were adrift at sea. After being adrift for 47 days, Zamperini and the other man remaining were taken as POWs to Japan. (Courtesy of Torrance Historical Society.)

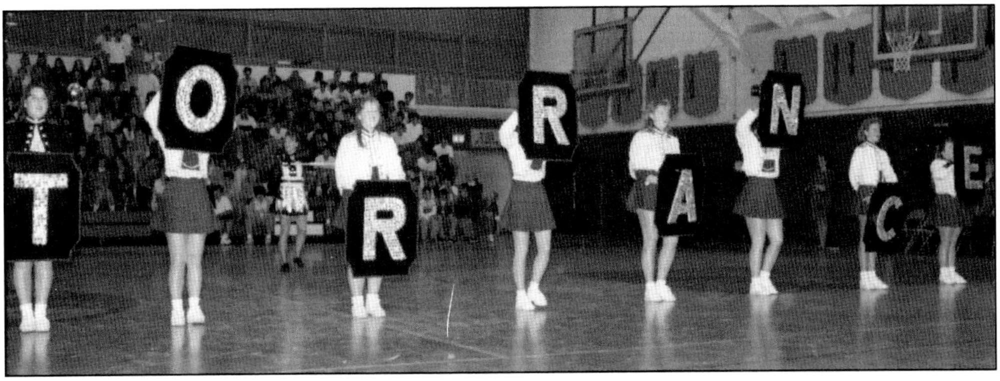

According to the *Torrance High School Torch*, the Torrance High Banner Squad was introduced in 1980. As this image from the early 1990s shows, each girl carried a different letter to spell out "Torrance." As the girls walked in parades or performed in competitions, they would spin the letters and twirl to choreographed routines. Sadly, by the end of the 1990s, the banner squad no longer performed. (Courtesy of Torrance High Associated Student Body.)

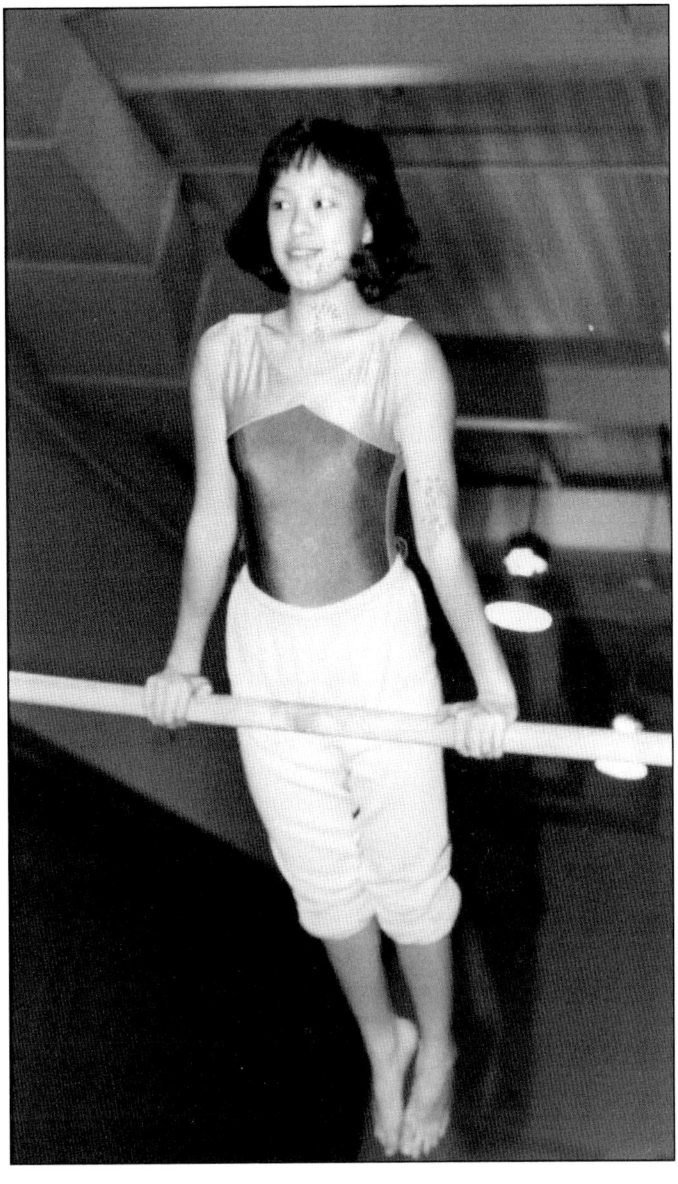

Gymnastics date back to the mid-1940s when Pete Zamperini coached a team of boys that competed on a rope that was too short and high bar and parallel bars that were too low and did not have enough mats. By the 1970s, gymnastics had become a sport for girls. This image shows Lila Paik on the uneven bars in 1988. Due to budget constraints, this was the last year of the program. (Courtesy of Torrance High Associated Student Body.)

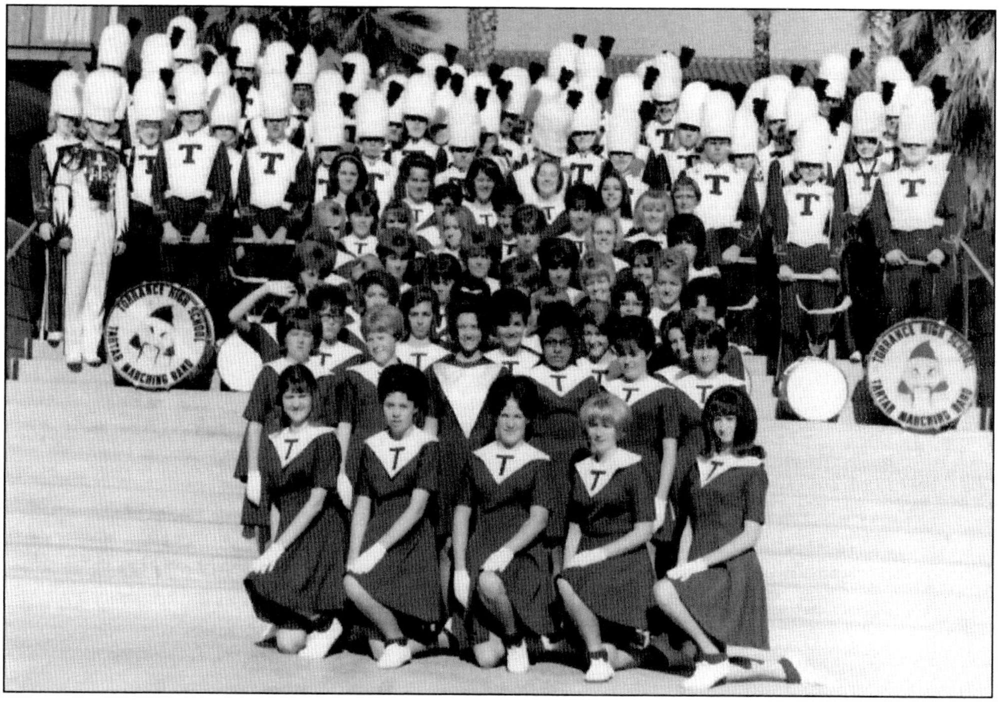

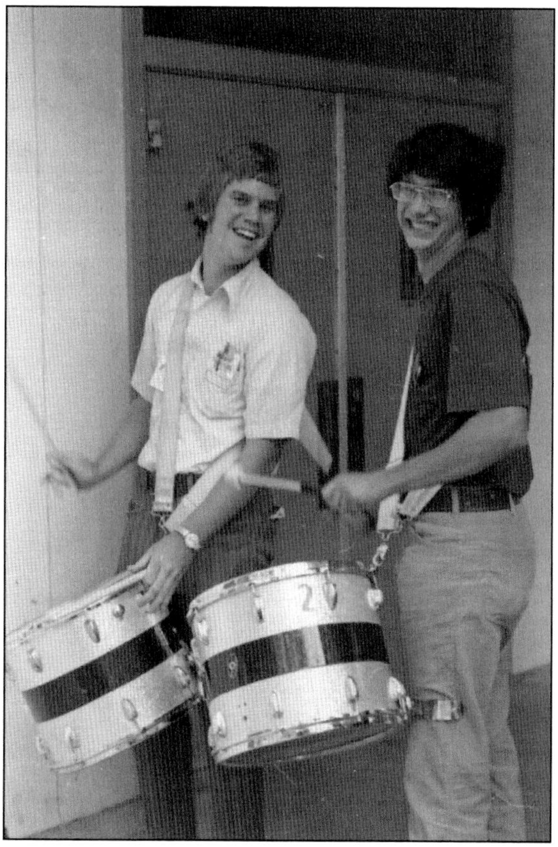

While the marching band was a long-standing program at Torrance High, in 1965, the drill team was added. This image shows the first drill team, along with the marching band. Drill took a short hiatus in the late 1990s and early 2000s, but it was reintroduced in 2011. (Courtesy of Torrance High Associated Student Body.)

In this 1975 photograph, Dennis St. Amour (left) and John Fontana demonstrate the role that percussion instruments play in the band. The Tartar band consists of the Marching Alliance, a jazz band, drumline, and color guard. They often perform together, but each unit is an award-winning team in its own right. (Courtesy of Torrance High Associated Student Body.)

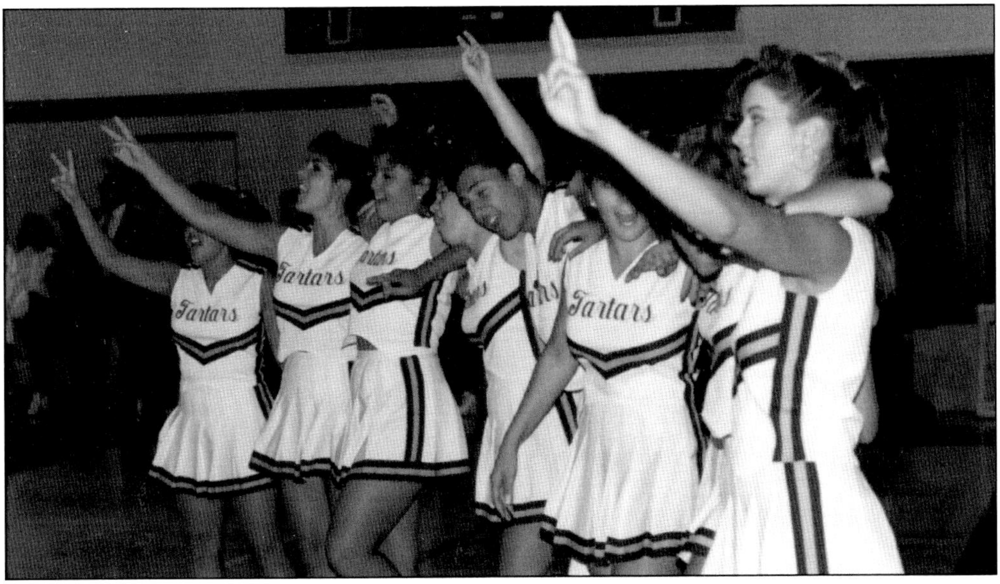

The Torrance High Pep Squad has a long-standing tradition of winning awards at competitions. Through the 1940s, it was rare to see females in the Pep Club, as it was called then. By the 1960s, it had become rare to see males on the squad. This 1980s photograph shows members of the pep squad leading students in the alma mater. (Courtesy of Torrance High Associated Student Body.)

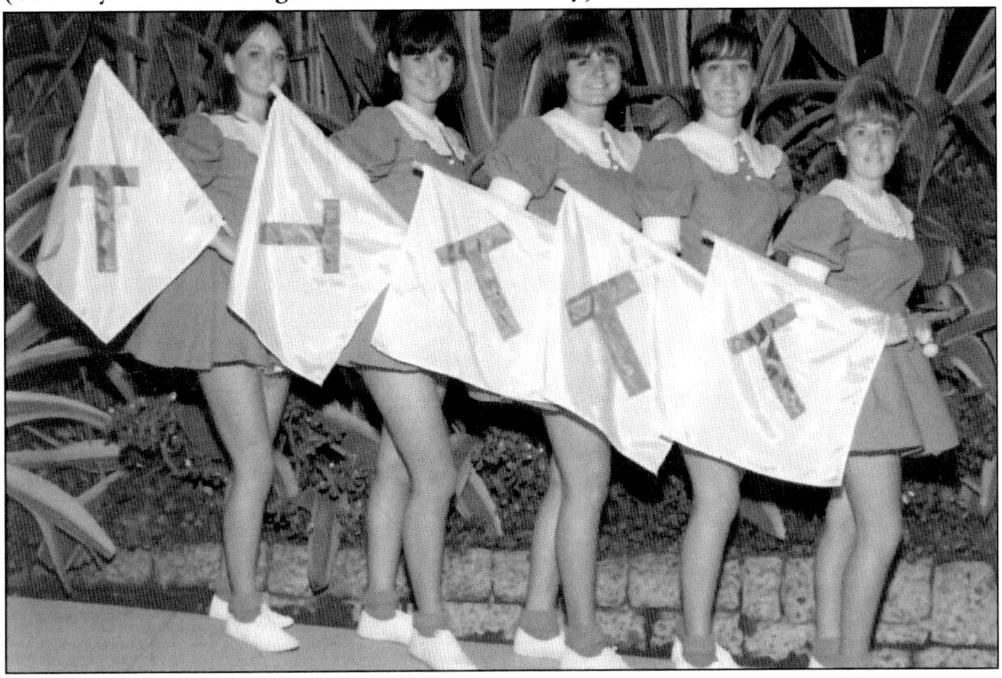

As early as the 1960s, short flags were added to the cheerleading program. Their intricate routines twirling the flags were an impressive display of coordination. Short flags were removed from the cheer program sometime in the late 1990s. This 1968 photograph shows, from left to right, Judy Engstrom, Mona Carlin, Connie Dearden, Laura Echols, and Georgia Potter. (Courtesy of Torrance High Associated Student Body.)

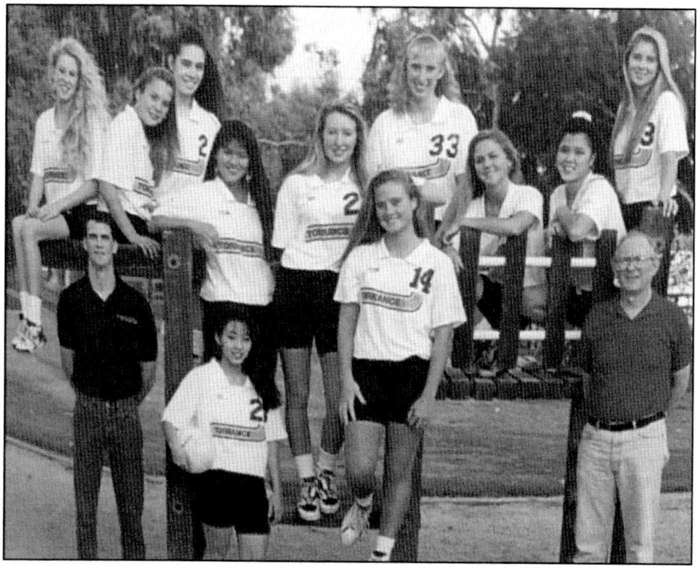

This photograph shows the 1992 CIF champions in girls' volleyball. The team included, from left to right, (first row) Brian Chartierre, Wendy Shimohara, Kim Blankinship, and John Radcliffe; (second row) Sunshine Van Wie, Circe Thompson, Vika Malu, Tiffany Fujimoto, Tammy Burchard, Sara Fauk, Kim Neuchterlein, Jenny Yokohama, and Suzanne Radcliffe (Courtesy of Torrance High School Associated Student Body.)

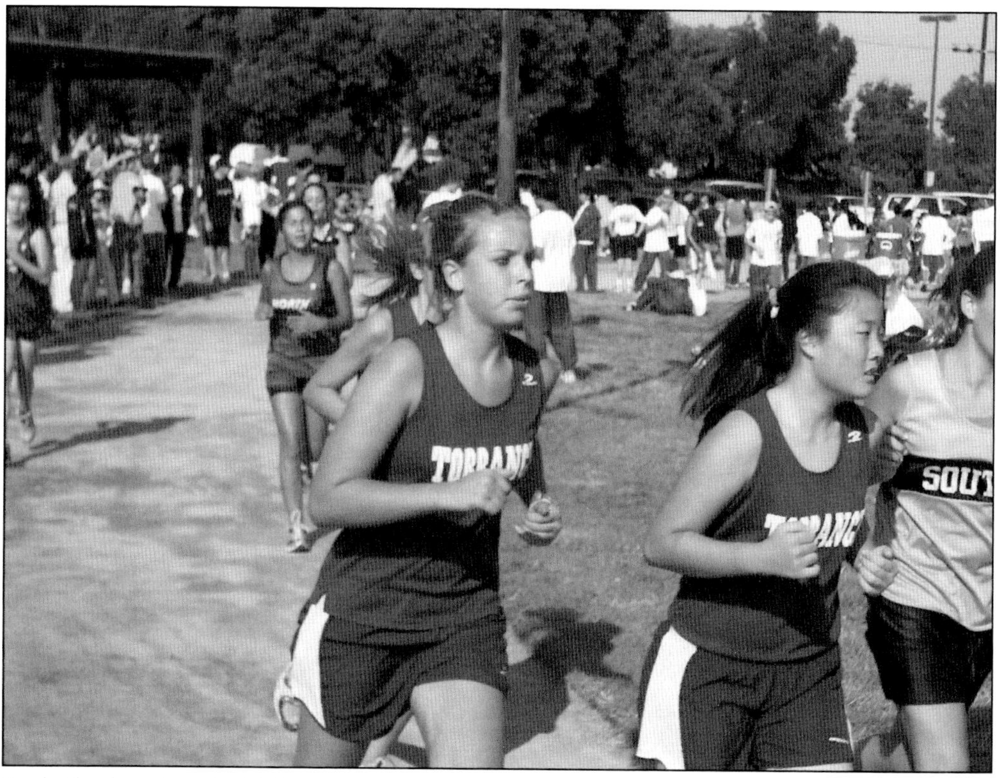

Both the boys' and girls' cross-country teams consistently do well. The varsity level is coached by Israel Pose, who was on the best long-distance high school runners in the early 1990s. In this image from 2009, Hailee Castro (center foreground) paces herself as she and Michelle Cho move past a runner from South High. (Courtesy of Traci Liston Castro.)

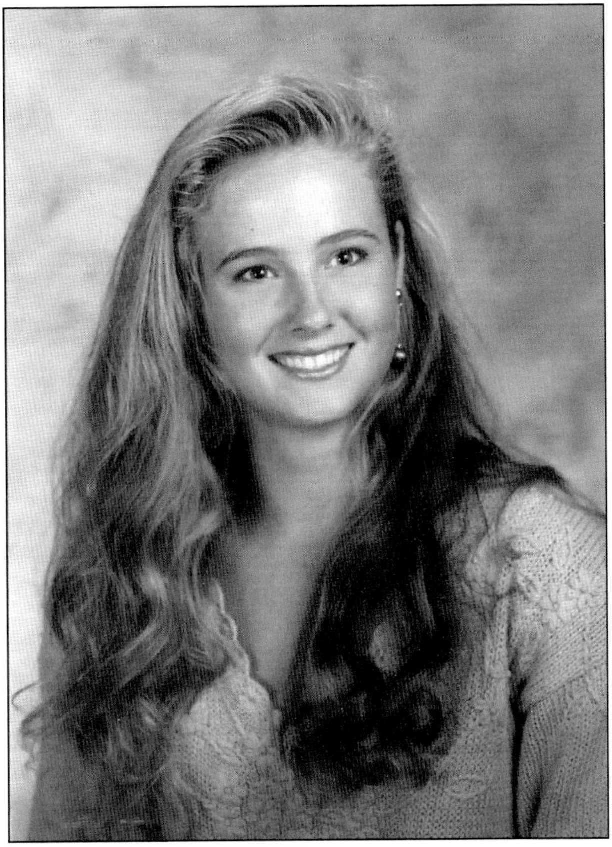

Kim Blankinship, as seen at right in her senior portrait, was arguably among the best female athletes at the high school level. The 1993 graduate earned a total of 12 varsity letters while at Torrance High, four each in volleyball, soccer, and track and field. During her senior year, the girls' volleyball team won the CIF championship but lost in the state final. Blankinship also was a 1993 CIF champion in the high jump. In 1991 and 1992, she was named All CIF in volleyball and soccer. In 1992, she also was chosen by *Volleyball Magazine* as a FAB 50 selection. Her senior year, Blankinship was one of the five finalists for the state's High School Girls Athlete of the Year. She went on to play volleyball at the collegiate level, at Loyola Marymount University. (Both, courtesy of Nathan Jones.)

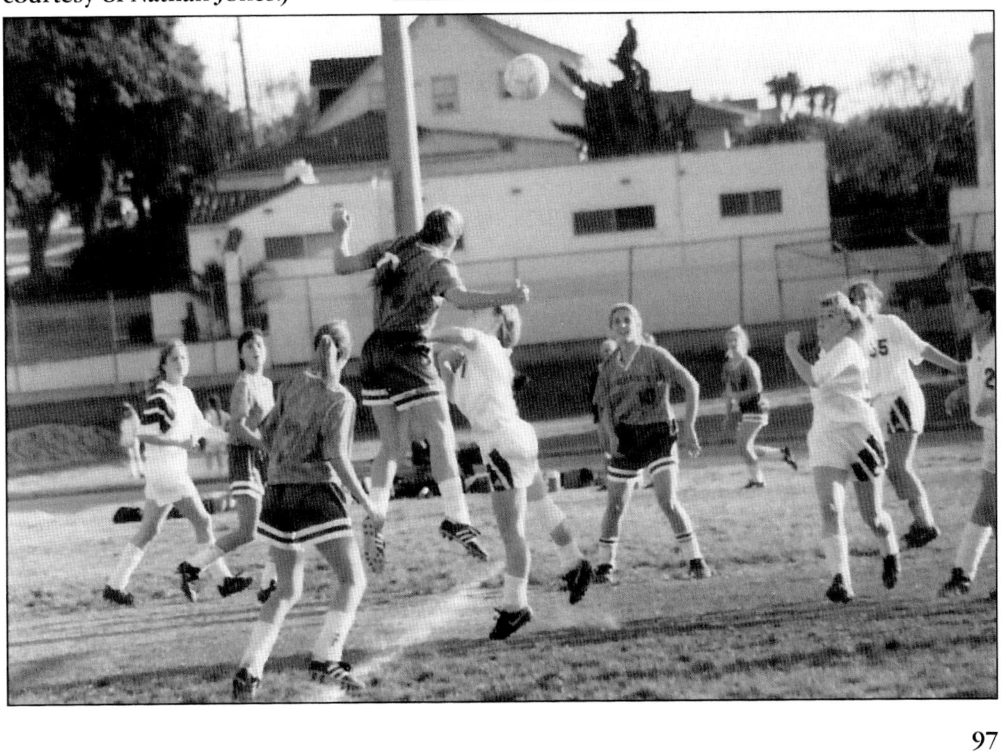

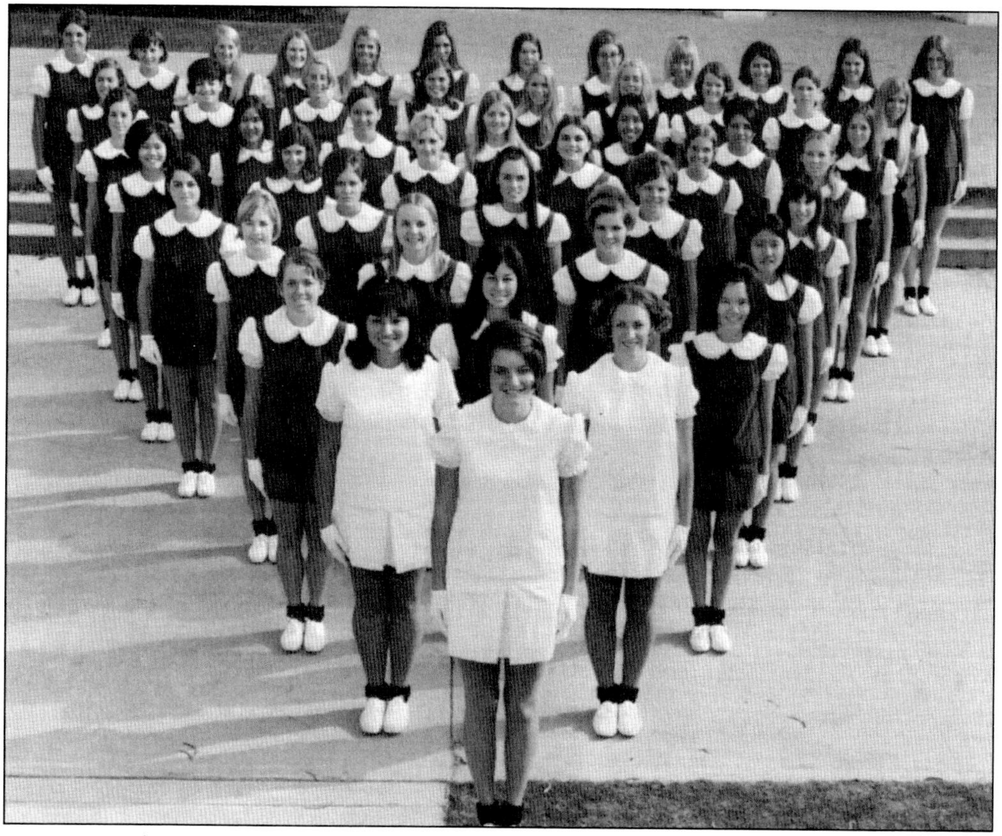

Between 1965 and 1970, the drill team continued to expand. The girls in white in this 1970 team photograph are, from left to right, captain and cocaptains Lisa Stanley, Diane Leon, and Margie Peterson. The drill team program was added through the auspices of the Girls' Athletic Association. (Courtesy of Torrance High Associated Student Body.)

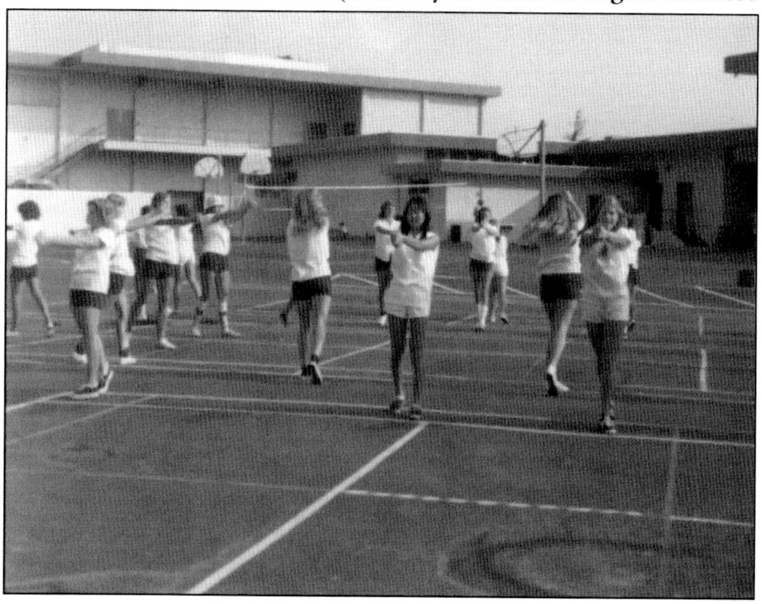

This 1976 image shows several members of the drill team rehearsing their routine. This photograph was taken behind the girls' gymnasium (now known as the small gym), added in 1965. To the back left, the second floor of the industrial arts building is visible. (Courtesy of Torrance High Associated Student Body.)

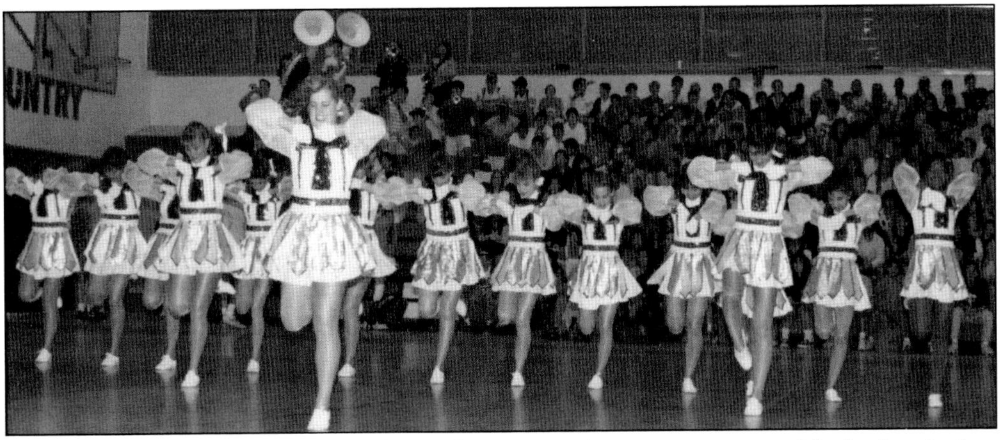

While the drill team performs at football games, either as a team or with the band, they also compete in competitions with other local schools. The drill team disbanded in the late 1990s but was reintroduced in the fall of 2011 by Kelly Gasset. In a very short time, the revived program has produced national winners. (Courtesy of Torrance High School Associated Student Body.)

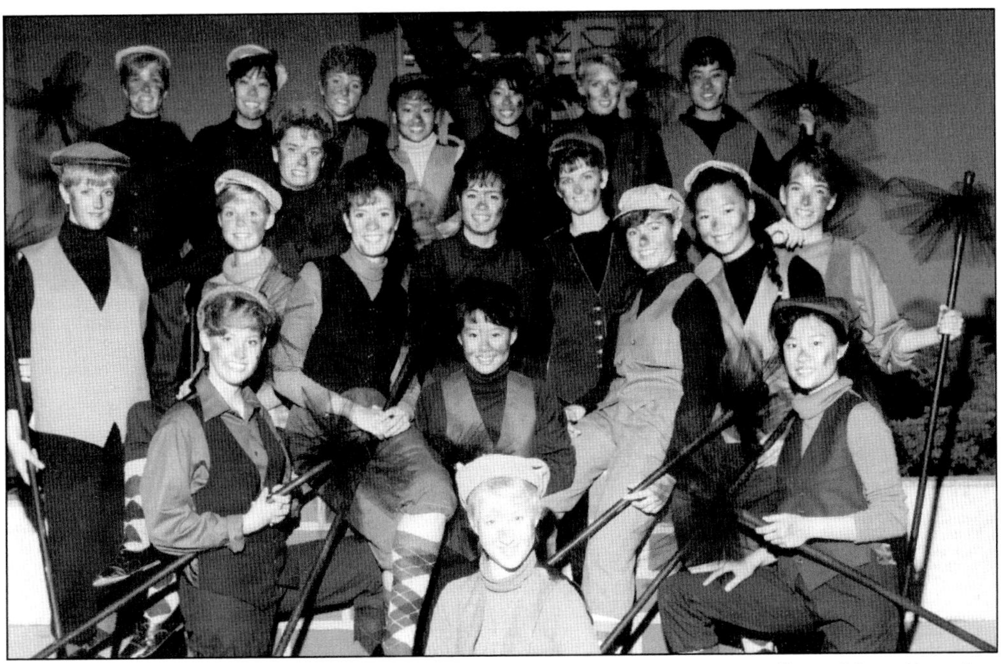

In this 1989 image of the drill team, the girls were chimney sweeps from *Mary Poppins*. The team is, from left to right, (first row) Toni Long; (second row) Kelly Meese, Kristina Fukazuki, and Helen Yu; (third row) Stacie Webster, Ruth Millar, Lesley Phelps, Stephanie Learman, Donna Irwin, Heidi Prophett, Jennifer Embree, Cathy Chen, and Keri Cornwell; (fourth row) Kathy Weingartner, Jennifer Taira, Cathy Smith, Sandra Kim, Joni Okinaka, Shelly Bly, and Cheryl Kawamoto. (Courtesy of Kelly Meese Gasset.)

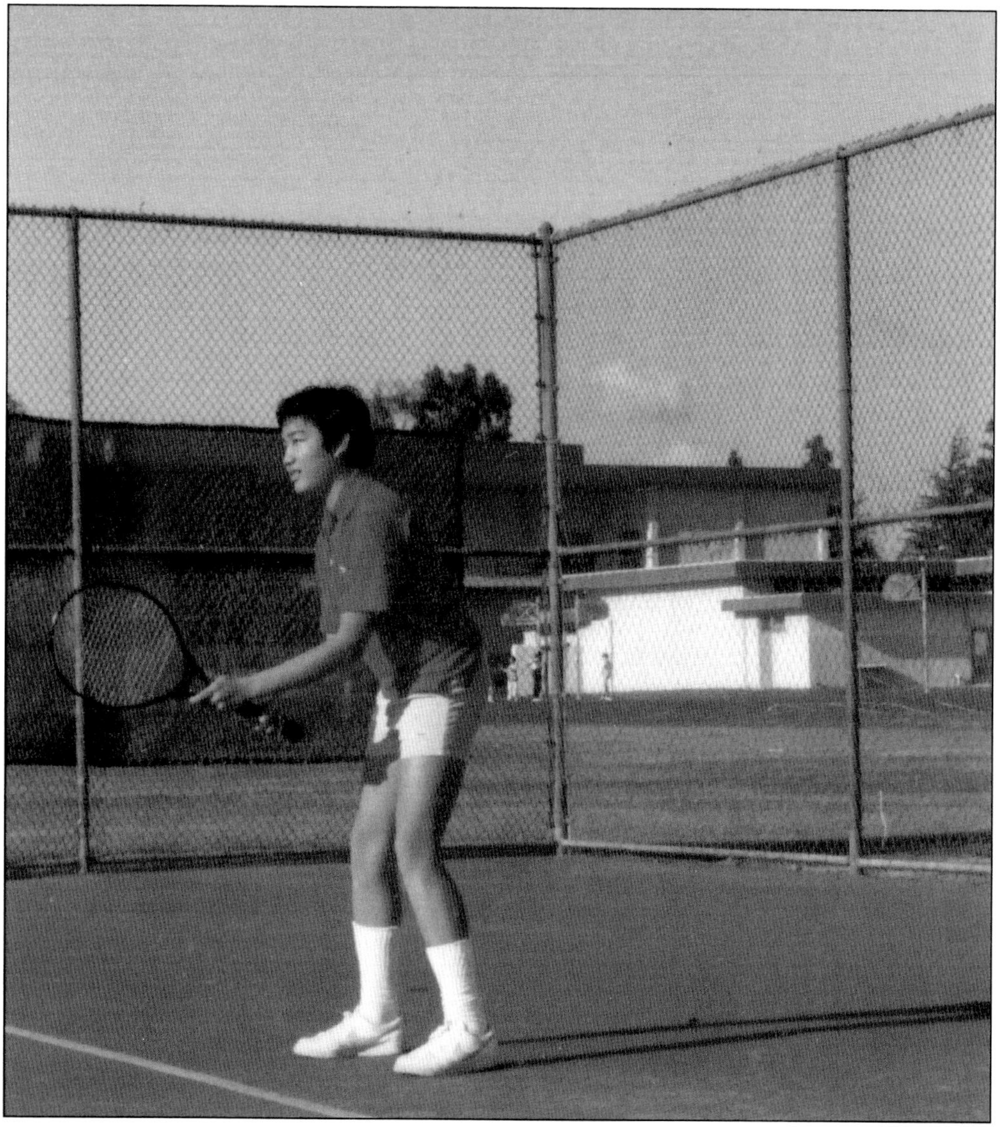

Boys' tennis was introduced in 1927. According to the 1928 yearbook, on October 27, 1927, "Tennis was accepted as an interclass sport." This 1988 photograph shows Kevin Mayetani waiting to return the ball. The tennis courts were originally located closer to the main building but were moved in the 1960s to their present location near the Annex. (Courtesy of Torrance High School Associated Student Body.)

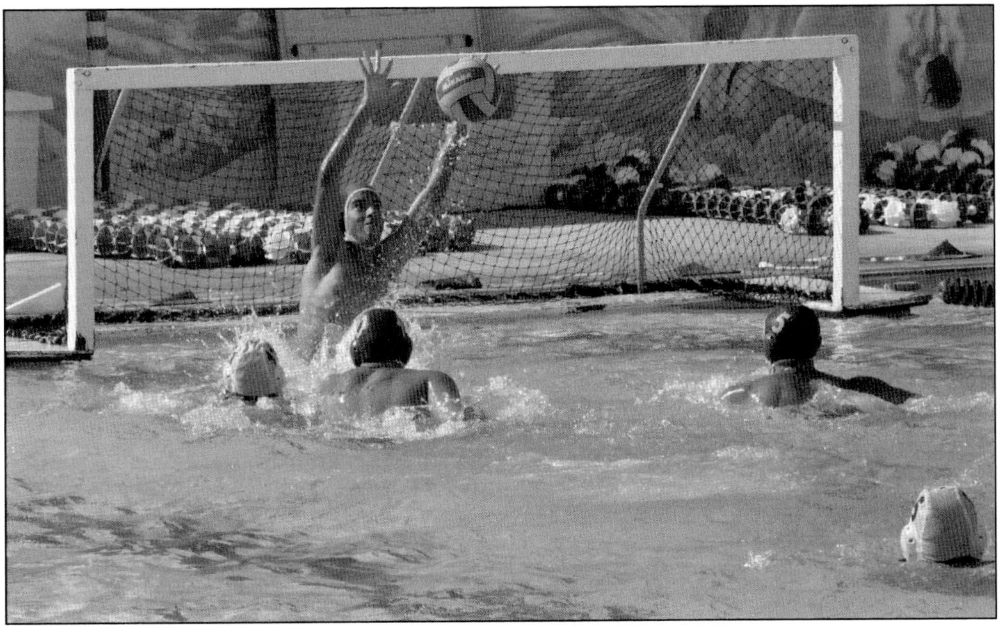

One of the recent additions to athletics at Torrance High is the aquatics program. Introduced at a district level in 2000, the program consisted of a district swim team. By 2002, each of the four high schools in Torrance had individual programs. In addition to the swim team, water polo was introduced and quickly became a popular sport for both boys and girls. The boys' swim team became CIF champions in 2009 and 2010. The four schools share the city of Torrance's public pool, the Plunge. In 2016, ground was broken for a new aquatics center near Wilson Park. This new district facility features a regulation Olympic-size pool. In the above image, Tanner Castro defends the goal. The below image shows the stamina and strength water polo players like Tanner Castro need to be successful. (Both, courtesy of Traci Liston Castro.)

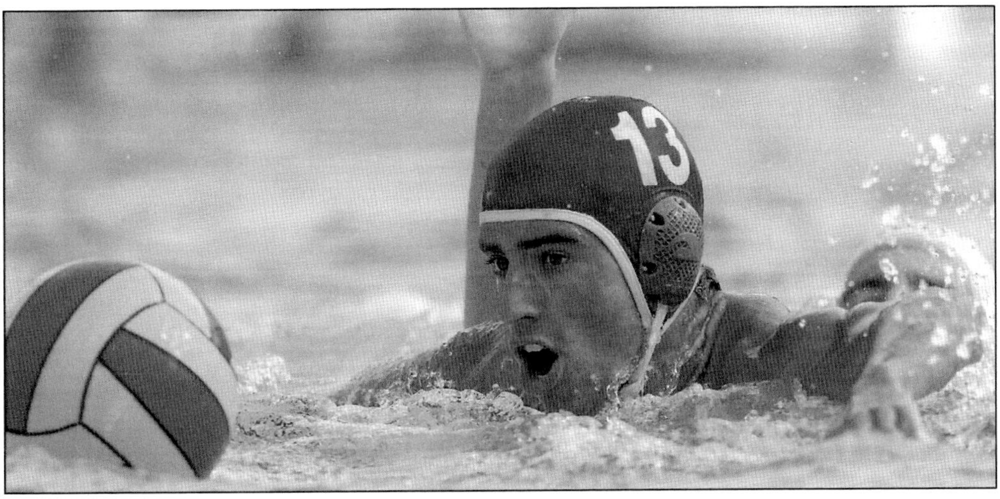

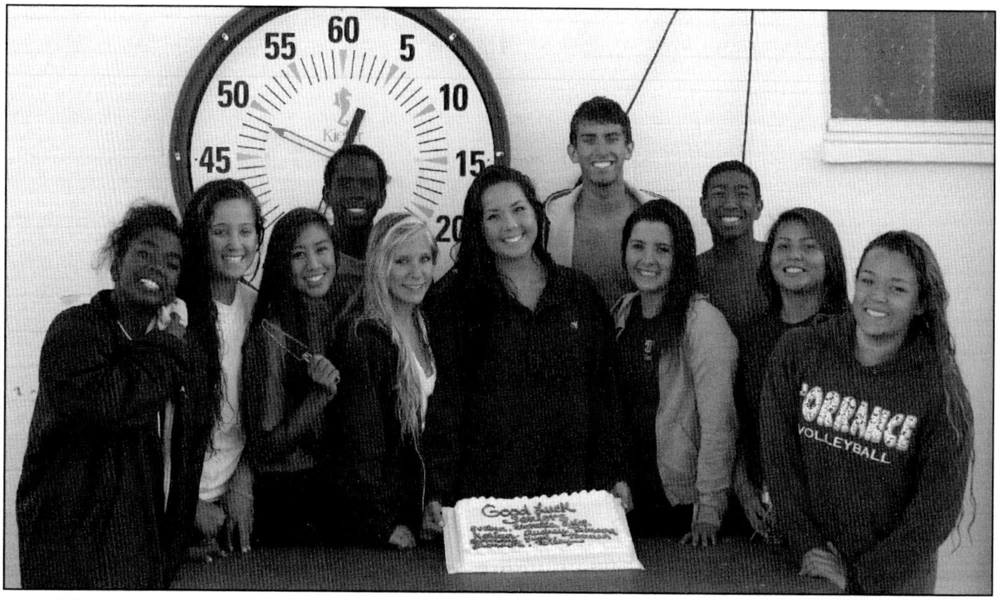

In addition to the water polo program, Tartar swimmers have continued to build a strong tradition. At the end of each season, the senior athletes are honored. In this 2009 photograph, the senior swimmers are, from left to right, Rochelle Walker, Brittney Kovacs, Andrea Alcatana, Leonard King, Tamara Thebidoux, Ariel Carillo, Yumi Gibson, Billy Sanders, Evelyn Siguenza, and Katelyn Vannieuwenhuyse. (Courtesy of Traci Liston Castro.)

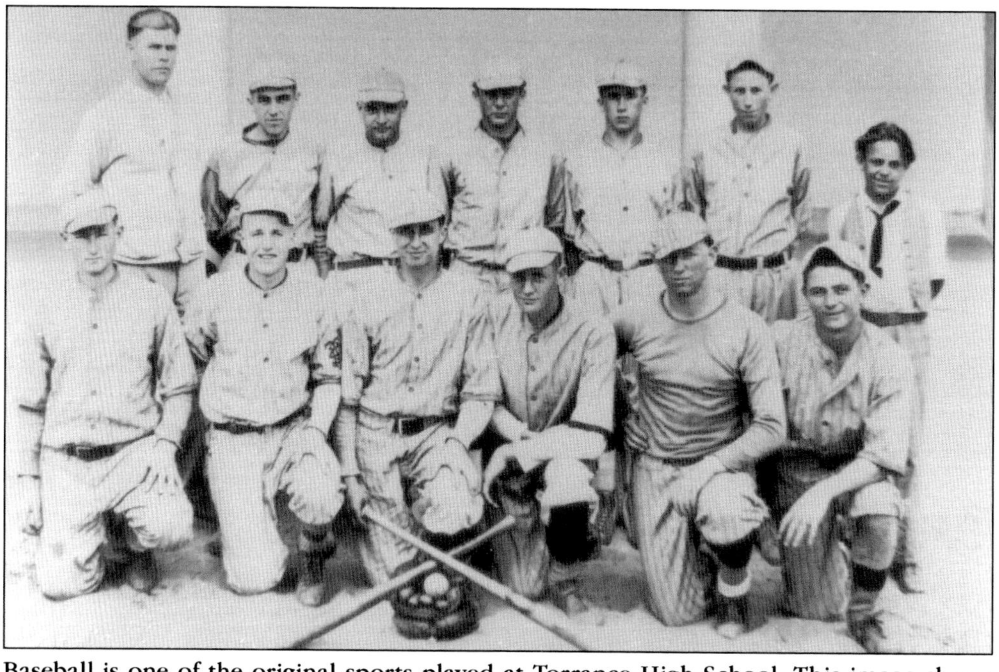

Baseball is one of the original sports played at Torrance High School. This image shows the team from 1926. Among the legendary coaches that have helped this program succeed were Will Boerger and John Radcliffe. In 2014, coach Ollie Turner, a former player, took his team to a CIF championship. (Courtesy of Torrance High School Alumni Association.)

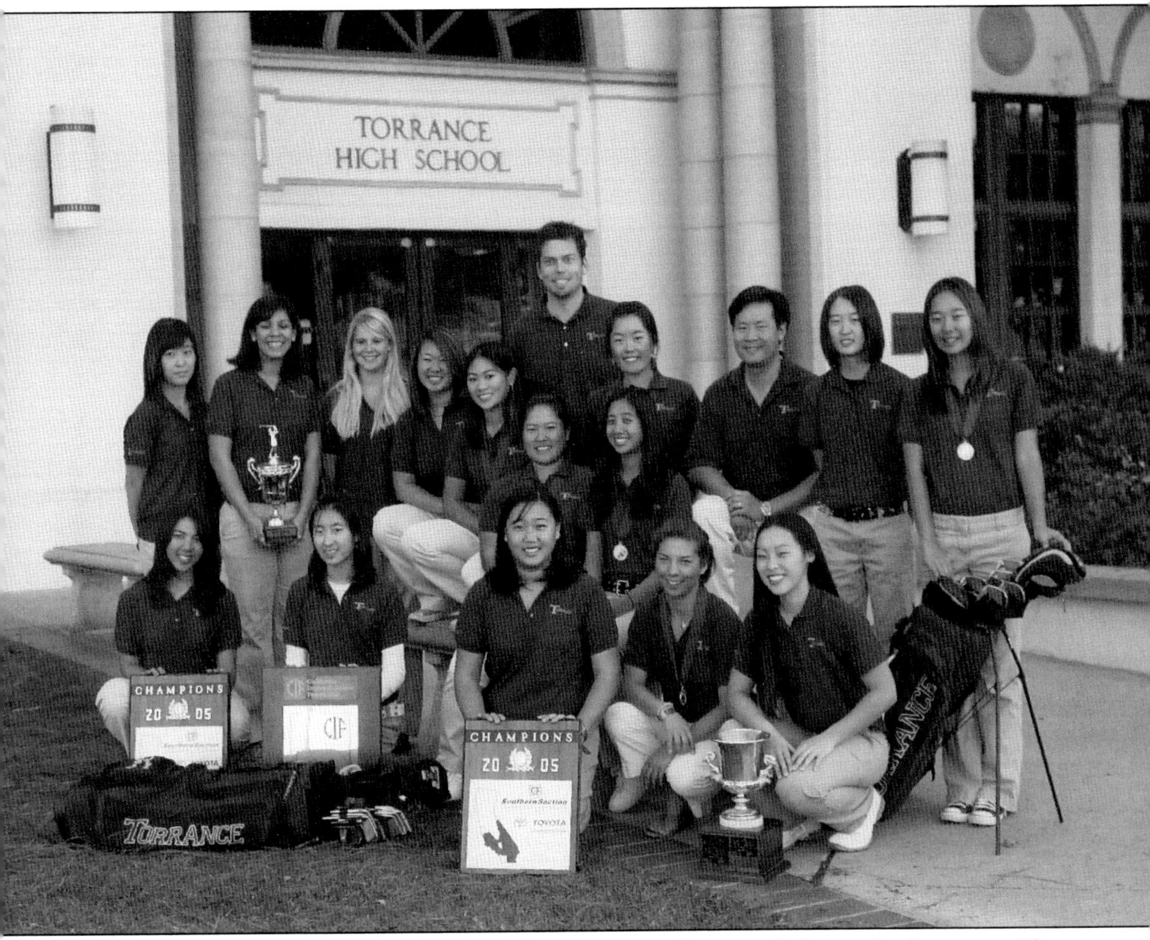

In 1988, the Torrance High golf program was almost eliminated due to budget cuts. The program was saved, and by the early 2000s, the girls' program dominated CIF. They appeared in seven consecutive CIF State Championships, bringing home the first-place trophy in 2005, 2007, 2008, and 2009. Individual players also earned state titles, such as Jane Rah (2005) and Jenny Shin (2008 and 2009). In this 2005 team photograph, the state champion golfers include, from left to right, (first row) Jennel Alexander, Alyssa Lee, Emily Chong, Dani Powell, and Lauren Kato; (second row, seated) Jane Rah and Christina Siew; (third row) Linda Hyun, Tiffany Andres, Chelsea Lawless, Annie Son, Demi Runas, head coach John Wurzer, Angela Park (standing), assistant coach Devin Kushi, Cindy Song, and Julie Cho. (Courtesy of Devin Kushi.)

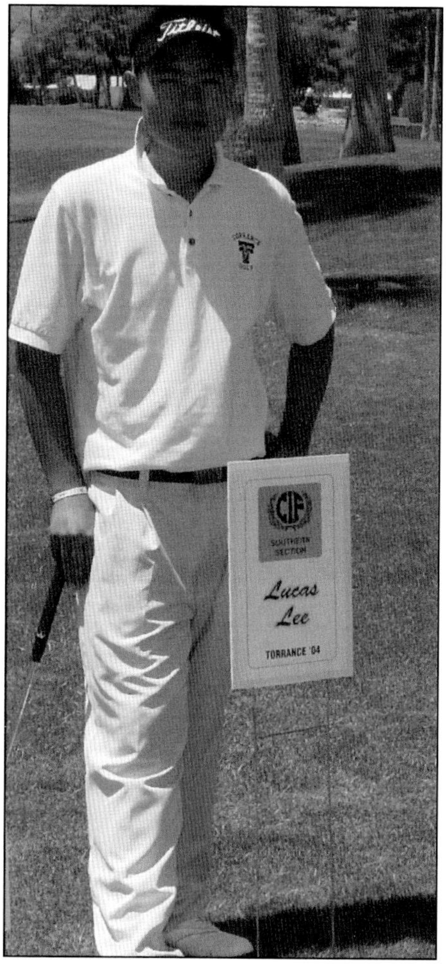

One of the standouts in boys' golf was Lucas Lee. He won the individual championship for the CIF Southern Section in 2004. During the competition, Lee shot under par and birdied in a sudden death playoff. Lucas Lee and fellow Tartar Ted Oh (1992) are the only South Bay boys to win individual championships since 1973. (Courtesy of Devin Kushi.)

In the fall of 1992, the Tartar Athletic Hall of Fame inducted their inaugural class. These Tartars represent the best of athleticism as well as character. Included in the first class were Fred Kendall, who played Major League Baseball, and Louis Zamperini (third from left). (Courtesy of Torrance High Associated Student Body.)

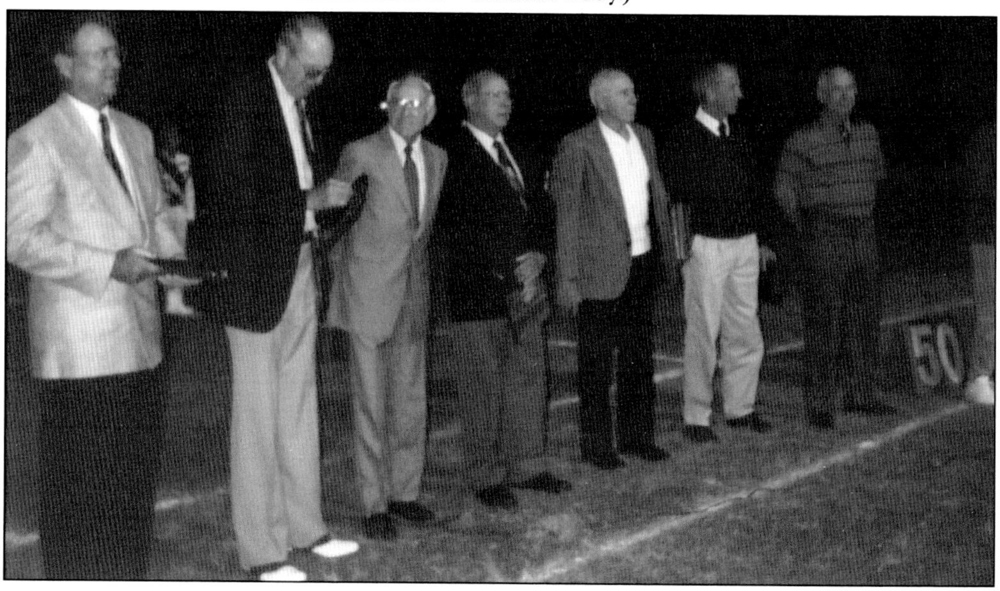

Jamie Sibley, pictured here in 1989, was a star pitcher for the Torrance High softball team. She clocked speeds as high as 61 miles per hour. She was recognized as the Player of the Year by the local newspaper and was named to the 1st Team All Bay League. That year, the team was Bay League Champions. (Courtesy of John and Norma Sibley.)

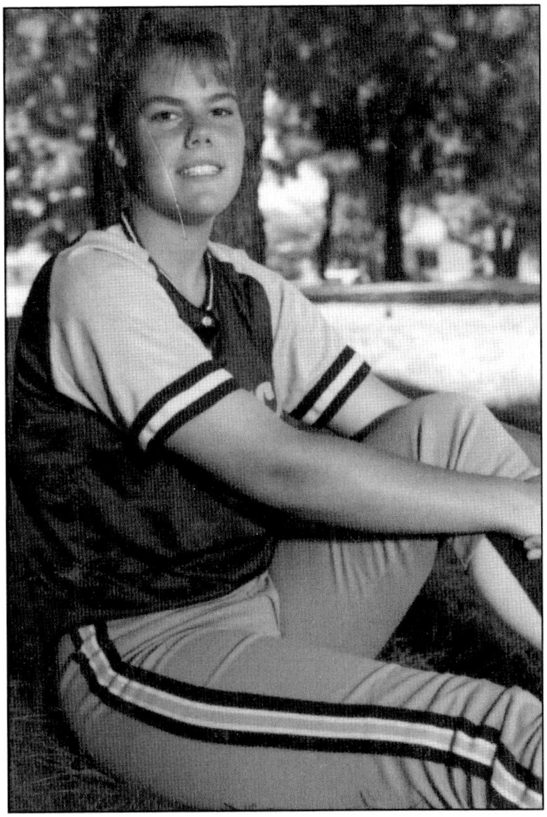

Rock Hollis graduated from Torrance High in 1971. He returned as an assistant football coach. He became the head coach of the varsity football team. He is pictured here with Louis Zamperini. (Courtesy of Theresa Fagan Hollis.)

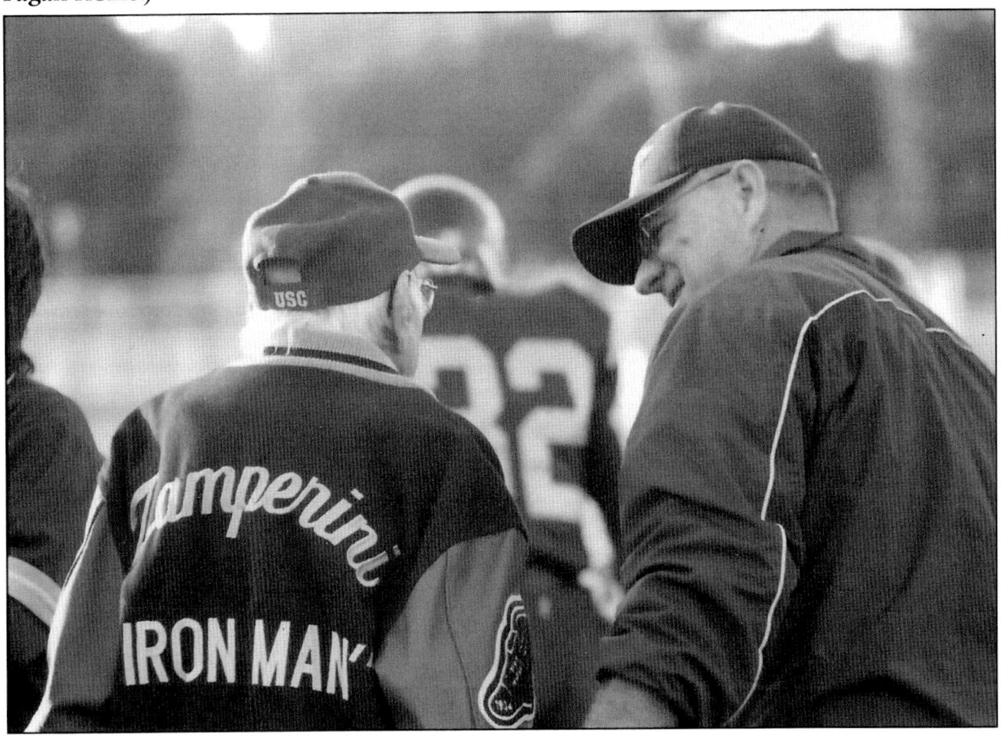

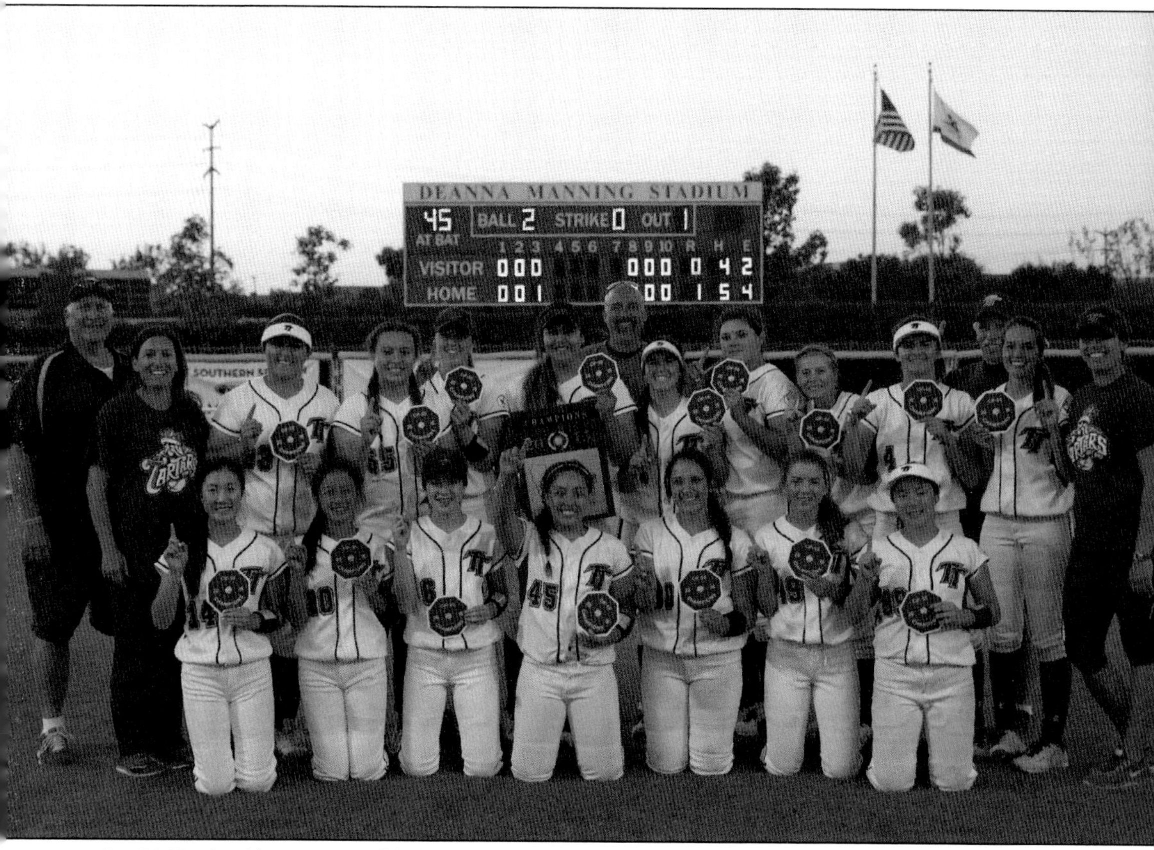

In 2015, the Torrance softball team made it to the CIF Southern Section Championship game in their division. The game took 13 innings and became the longest game in CIF history, as neither pitcher was willing to give up a hit. The Tartars emerged with the victory, their first CIF championship in softball, and an overall record of 27-9. Pictured from left to right are (first row) Abby Yamamoto, Jen Lew, Erin Alvarado, Britny Jumalon, Desiree Medina, Sydney "Squid" Lima, and Kayla Yoshioka; (second row) assistant coach Dan Cowden, assistant coach Mary Pecotich, Alyssa Loza, Jenna Wilson, Katelyn Christian, Marissa Moreno, head coach Don Glavich, Jade Arslanian, CeCe DeCosta, Bridget Shaw, Kayla Aros, assistant coach Mike Effler, Samantha Pollock, and assistant coach Lauren DeCastro. (Courtesy of Don Glavich.)

Five

Go Forth to Serve

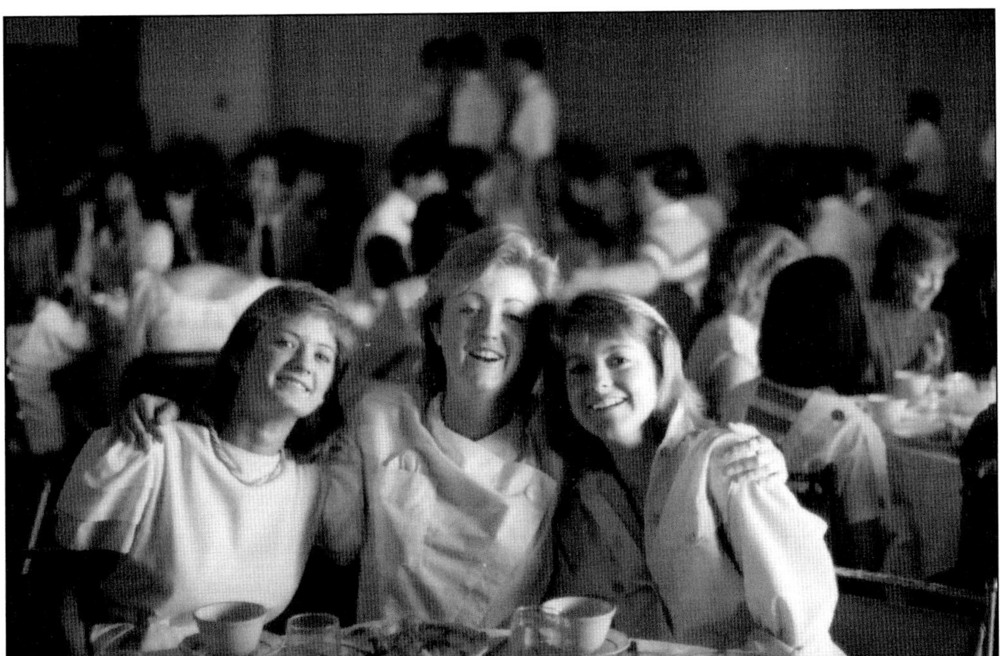

Each year in June, the senior class is invited to a catered luncheon at a local hotel. Started in 1928, the tradition of the senior luncheon typically occurs the day before graduation and is one of the last few times the seniors will be together. In this 1984 photograph, from left to right, Jennifer Schwartz, Erica Marcroft, and Karen Schooly share their memories. (Courtesy of Alice Sun Davis.)

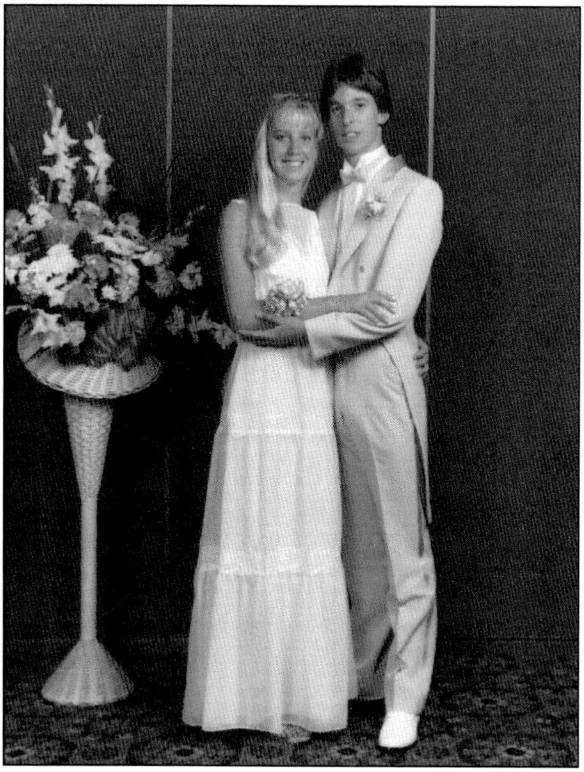

Prom is the highlight of senior year. Through the 1990s, proms were typically held in ballrooms in hotels with sit-down dinner service. By the 2000s, locations like Universal Studios or the Space Shuttle Endeavor have been used as sites. Instead of sit-down dinners, the meal is served as buffet. At left, Traci Liston poses with Ted Allison at the 1981 prom held at the Disneyland Hotel. In the image below, Brian Spradlin with his date Christy Gustafson (left) and Russell Watanabe with his date Lori Spradlin (right) pose together at the 1993 prom. (Left, courtesy of Traci Liston Castro; below, courtesy of Christy Gustafson.)

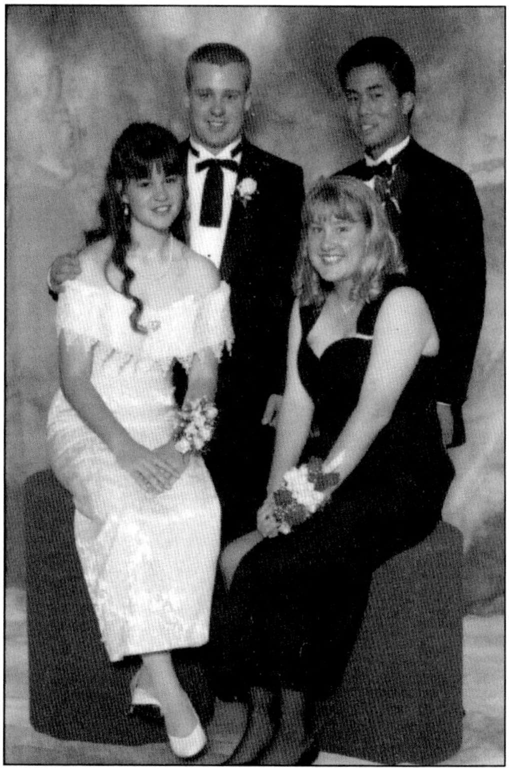

For many years, the baccalaureate service was a religious-based part of commencement held the Sunday before graduation. Over the years, the non-mandatory service was moved to Saturday evening. The highlight of the evening is the senior slide show. This photograph shows the cover of the baccalaureate program for 1957. (Courtesy of Torrance High Associated Student Body.)

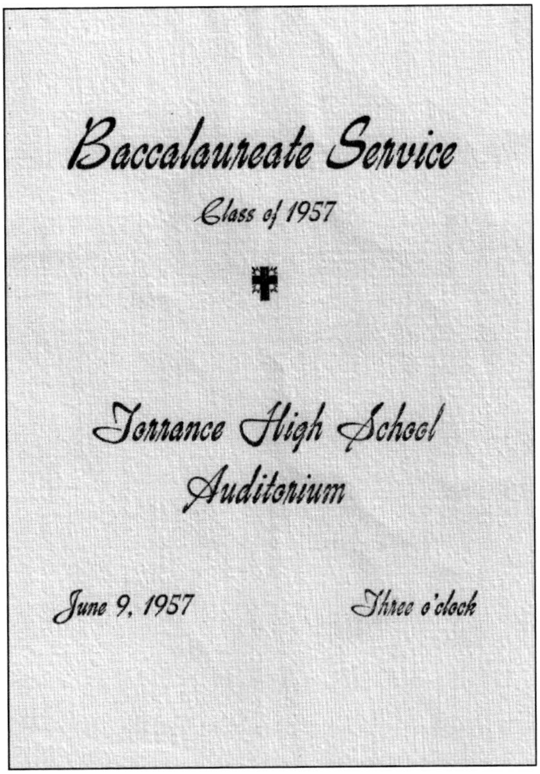
Baccalaureate Service

Class of 1957

Torrance High School
Auditorium

June 9, 1957 Three o'clock

Pictured from left to right are Kirk Krause, Hailee Castro, and Riley Popp. Hailee and Riley are cousins. Their mothers attended Torrance High School, as did much of their extended families. Hailee followed in her the footsteps of her mother, Traci, and became a teacher, but at the elementary level. (Courtesy of Traci Liston Castro.)

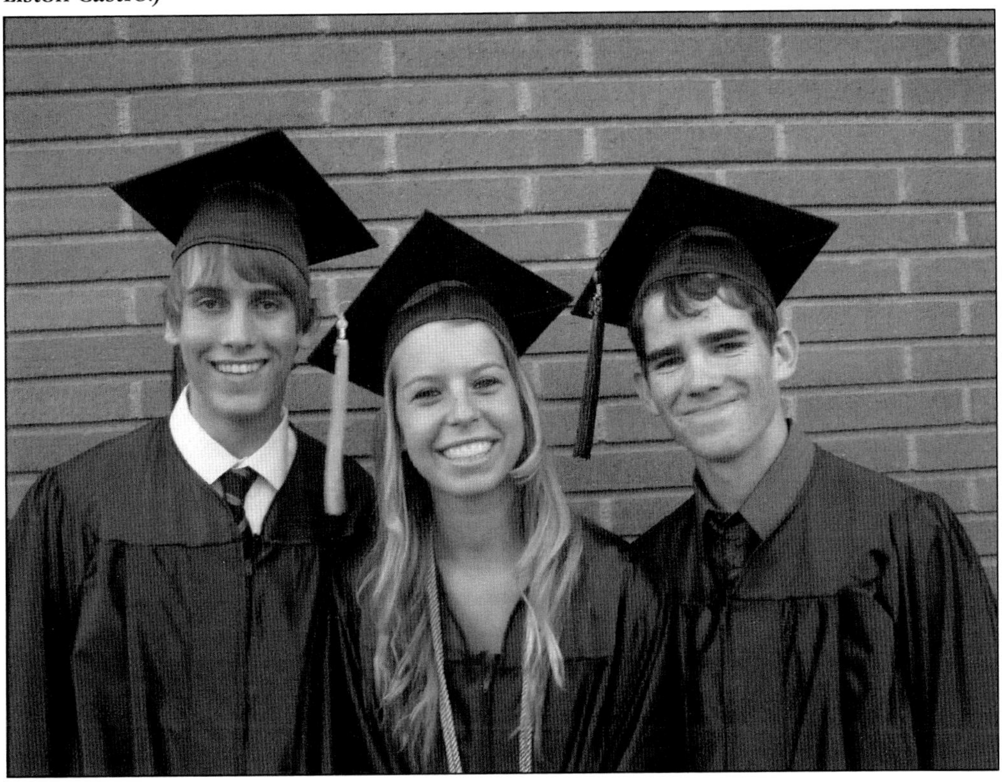

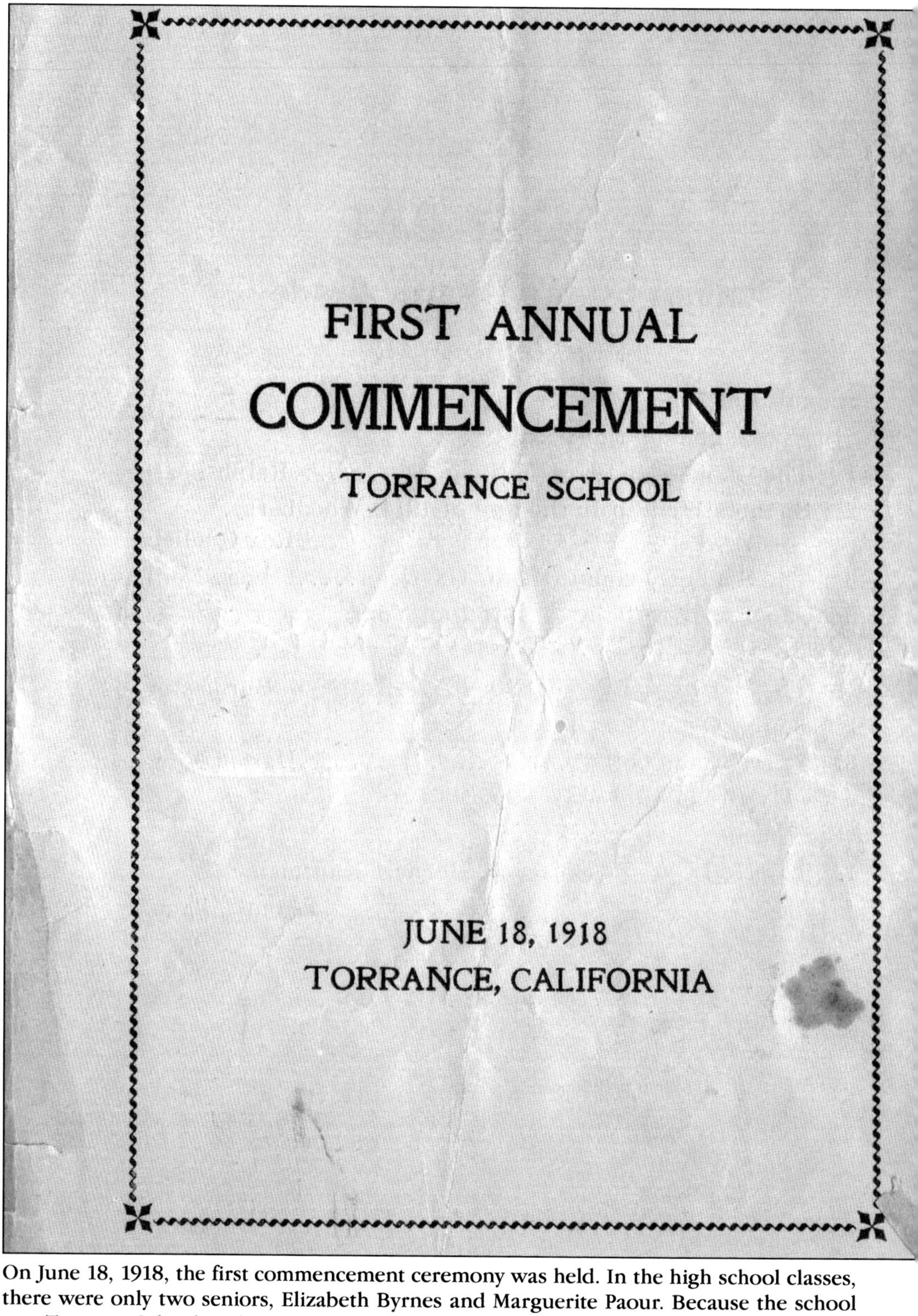

On June 18, 1918, the first commencement ceremony was held. In the high school classes, there were only two seniors, Elizabeth Byrnes and Marguerite Paour. Because the school was Torrance School at the time, eighth graders also received recognition for promotion

GRADUATES

HIGH SCHOOL

Elizabeth Byrnes

Marguerite Paour

EIGHTH GRADE

Linus Adams

Ralph Beall

Kathryn Burmaster

Mable Davis

Rex Guelich

Harold King

Muriel Munson

Helen Neill

Dewey Quigley

Curtis Tolson

Virginia Watson

to high school. The theme of the evening was World War I, as organized by the eighth graders. All 10 of the eighth graders performed some portion of the program, from songs to orations. (Courtesy of Torrance Historical Society.)

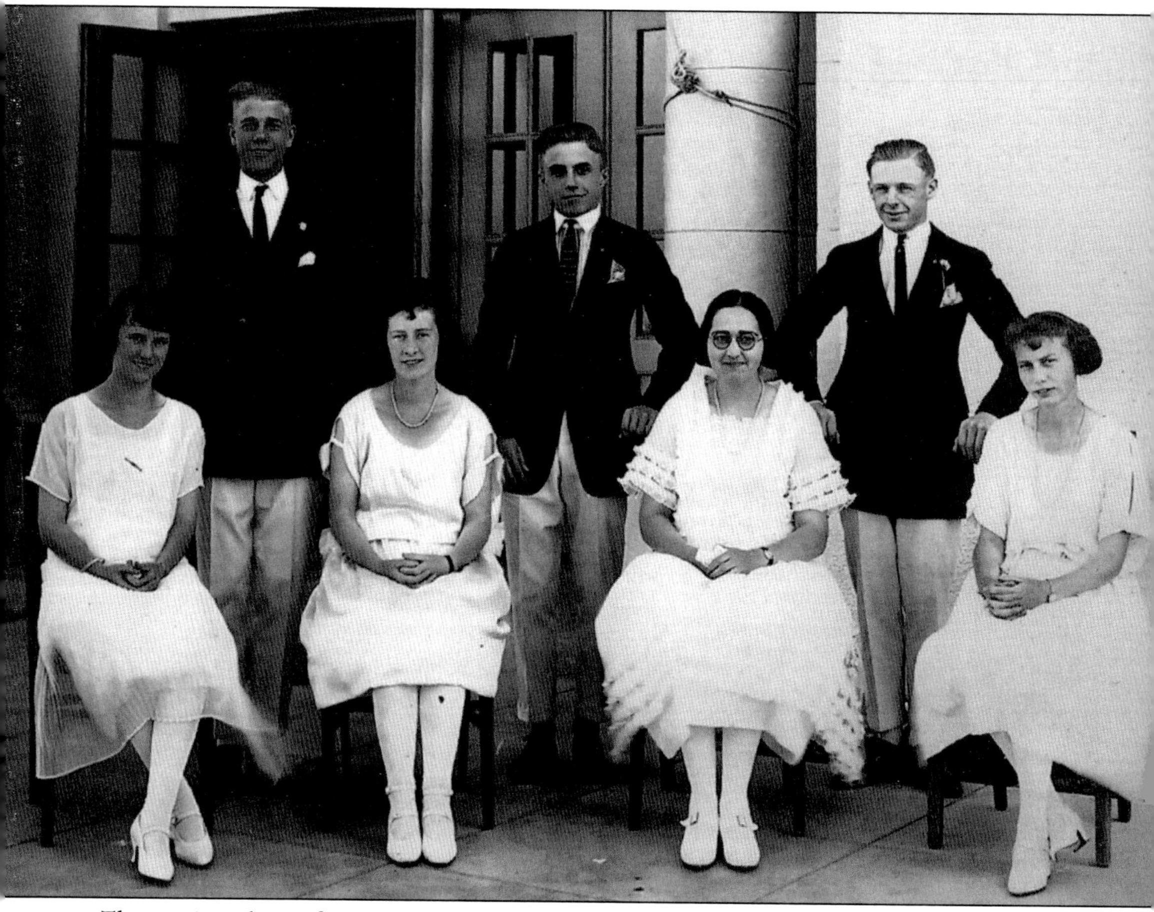

The senior class of 1922 included only seven students. The gentlemen, from left to right, are Karl Von Hagen, Ralph Beall, and Dewey Quegley. The young ladies are, from left to right, Katherine Burmaster, Virginia Watson, Virgie Pratt, and Helen Neill. Beall, Quegley, Burmaster, and Neill are part of the original 1918 eighth-grade graduating class. The students are posed in front of the main building of Torrance High. It is interesting to note that the boys are all wearing dark jackets with light colored pants, while the girls are all in white dresses. This attire was typical for the time. (Courtesy of Torrance Historical Society.)

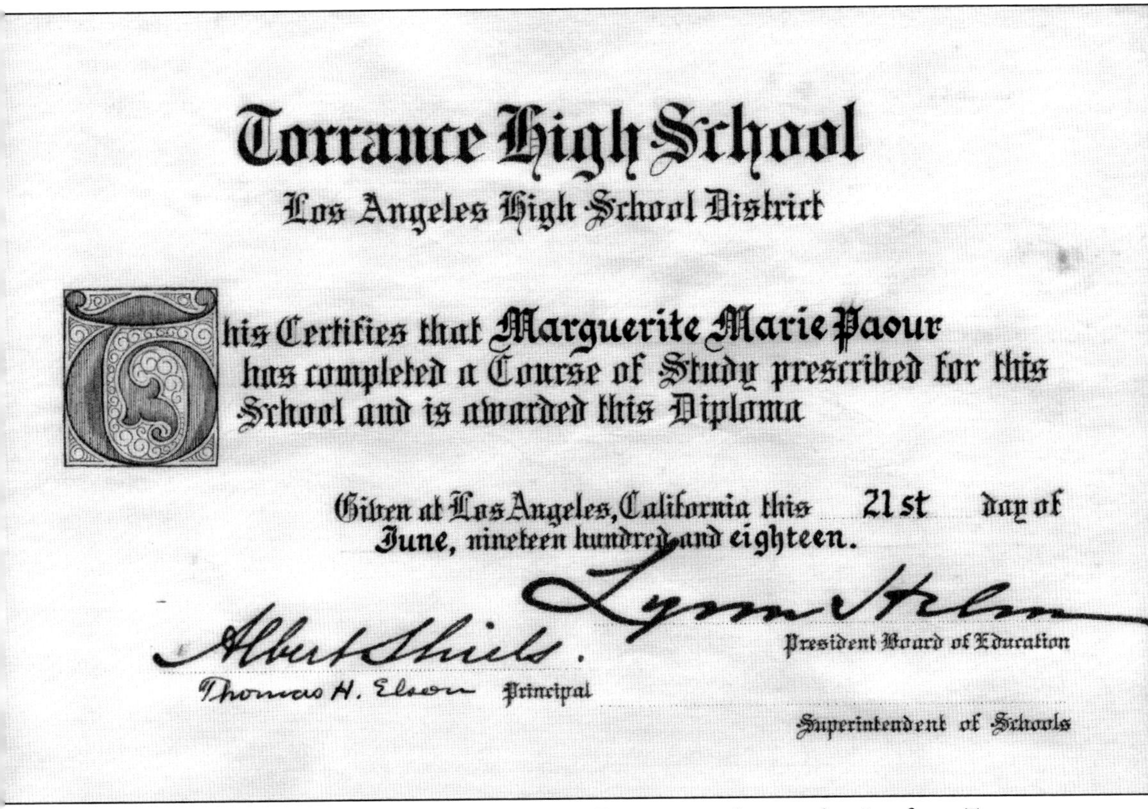

Torrance High School

Los Angeles High School District

This Certifies that Marguerite Marie Paour has completed a Course of Study prescribed for this School and is awarded this Diploma

Given at Los Angeles, California this 21st day of June, nineteen hundred and eighteen.

President Board of Education

Principal

Superintendent of Schools

Shown here is the diploma given to Marguerite Paour upon her graduation from Torrance School. The diploma is dated three days after the commencement ceremony took place. Paour was the first known alumnus to have a child attend and graduate from Torrance High School. Her daughter June Nuckles graduated in 1940. Because Torrance School was under the auspices of Los Angeles High School District, it was their officials who authorized the diploma. (Courtesy of Torrance Historical Society.)

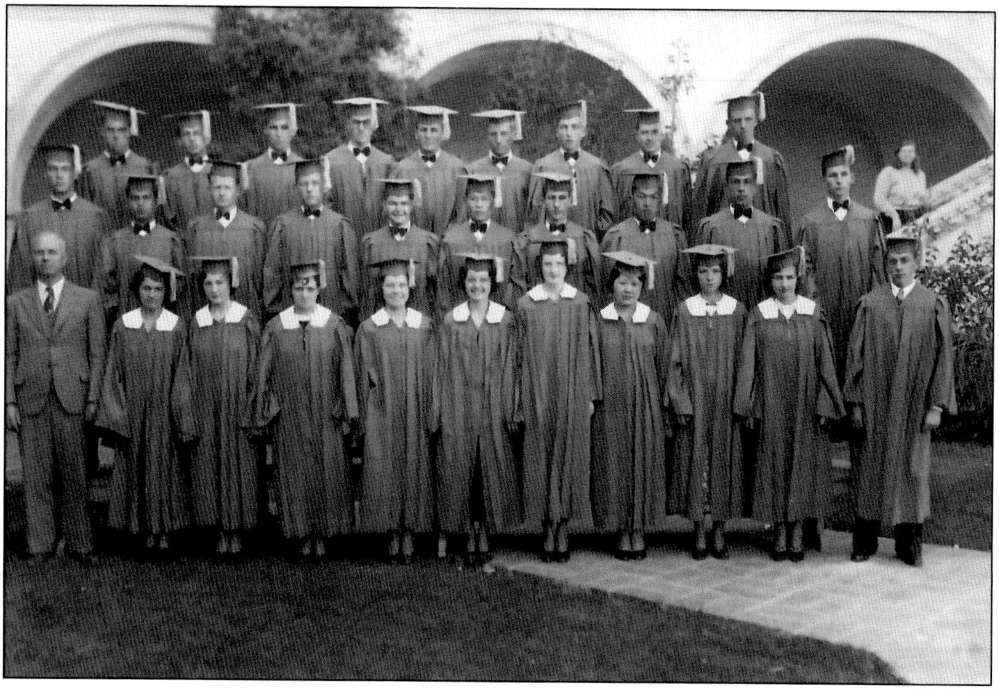

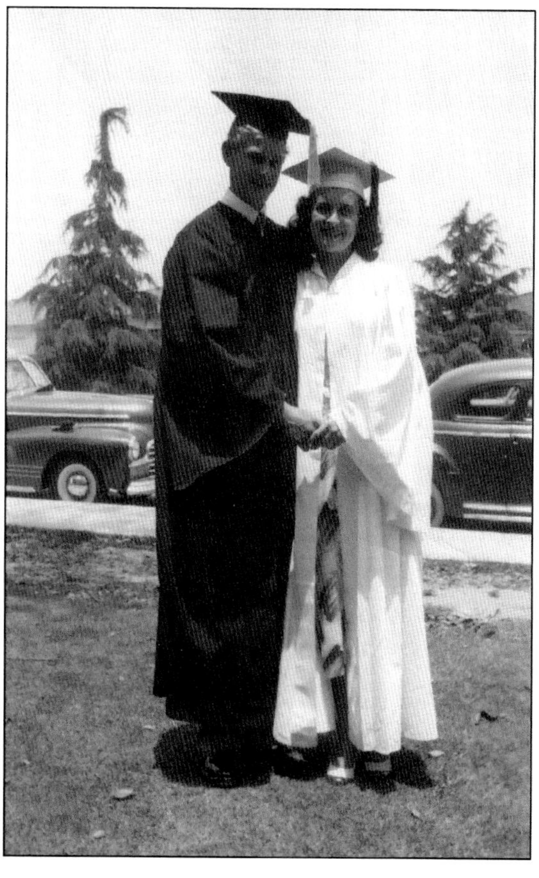

For many years, Torrance High School had both a summer and winter graduating class. Torrance High's winter class of 1934 is pictured here. This photograph was taken on the senior patio. Behind them is an exterior staircase with graduated arches leading to the second floor of the main building. (Courtesy of Torrance High Alumni Association.)

This 1949 photograph shows Milo Goettsch and Anna Jane Kelley ready for graduation. Milo and Anna Jane were active on campus. Their children also attended Torrance High. Milo was the cocaptain of the varsity football team and an integral part of the track team. Anna Jane was part of the yearbook staff and active in clubs. (Courtesy of Janis Gragg.)

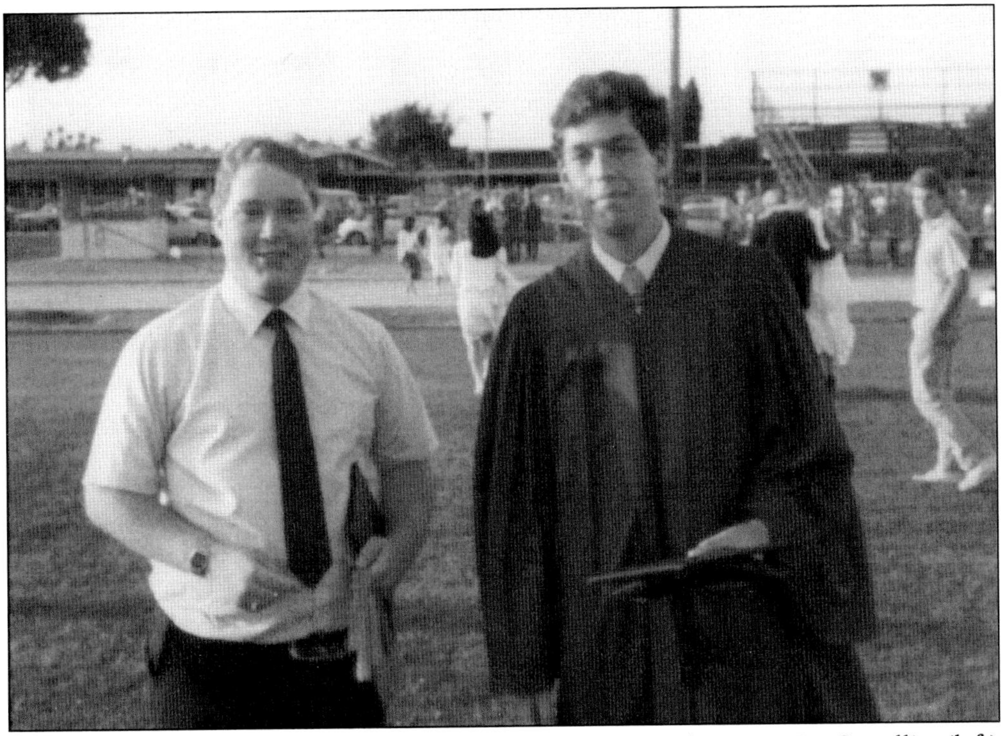

High school can create lifelong friendships, like the one between Jay Spradlin (left) and Michael Shapiro, seen here on graduation day in 1984. They became friends their freshman year. Both Spradlin and Shapiro attended California State University, Long Beach. For several years after high school, both men worked for the Torrance Public Library. (Courtesy of Charlene Spradlin.)

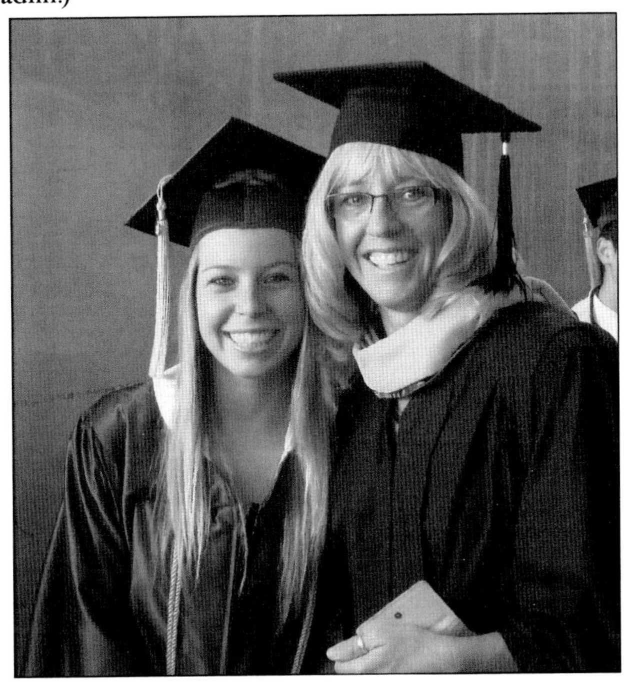

In 2009, all four of the high school stadiums in Torrance were undergoing renovations. Each ceremony took place at the Home Depot Center (now StubHub) where the Los Angeles Galaxy Major League Soccer team plays. Graduate Hailee Castro is seen here with her mother, Traci Castro, a math teacher at Torrance High. (Courtesy of Traci Liston Castro.)

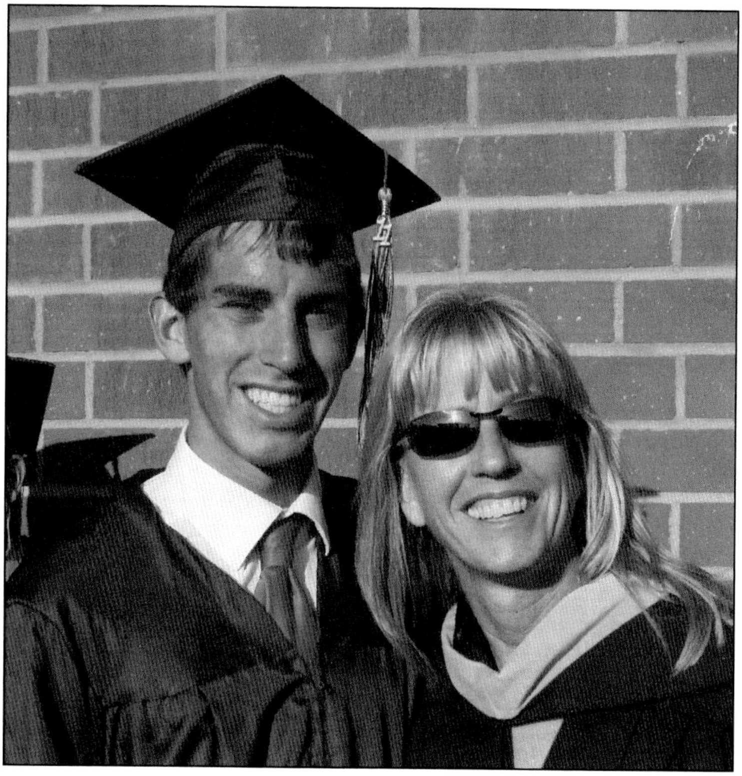

All teachers are required to attend graduation. Several teachers escort the lines of students to the field and then join them as they take their seats. Those teachers that accompany the graduates wear caps and gowns reflecting their degrees and universities. In this image from 2011, graduate Tanner Castro is with his mother, Traci Castro. (Courtesy of Traci Liston Castro.)

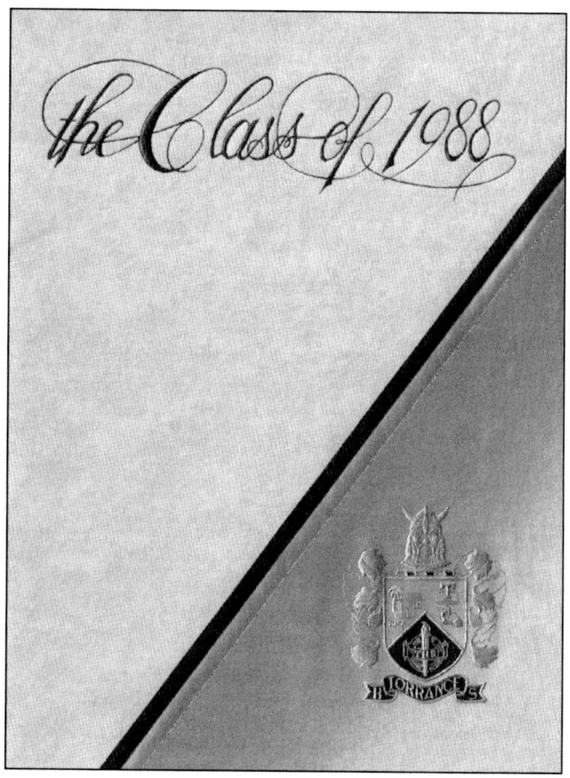

Another common graduation practice is to send out announcements to family and friends, especially those that cannot attend the commencement ceremony. The announcements, like this one from 1988, share information about the graduation ceremony. The announcements are typically printed in school colors, and students include a wallet-sized image of their senior portrait. (Courtesy of Charlene Spradlin.)

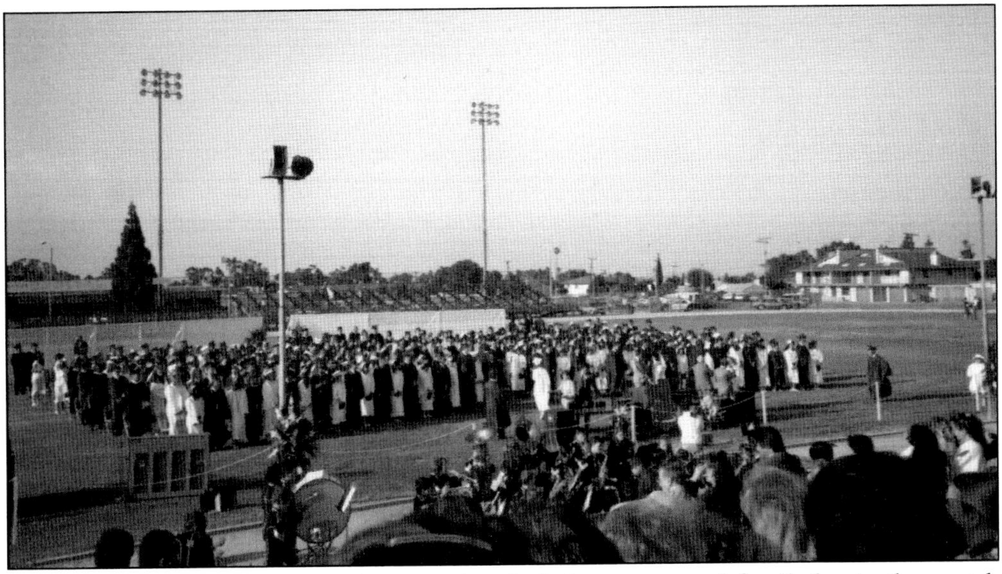

As the students participate in the recessional, their parents and family begin the search for their graduate. In this photograph from the 1988 graduation, it is evident that the graduates face only the home side of the stadium bleachers. Class sizes have increased so much in 20 years that both sides of the bleachers are needed, so graduates proceed along the edge of the field and face east. (Courtesy of Charlene Spradlin.)

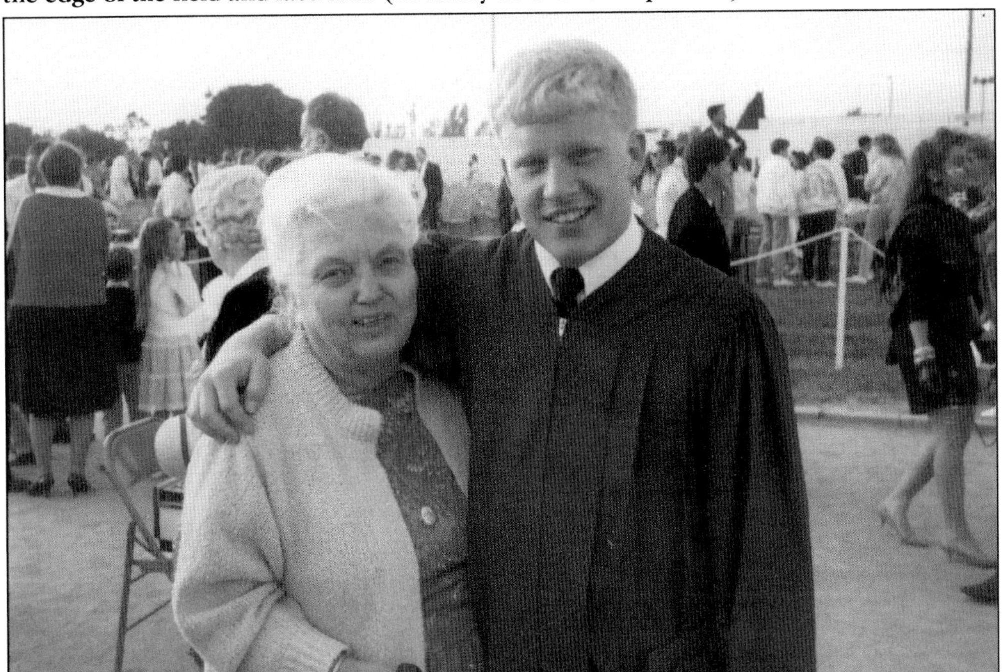

Graduations are not just for seniors to celebrate their accomplishments. These ceremonies are also a chance for family to honor their senior. Jeff Spradlin, graduate from 1988, is shown here with his grandmother Karlene Atkins following the commencement ceremony. As the student population has grown, more extended families often attend graduations. (Courtesy of Charlene Spradlin.)

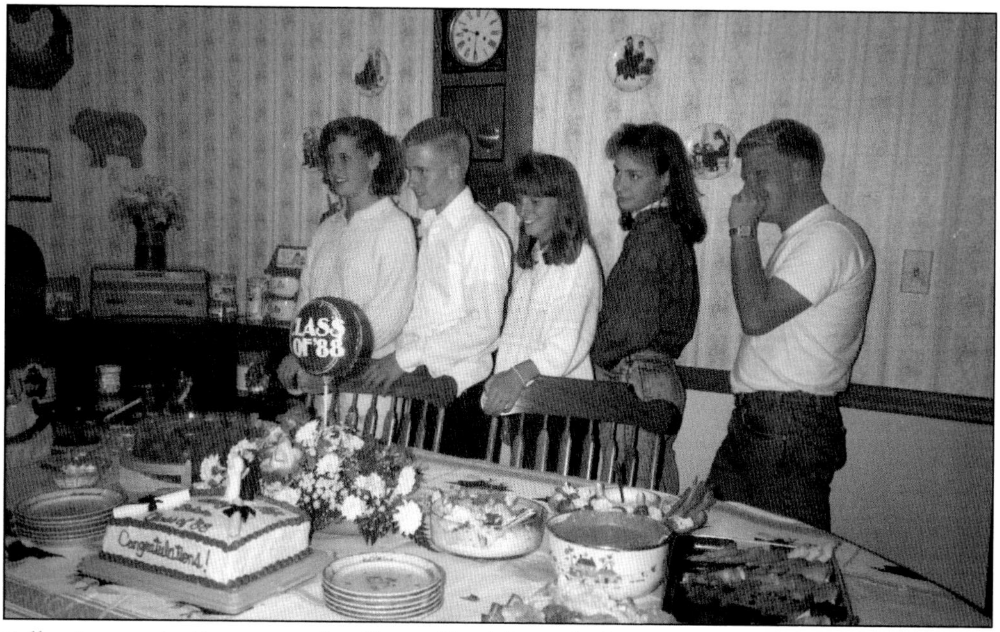

Following graduation, many families will celebrate before the Grad Nite party begins. In this photograph, from left to right, Kelly Meese, Brian Spradlin, and Patty Rhoades are celebrating their graduation from eighth grade and becoming Tartars, while Sharon Rhoades and Jeff Spradlin celebrate their graduation from Torrance High School. (Courtesy of Charlene Spradlin.)

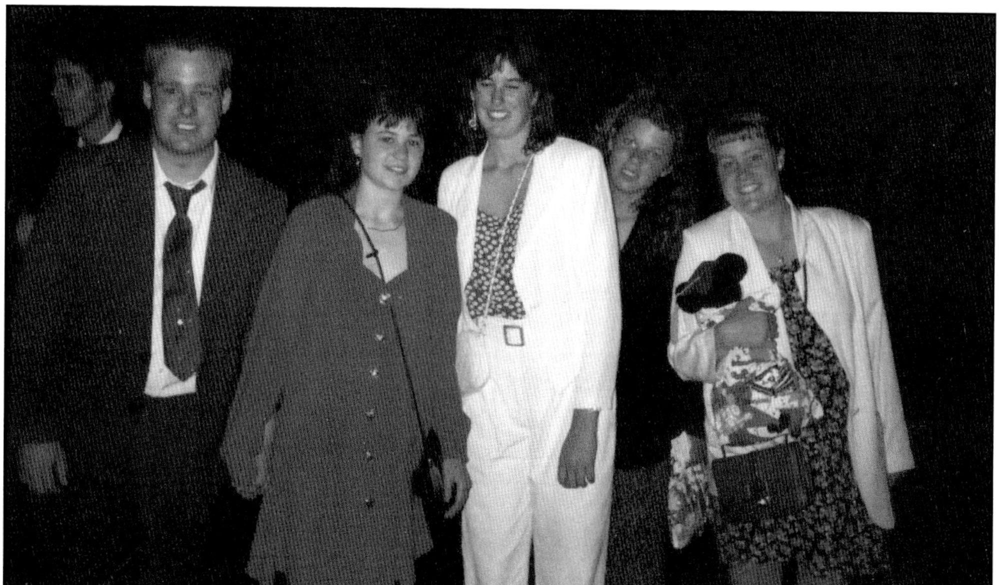

Pictured from left to right, Brian Spradlin (class of 1992), Christy Gustafson, Jennifer Baldwin, Kristen White, and Lori Spradlin celebrate Grad Nite at Disneyland. This was one of the last years that Torrance High celebrated Grad Nite at Disneyland. Through the early 2000s, the celebration was held on campus. PTSA brought in games, entertainment, and plenty of food. In recent years, Grad Nite parties have been held at Knott's Berry Farm and Dave & Buster's. (Courtesy of Christy Gustafson.)

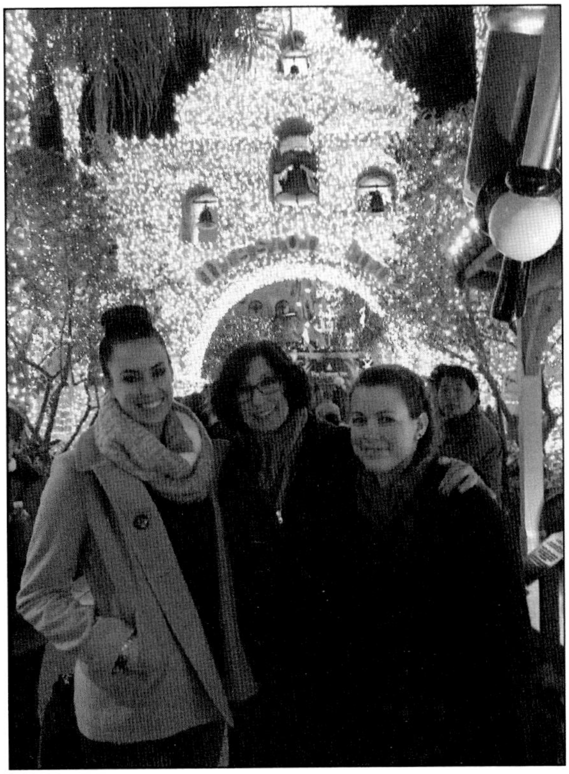

Many multigenerational families have attended Torrance High School. Ann Lujan Strong (center) graduated in 1979 and is an elementary teacher at Howard Wood Elementary school in Torrance. Her daughter Erika (left) graduated in 2010 and was a member of the cheerleading team; she is now a teacher with her mom. Sydney (right) is a talented musician who played in the Tartar band. She graduated in 2012. Ann's brother Rich graduated in 1984, and his son Nick graduated in 2016. (Both, courtesy of Ann Strong.)

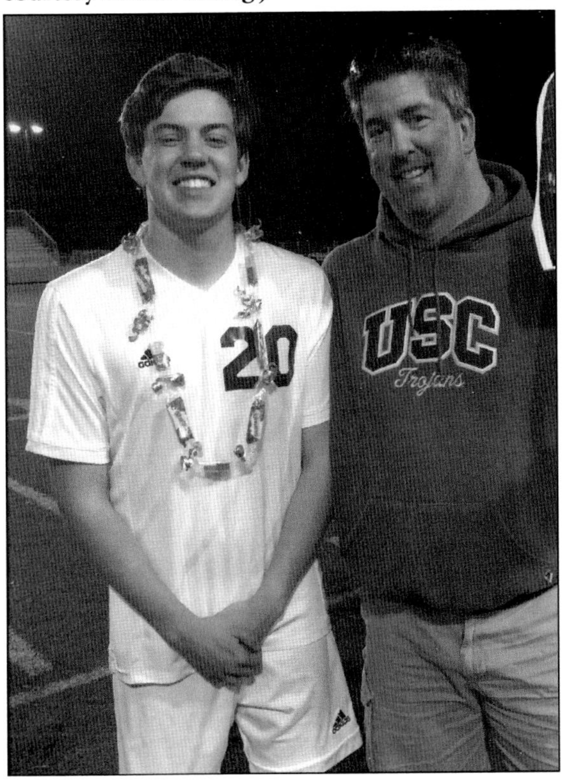

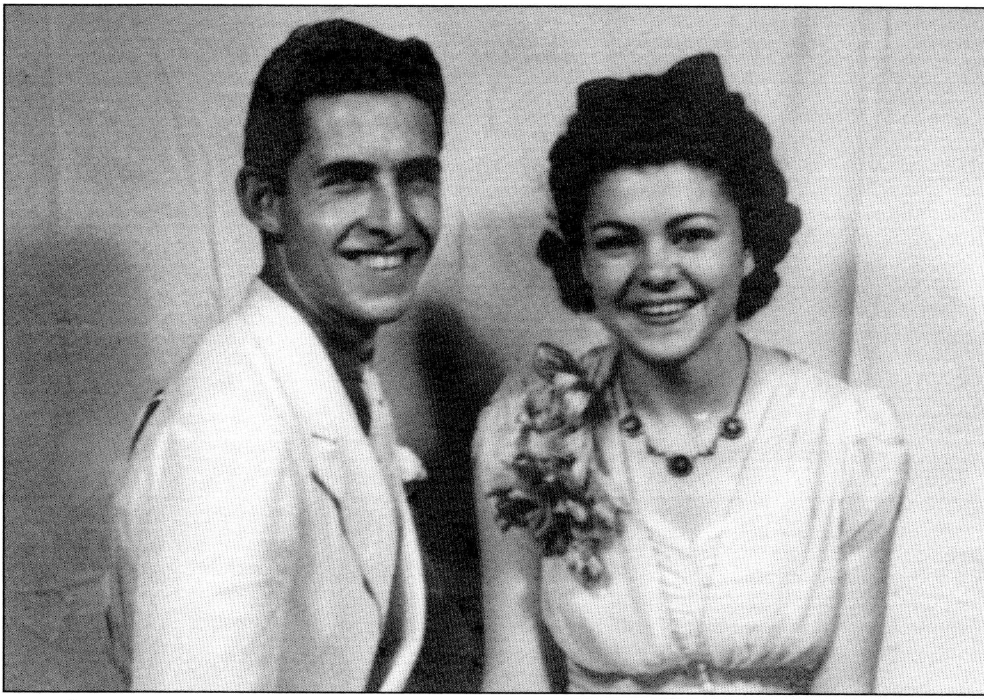

In 1941, Howard Foster and Margaret Moon attended the Spring Prom, above. Their children, including daughter Sharyn, also attended Torrance High, as did her daughter Wendy. In the below photograph, Sharyn (center) and Margaret (right) attend the alumni association's multi-class reunion. Sharyn's daughter Wendy, a Tartar Lady, was there to help with the event. (Both, courtesy of Sharyn Foster McCamish.)

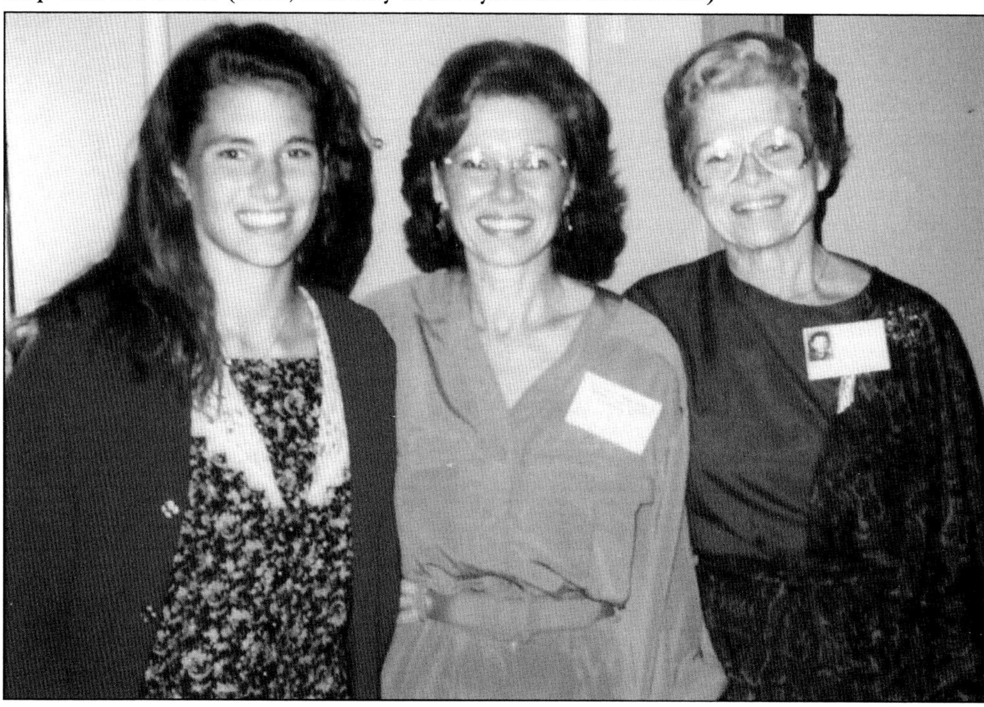

This photograph shows Margaret Moon Foster with her daughter Sharyn Foster McCamish and granddaughter Noelle McCamish. In addition to this branch of the family tree, Sharyn's sister's children also attended Torrance High. (Courtesy of Sharyn Foster McCamish.)

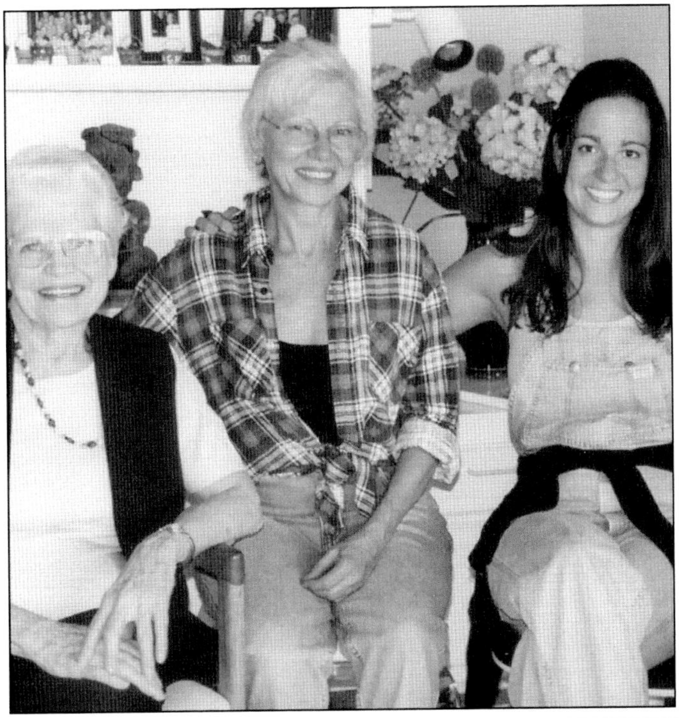

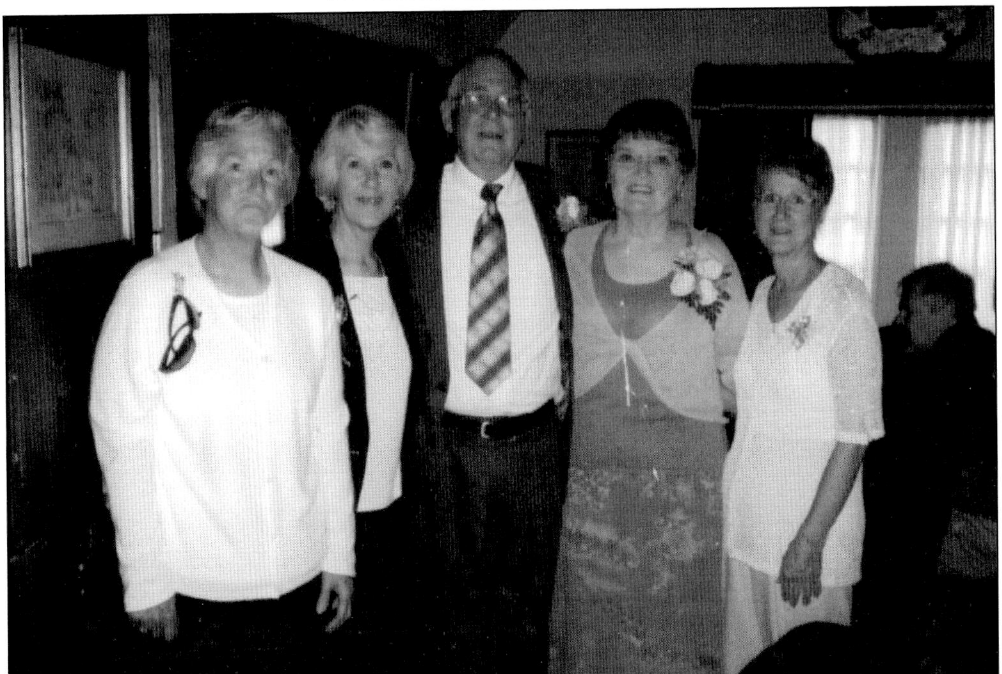

From left to right, twins Joy and Jill Drazkowski (class of 1962) are pictured with their brother David (class of 1954), his wife Patricia Merritt (class of 1954), and their other sister Mary (class of 1959). Jill's children Denise (class of 1985) and Howie (class of 1989) graduated from Torrance High, as did Denise's children Dominique (class of 2012) and Dante (class of 2017). (Courtesy of Jill Kingsmill.)

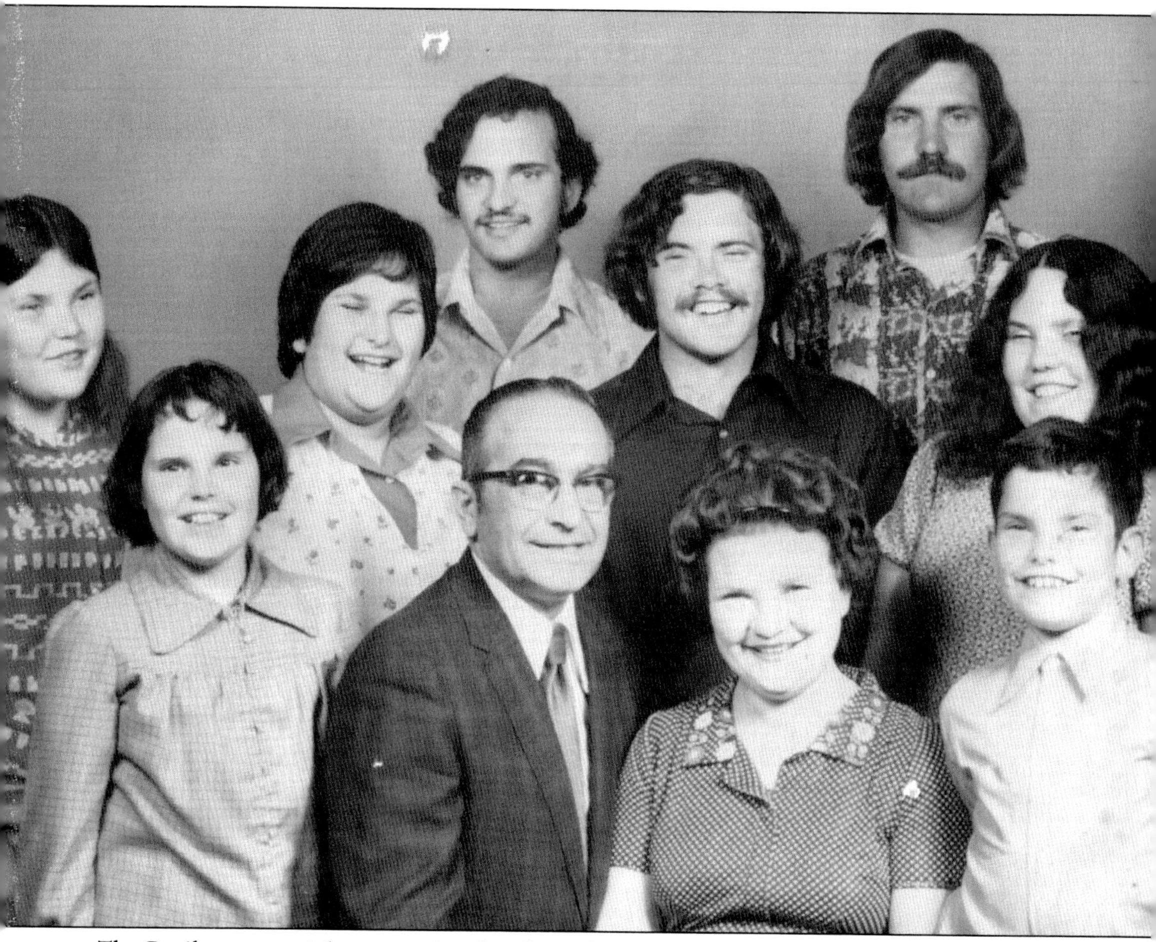

The Basiles are a triple-generation family. Father Joseph attended Torrance High School in the 1930s. Joseph's children Patricia, Vince, Peggy, Greg, Larry, Anne, Carolyn, Steve, and Mary all graduated from Torrance High as well. Larry's daughter Elizabeth will graduate from Torrance High in 2018. Pictured from left to right are (first row) Mary, Joseph, Barbara, and Steve; (second row) Carolyn, Peggy, Larry, Greg, Vince, and Anne. (Courtesy of Mary Basile.)

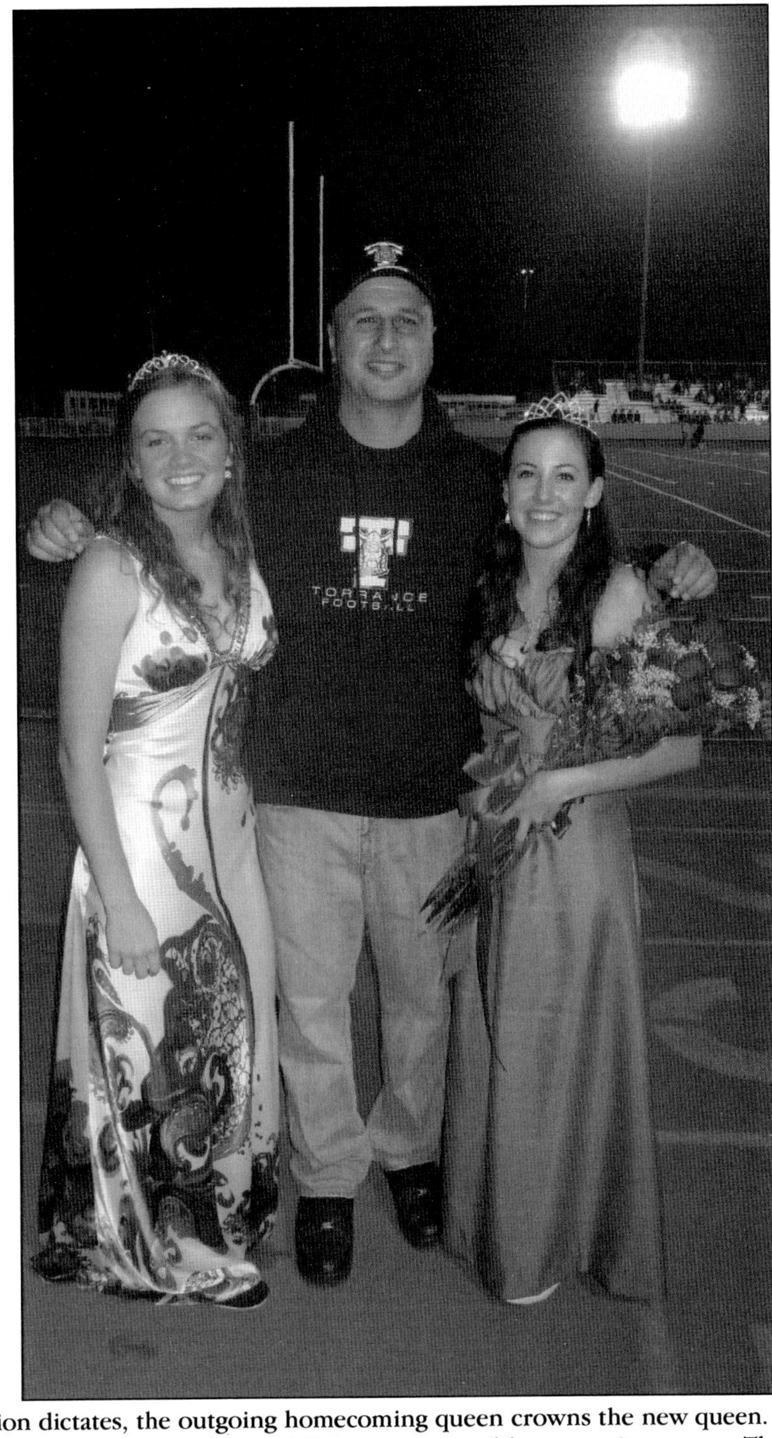

As tradition dictates, the outgoing homecoming queen crowns the new queen. In October 2010, graduate Amy Carr (class of 2011) was crowned homecoming queen. The following year, Amy placed the crown on her sister Tracy's head, in the first back-to-back sibling queens. In this photograph from 2011, Amy (left) and Tracy (right) are with principal Karim Girgis. (Courtesy of Graham and Sherri Carr.)

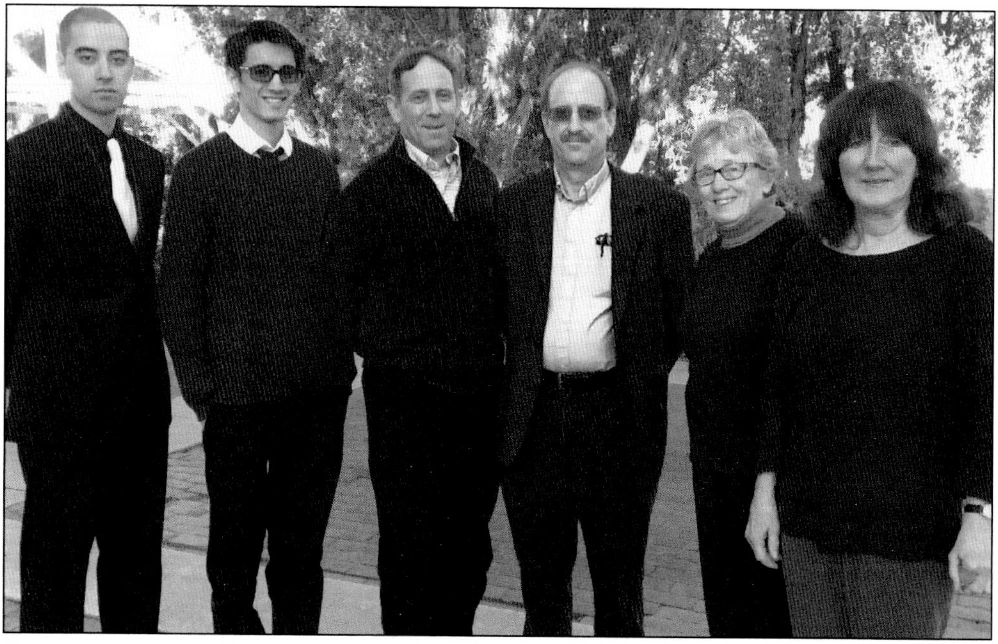

Four generations of the Wolverton family have attended Torrance High School. Rose Paige King graduated in 1928, while her daughters Claudia and Lorna graduated in 1955 and 1971, respectively. Claudia married Dick Wolverton, and their sons Scott (class of 1980) and Gary (class of 1982) attended Torrance High. Scott's two sons, Andrew and Adam graduated in 2011 and 2013, respectively. The photograph shows from left to right, Andrew, Adam, Gary, Scott, Claudia, and Lorna King, Claudia's sister. (Courtesy of Leah Wolverton.)

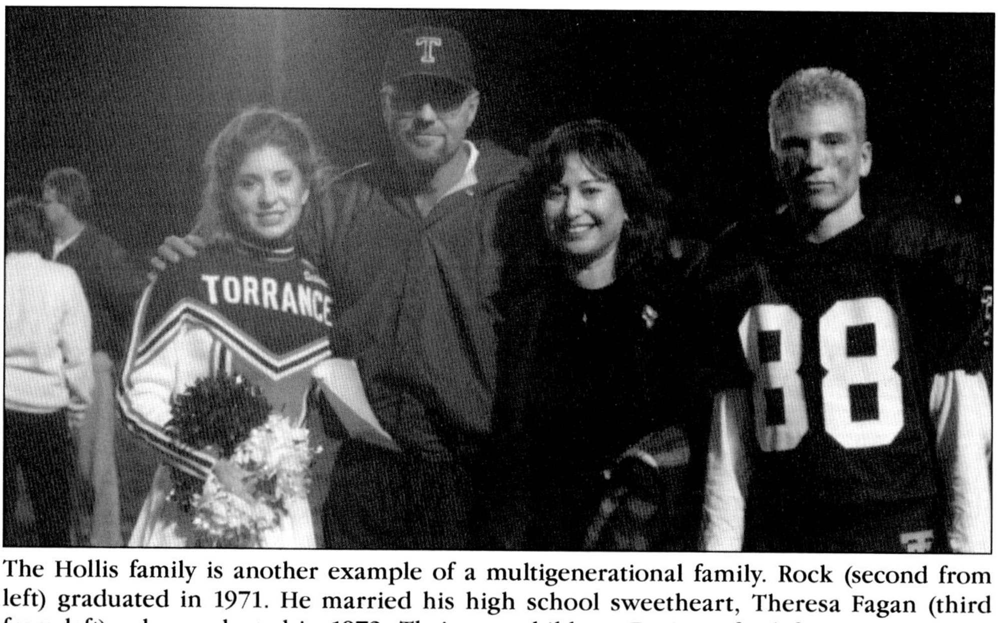

The Hollis family is another example of a multigenerational family. Rock (second from left) graduated in 1971. He married his high school sweetheart, Theresa Fagan (third from left), who graduated in 1972. Their two children, Desiree (far left) and Rocky (far right), graduated from Torrance High in 1997 and 1998, respectively. (Courtesy of Theresa Fagan Hollis.)

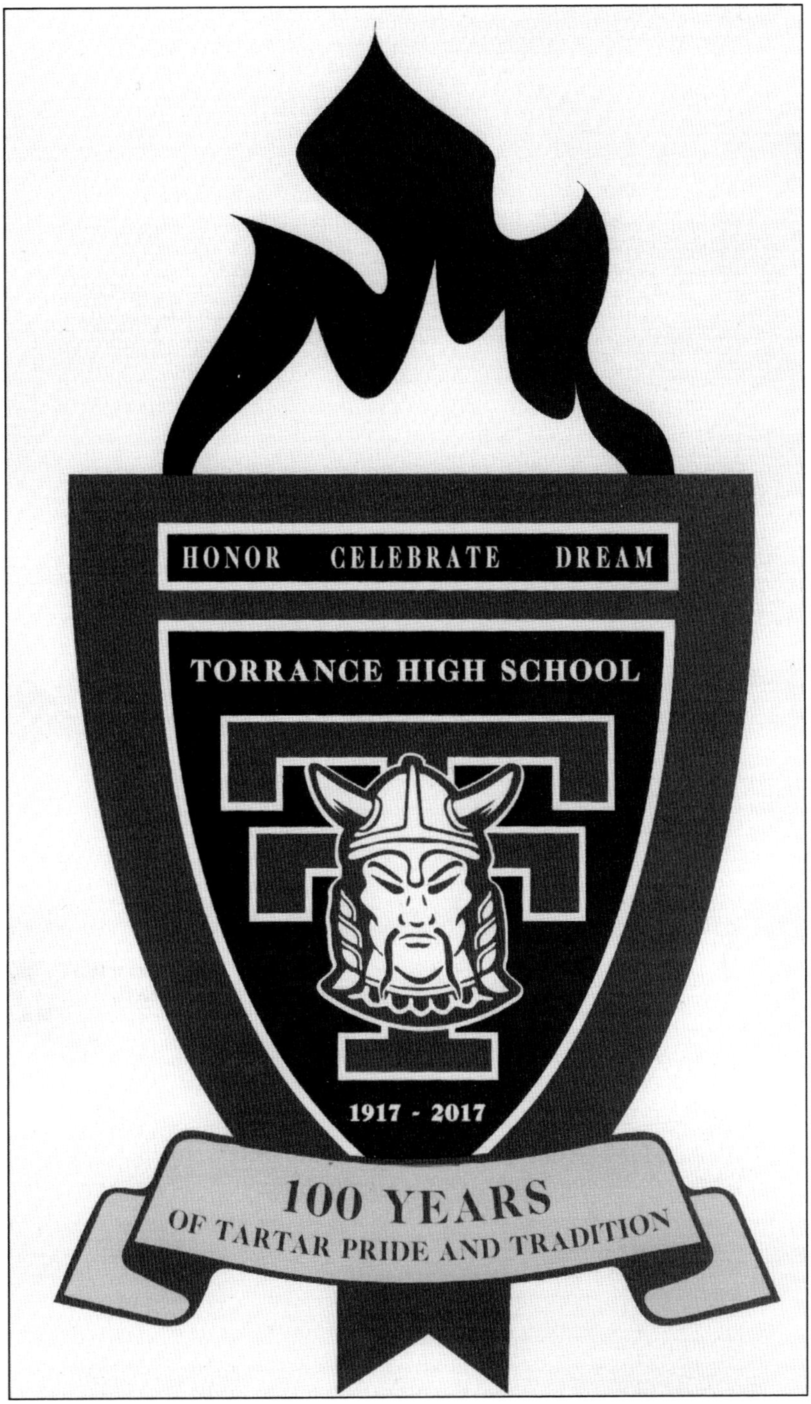

The centennial logo was designed by Jonathan Cordova, a 2015 graduate. Trisha Matoba, an alumnus, helped refine the initial proposal, leading to this final rendition. Torrance High is an exceptional institution, and Tartars should be proud to claim this school as their own and honor the past, celebrate the present, and dream of the future. (Courtesy of Torrance High School Associated Student Body.)

About the Torrance Historical Society and Museum

The Torrance Historical Society and Museum is a jewel. Located in Old Torrance in the site of the old public library, the museum houses many artifacts that visually represent the history of the city of Torrance. Current exhibits include the ranchos of the 18th and 19th centuries, the development of the city, including the police and fire departments, and local military service. It hosts a truly impressive collection of mementos and artifacts from hometown hero Louis Zamperini. In addition to the museum's thoughtful displays, the Torrance Historical Society has a large archive of photographs depicting the city's history. The society works tirelessly to share its love of the city's history and host many annual events, like the Rock Around the Block celebration in July. The volunteer staff encourages research and will put together information to aid in the research process.

The Torrance Historical Society and Museum
1345 Post Avenue
Torrance, CA 90501
(310) 328-5392
www.torrancehistoricalsociety.org

About the Torrance High School Alumni Association

Formed in 1971, the Torrance High School Alumni Association helps promote the history of Torrance High. The association is the caretaker of numerous items donated by Tartars through the decades. In addition to the old yearbooks, there is a beautiful collection of paintings done by alumni and numerous awards and trophies. Members of the association were instrumental in helping secure a listing in the National Register of Historic Landmarks. The Torrance High School Alumni Association has contributed to the refurbishment of the Senior Fountain as well as restoration of the mural and new seats in the auditorium. Each year, the association displays memorabilia and hosts a car show on the school's campus as a fundraising event for the school and clubs. It was an integral player in the creation of the Ted Tanouye Memorial, located across the road from the main building. Donations have been made to teams and organizations to help defray the cost of uniforms. Numerous scholarships have been given to deserving seniors.

Torrance High School Alumni Association
PO Box 535
Torrance, CA 90508